## Forthcoming in the series:

# Travel

Living in a world that is increasingly 'on the move' means that many of us now rely on mobile devices, social media and networking technologies to coordinate togetherness with our social networks even when we are apart. Nowhere is this phenomenon more evident than in the emerging practices of 'interactive travel'. Today's travellers are more likely than ever to pack a laptop or a mobile phone and to use these devices to stay in touch with friends and family members – as well as to connect with strangers and other travellers – while they are on the road. New practices such as location-aware navigating, travel blogging, flashpacking and couchsurfing now shape the way travellers engage with each other, with their social networks and with the world around them.

*Travel Connections* prompts a rethinking of the key paradigms in tourism studies in the digital age. Interactive travel calls into question longstanding tourism concepts such as landscape, the tourist gaze, hospitality, authenticity and escape. The book proposes a range of new concepts to describe the way tourists inhabit the world and engage with their social networks in the twenty-first century: smart tourism, the mediated gaze, mobile conviviality, re-enchantment and embrace.

Based on intensive fieldwork with interactive travellers, *Travel Connections* offers a detailed account of this emerging phenomenon and uncovers the new forms of mediated and face-to-face togetherness that become possible in a mobile world. This book will be of interest to students and scholars of sociology, tourism and hospitality, new media, cosmopolitanism studies, mobility studies and cultural studies.

**Jennie Germann Molz** is an Assistant Professor of Sociology at the College of the Holy Cross in Massachusetts, USA. Her research focuses on the social and civic implications of tourism mobilities and technology. She is the co-editor of *Mobilizing Hospitality* and an editor of the journal *Hospitality & Society*. She has published extensively on the topics of tourism, mobility, hospitality, globalization, cosmopolitanism and new technologies.

## International Library of Sociology
Founded by Karl Mannheim
Editor: John Urry, Lancaster University

## Recent publications in this series include:

**Risk and Technological Culture**
Towards a sociology of virulence
*Joost Van Loon*

**Reconnecting Culture, Technology and Nature**
*Mike Michael*

**Advertising Myths**
The strange half lives of images and commodities
*Anne M. Cronin*

**Adorno on Popular Culture**
*Robert R. Witkin*

**Consuming the Caribbean**
From arkwarks to zombies
*Mimi Sheller*

**Between Sex and Power**
Family in the world, 1900–2000
*Goran Therborn*

**States of Knowledge**
The co-production of social science and social order
*Sheila Jasanoff*

**After Method**
Mess in social science research
*John Law*

**Brands**
Logos of the global economy
*Celia Lury*

**The Culture of Exception**
Sociology facing the camp
*Bülent Diken and Carsten Bagge Laustsen*

**Visual Worlds**
*John Hall, Blake Stimson and Lisa Tamiris Becker*

**Time, Innovation and Mobilities**
Travel in technological cultures
*Peter Frank Peters*

**Complexity and Social Movements**
Multitudes acting at the edge of chaos
*Ian Welsh and Graeme Chesters*

**Qualitative Complexity**
Ecology, cognitive processes and the re-emergence of structures in post-humanist social theory
*Chris Jenks and John Smith*

**Theories of the Information Society,**
3rd Edition
*Frank Webster*

**Crime and Punishment in Contemporary Culture**
*Claire Grant*

**Mediating Nature**
*Nils Lindahl Elliot*

# Travel Connections

Tourism, technology and
togetherness in a mobile world

**Jennie Germann Molz**

Routledge
Taylor & Francis Group

LONDON AND NEW YORK

First published 2012
by Routledge
2 Park Square, Milton Park, Abingdon, Oxfordshire OX14 4RN

Simultaneously published in the USA and Canada
by Routledge
711 Third Avenue, New York, NY 10017
First issued in paperback 2014

*Routledge is an imprint of the Taylor and Francis Group, an informa business*

*British Library Cataloguing in Publication Data*
A catalogue record for this book is available from the British Library

*Library of Congress Cataloging-in-Publication Data*
Molz, Jennie Germann, 1969–
    Travel connections: tourism, technology and togetherness in a
    mobile world/by Jennie Germann Molz. – 1st ed.
    p. cm. – (International library of sociology)
    Includes bibliographical references and index.
    1. Online social networks. 2. Tourism–Social aspects.
    3. Tourism–Technological innovations. 4. Culture and tourism.
    I. Title.
HM742.M65 2012
306.4'819–dc23                                              2011040534

ISBN 978-0-415-68285-5 (hbk)
ISBN 978-1-138-02006-1 (pbk)
ISBN 978-0-203-12309-6 (ebk)

Typeset in Times New Roman
by Sunrise Setting Ltd, Torquay, UK

To Martin and Elliot, the best travel
companions I could ever hope for.

# Contents

# Illustrations

**Figures**

**Table**

# Acknowledgements

I am grateful to everyone who engaged with this project, first at the Centre for Mobilities Research at Lancaster University, where these ideas first took root, and then later as they were routed across two continents, through several conferences and into the hands of friends and colleagues around the world. While I was writing the book, I presented working drafts at a number of conferences and seminars. I would like to thank all of the conference organizers and participants for invigorating conversations and valuable feedback, with a special note of thanks to David Bissel, Sonja Buchberger, De-Jung Chen, Jim Conley, Matilde Cordoba Azcarate, Tim Cresswell, Timothy Dallen, Adriana de Souza e Silva, Tim Edensor, Christian Fisker, Malene Freudendal-Pedersen, Nelson H. H. Graburn, Maria Gravari-Barbas, Juliet Jain, Ole B. Jensen, Paola Jiron, Hillary Kaell, Sven Kesselring, Chia-ling Lai, Daniel Olson, Cody Paris, Noel Salazar, Mimi Sheller, Jen Southern, Vicky Steylaerts, Jennifer Sweda, Phillip Vannini and Dennis Zuev. I am especially grateful to John Urry for his unfailing support of this project from the very beginning, and for his helpful guidance along the way. Thanks are due to Anne-Marie Fortier, Michael Haldrup, Sven Kesselring, Mimi Sheller and Soile Veijola for their generous intellectual hospitality, especially during the early stages of this project. I would also like to express my appreciation to Monika Büscher, Michael Epstein, Adi Kuntsman and Peggy Schyns for their astute comments and words of encouragement on early chapter drafts, as well as to Lydia Brauer, Jonas Larsen and Mary McGlynn for their valuable advice. Thank you also to Gerhard Boomgaarden, Jennifer Dodd and Emily Briggs at Routledge for their enthusiasm about this project and for their editorial assistance.

At Holy Cross, I would like to thank the Charles and Rosanna Batchelor (Ford) Foundation Grant, the Michael C. and Maureen Ruetggers Research Fund and the Committee on Faculty Scholarship for providing financial support for fieldwork, conference travel and research assistance. Heartfelt thanks are due to Michele Latour, Lia McCarthy and Kristen Troy for their invaluable research and administrative assistance, as well as to my students whose smart questions and creative observations helped me think about travel and technology in new ways. Many of my department colleagues commented on this project at various stages, and I would like to thank them for their time, insights and encouragement: Renée

Beard, Susan Crawford Sullivan, Susan Cunningham, Jeffrey Dixon, Ara Francis, Dave Hummon, Ellis Jones, Tom Landy, Jerry Lembcke, Ann Marie Leshkowich, Sasha Newell, Susan Rodgers, Royce Singleton, Ed Thompson and Caroline Yezer.

I am extremely grateful to all of the people who participated in this research and shared their stories and experiences of interactive travel with me. Thank you especially to Simon Dao, Michael Epstein, Richard Paik and Nicholas Tommarello, to the travel bloggers who allowed me follow and analyse their blogs and agreed to let me interview them, and to the dozens of CouchSurfers who welcomed me into their homes and their lives.

Thank you to my dispersed networks of dear friends and family members, whom I see only intermittently (and mostly online!), but whose support for this project has been tangible and constant. Thanks also to my neighbours in Massachusetts and Italy for food and laughter, for filling in at the last minute, for sharing the garden duties and the harvest, for snow-blowing the driveway and for caring about the progress on this book! I am indebted to Susie Masters, yoga instructor extraordinaire, whose expertise on flow and movement rejuvenated and grounded me on a weekly basis.

And of course my deepest appreciation goes to my husband, Martin Molz, and my son, Elliot Molz, for making this book *possible*, in every sense, with their patience and understanding, their creativity and fearlessness, their warm hospitality to the CouchSurfers I brought home, their good sense to put my phone on the charger and their love of travel. They are my mooring in the midst of mobility, for which I am always grateful.

JGM

Wired and wireless communication at the airport in Cusco, Peru.
Source: Photograph taken by the author.

*travel*: to go on or as if on a trip or tour; to move or undergo transmission from one place to another; to journey through or over; to move in a given direction or path or through a given distance; to move rapidly.

*connection*: a link; a relation of personal intimacy; a means of communication or transport; a political, social, professional, or commercial relationship; rapport; tie; bond.

# 1 Introduction

## Tourism, technology and togetherness in a mobile world

Yogyakarta, Indonesia, 1994

The rooms in the Sumaryo Guest House where I was staying opened onto a sunny central courtyard blooming with hibiscus bushes and furnished with low-slung lawn chairs. Small clusters of three or four travellers, mostly young Western backpackers, would sit in the lawn chairs late into the night engaging in that casual banter and story swapping that tends to characterize backpacker socializing. Mark made an odd exception to this social choreography. I noticed that he had pulled one of those lawn chairs up against a wall and was sitting there alone, hunched over a black portable computer. Wires spilled out of the side of his computer and snaked up the wall where he had rigged a power converter to plug his computer into an outlet. When I asked him what he was doing, he slowly peeled his gaze away from the screen to look at me and then patiently explained that he was keeping a digital travel journal and writing articles about travelling around the world with a computer. These articles were intended as a kind of 'how-to' guide for other travellers who might want to bring their computers along, but were worried about security or weight or voltage. He gestured to one of the wires, which led to a phone jack, and explained that he was occasionally able to connect his modem to the phone line in the guest house to transmit his travel journal to friends back home. 'All my friends get is a postcard', I joked. But, I quickly figured out that his friends were not like my friends. They were tech-savvy computer nerds who spent most of their time in a university lab and knew how to make computers on opposite sides of the world talk to one another. He clearly wanted to get back to the task at hand, so I wandered off, fascinated and confused by this guy in a guest house in Indonesia communicating, somehow, with his friends on another continent.

## Introduction

I did not realize it then, but I had encountered my first 'flashpacker'. Of course, in 1994, that term did not exist and would not be coined for another decade or so. At the time, I thought of Mark rather prosaically as the guy with the computer. Like me, he was in his early twenties, from the United States, and taking a few months off to backpack around the world. Unlike me, or any other backpacker I had met so far on my journey, Mark was hauling a heavy, expensive laptop computer everywhere he went. It is difficult to capture in retrospect my initial reactions to Mark and his computer. It helps to remember that, at the time, few people were using email let alone mobile phones or social networking sites for daily communication. There was no Yahoo! and certainly no Facebook. There was no Google. I had still not heard of a browser. The word 'blog' did not yet exist. I knew people who owned laptop computers, but it would never occur to them to lug their laptops around the world in a backpack. What Mark was doing with his computer in the courtyard of the Sumaryo Guest House seemed uncanny to me. There he was, his face buried in a computer screen, his back to the communal space of the guest house, apparently alone and yet, at the same time, connected across time and space to distant friends.

The image of Mark bent over his laptop computer and the sense I had that he was both connected *and* disconnected – socially, digitally, physically – piqued a curiosity that has motivated much of my scholarly research over the past fifteen years. Since then, I have been exploring the way travellers integrate portable computers and the Internet, and more recently mobile phones and social media, into their travel and tourism practices, a trend I refer to as 'interactive travel'. In this book, I explore some of the questions that Mark and his laptop computer prompted all those years ago. How do we 'do togetherness' at a distance? What kinds of connections – and disconnections – do new technologies make available to travellers? What do we gain by being able to connect to places in new ways or stay in touch with loved ones while on the road, and what do we give up? These new patterns of togetherness and sociality that emerge when physical travel intersects with communication technologies are the topic of this book.

In this introductory chapter, I describe the growing trend of 'interactive travel' and locate it within the larger debates surrounding mobility, technology and sociality. I begin by showing how the rapidly evolving context of new mobile and media technologies has made interactive travel an ever more significant element of modern social life, especially in a mobile world. As interactive travellers use mobile phones and the Internet to upload blogs, post photos and videos, network with other travellers or navigate through tourist spaces, they are not merely rewriting the social and spatial significance of travel, they are pointing to significant shifts in how we use mobile technologies every day to engage with each other and the world while on the move. I then situate this discussion within the debate between social cohesion and fragmentation that often arises when new technologies appear on the social scene. Here, I expand in particular on Andreas Wittel's notion of 'network sociality' and Zygmunt Bauman's concept of 'liquid love', using their critiques of the frail and fleeting nature of social life to frame the questions I ask about mobile sociality. I conclude the chapter by considering how new communication technologies afford certain forms of togetherness on the move, and how the anxieties and aspirations travellers attach to these new technologies shed light on the imagined limits and possibilities of this mobile sociality.

## Taking technology on the road: the rise of 'interactive travel'

Interactive travel looks quite different today than it did when I met Mark at that guest house in Indonesia. Mark's seemingly idiosyncratic travel hobby has, in fact, become a massive trend. What began as a marginal activity is now central to back-packers' experiences, and to the general practice of travel. By 2000, hundreds of round-the-world travellers were publishing websites similar to Mark's digital travel journal. By 2011, the term 'round-the-world travel blog' had become so commonplace that a Google search returned more than 89 million results for this keyword. According to the annual 'State of the American Traveler Survey' from Destination Analysts, Inc. (2009, 2010, 2011), travellers in the United States have become increasingly likely to use the Internet and mobile technologies to plan and coordinate their journeys. In 2011, more than 43 per cent of travellers surveyed reported that they consulted user-generated online content, up from 30 per cent in 2009. In 2009, only 8.5 per cent of respondents used social media and photo sharing sites while planning their trips. By 2011, this number had risen to 25.8 per cent. That same year, significant numbers of respondents reported taking laptops with them on leisure trips, as well as using mobile devices to access travel or desti-nation information online and to download destination-specific podcasts, locative tools and interactive guides.

Over the past decade, the proliferation of Internet cafés, portable computers, mobile smartphones, wireless Internet, connected hotspots, online social net-working sites, user-friendly social media platforms and photo sharing sites has normalized ubiquitous access to the Internet among mobile and geographically-dispersed social groups, not least of all interactive travellers. Travellers' tales from the road reveal the assumption that blogging and flashpacking, a neologism that refers to packing digital devices like laptops and smartphones in your back-pack, have become ordinary aspects of most travellers' journeys. Logging onto Facebook, emailing home, uploading photos or texting friends are now normal, everyday aspects of a travelling lifestyle. *BootsnAll.com*, an online network for independent travellers, notes that 'To blog or not to blog?' is now a common ques-tion for prospective round-the-world travellers.[1] It is so common, in fact, that the website has published a guide to help travellers decide which blogging tools and smartphone applications to use while on the road. The author of *Nomadic Matt's Travel Site*, a popular travel blog that I will discuss in depth later in the book, observes that most of the backpackers he encounters are toting iPods, smartphones and laptop computers. He asks on his blog, 'Are we all flashpackers now?' As we will see, the answer to this question is less about the statistical significance of a trend than it is about the new patterns of sociality that emerge when movement, communication and technology converge.

To explore these new social configurations, I focus in this book on three inter-related practices of interactive travel, each one a point of intersection between technology and tourism. I describe my methodological approach to these prac-tices in more detail in Chapter 2, but I want to introduce briefly here the three case studies that make up the empirical context of the book. First is a study of mediated walking tours in the nearby cities of Boston and Cambridge. Curious about the way interactive technologies shape visitors' connections to the urban landscape, I downloaded several of these mobile guides to my iPod and iPhone[2] and followed them around the city. Afterwards, I contacted the developers who had created these guides and interviewed them about their vision for mobile technologies in urban tourism. In Chapter 3, I describe my experiences with these mediated and interactive walking tours and recount my conversations with the developers, highlighting in particular the way these mediated guides produce a hybrid geography of digital and physical landscapes and reflect the tension between commercial and civic applications of mobile technologies.

The second instance of interactive travel involves the interrelated practices of flashpacking and travel blogging. As I mentioned earlier, flashpacking refers to the relatively new practice of bringing digital devices along on a trip and using them to stay in touch while on the road. The flashpackers I focused on in my study were ones who used those devices to publish travel blogs as they travelled around the world. For several months, I followed these travel blogs online, regularly reading the stories travellers published online, looking at their photographs, watching their videos and paying careful attention to the back-and-forth comments posted by other readers. In Chapter 4, I describe my interactions with these blogs and introduce some of the travellers who published them. For example, I describe *The World Effect*, a blog published by Beau and Meggan, a couple from Colorado who set off on their round-the-world journey in 2008. Like most of the travellers in my study, Beau packed so many gadgets, converters, chargers and power cords that the inside of his backpack resembled, as he put it, 'a bowl of spaghetti'. The reason he packed all those devices, Beau explains on the blog, was not just to record his and Meggan's experiences, but also to share the trip – as it happened – with friends, family members and other travellers. In Chapter 4, I examine the implications of this impulse to stay in continuous touch with a dispersed and distant social group while on the move.

In order to address the specific kinds of sociality that emerge around social networking sites, I selected as my third case study an online network aimed specifically at travellers: *CouchSurfing.org*. CouchSurfing is an online hospitality exchange network that connects travellers in need of a couch to crash on with people willing to host them for a night or two. Like other interactive travel practices, CouchSurfing has grown exponentially in the past several years. It developed from a handful of founding members in 2003 to a worldwide network of more than 3 million members by the summer of 2011.[3] In this case, my fieldwork took place both online and offline. Online, I analysed the CouchSurfing website, browsed member profiles and participated in virtual community groups. At the same time, I surfed with, hosted and interviewed dozens of CouchSurfers in person. In Chapter 5, I describe my experiences as a CouchSurfer and introduce some of the people I met along the way, including Noelle and Marise who hosted me in Montreal, the eclectic group of CouchSurfers I hung out with at an organic farm in New Mexico, and Nico, an Italian artist, who sees CouchSurfing as fulfilling the revolutionary potential of the Internet. My interactions with these CouchSurfers reveal the new possibilities social networking technologies pose for interacting not just with friends, but also with strangers.

Throughout the book, I explore these intersections between tourism and technology in detail, in each case asking how travellers use mobile technologies, social media and online social networking to connect to – and disconnect from – people and places while on the move. My aim is to provide a textured account of mobile sociality as an increasingly predominant form of social life in an ever more mobile world.

## Connecting in a mobile world

By most accounts, we now live in a mobile world crisscrossed by intersecting trajectories of people, media, data, goods and risks. Travellers and tourists, satellite images and digitized photos, soldiers and refugees, currencies and debt, voice messages and email, food and clothing, and disease and pollution are constantly on the move. Most people in the world now find themselves living 'mobile lives' (Elliott and Urry 2010), whether they have chosen a mobile lifestyle (like many middle-class professionals, including the travellers I introduce in this book) or had mobility thrust upon them (like many asylum seekers, refugees and involuntary migrants). Questions of who moves and who does not, how movement is chosen, enforced or blocked, and the uneven conditions of movement are thus central to contemporary life (Sheller and Urry 2006). Based on sheer numbers, tourism mobilities are certainly implicated in these questions. The travel and tourism industry alone is worth more than US$7 trillion per year and is arguably the largest industry in the world (Elliott and Urry 2010: ix). Tourism accounts for close to one billion international arrivals annually, a number predicted to rise to 1.6 billion by the year 2020. Tourism is also implicated in the power-geometry of this mobile world (Massey 1993). As theorists have carefully pointed out, the mobility of some is often predicated on the immobility of others, and the fairly comfortable conditions of movement enjoyed by most of the travellers in this study rely heavily on privileges afforded by factors such as race, social class, gender, ethnicity and national citizenship.

If mobility itself is not exactly new, its particular salience within modern society certainly seems to be. The speed and scale of physical and virtual mobilities, the diversity and complexity of mobility systems, the ubiquity of movement in our everyday lives, and the new forms of communication, consumption, citizenship, space, selfhood and sociality that emerge through these mobilities are remarkable. What is also new, or so it seems, is the significance scholars now attribute to mobility. From 'scapes' (Appadurai 1990), 'flows' (Castells 1996), and 'acceleration' (Rosa and Scheuerman 2008) to 'turbulence' (Cresswell 2010), 'stillness' (Bissell and Fuller 2010) and 'moorings' (Hannam, Sheller and Urry 2006), a rich conceptual lexicon has emerged to describe the way contemporary social life is fundamentally organized around various mobilities and immobilities. These concepts signal a 'mobilities turn' in the social sciences that aims to make sense of social networks that are increasingly stretched across space, social relations that are ever more reliant on mediated communication, and social inequalities that are entrenched in access to or exclusion from physical and virtual mobilities.

In their analysis of the mobile lives that many people now lead, Elliott and Urry (2010: 5) observe that 'the emergence of complex global mobility systems involves the creation of new forms of mobile social life, new kinds of daily experience, and new forms of social interaction'. Central to the mobile lifeworlds they describe are the information and communication technologies people use to order, arrange and mediate life on the move. Especially for middle-class citizens living in wealthy societies, 'modern' lifestyles are only made liveable by virtue of the various mobility systems that whir ceaselessly in the background. One of the most striking aspects of this mobile, mediated and networked world is the extent to which physical movement and communication technologies intersect in new articulations of self and sociability. As networks of colleagues, friends and families extend and move across geographical space, social life now involves multiple forms of co-presence established through physical travel, online interactions and mobile communications (Larsen, Urry and Axhausen 2006). We see this in concentrated form in interactive travel, where travellers experiment with technology to engage in new mobile lifestyles, establish new ties to space and place, and navigate new modes of co-presence with friends and family members while on the road and far away. Physical travel and mediated communication are the 'social glue' (Vertovec 2004) that holds these dispersed and mobile social networks together. This hybrid sociality is impossible apart from the technologies of travel and communication that enable it, and yet, as we will see, it is not reducible to these technologies.

## Connecting

As I explore the contours, qualities and textures of togetherness in this mobile world, I return again and again to the concept of connection. I argue that connectivity, and especially the dialectic between connecting and disconnecting, lies at the heart of mobile sociality. In many ways, interactive travel conflates social, spatial and digital connectivity, and the title of this book is meant to capture precisely these overlaps. The phrase from which the book's title derives – 'travel connections' – conjures up many images: passengers rushing through airport terminals or train stations to catch the next leg of their itinerary; subway maps and airline routes built around hubs and spokes; and cartographies of the Internet or cellular networks depicting the wired and wireless routes that data travel along as they move between transmitters, servers and computers. These kinds of travel connections are predicated on complex mobility systems composed of interconnected infrastructures, services and modes of transportation and communication. But, 'travel connections' also connotes the social, intimate and interpersonal relations that emerge in the midst of all this mobility.

In public discourse about mobile technologies and social media, the term 'connect' often gets used in such unselfconscious ways that we rarely ask how we get from the digital to the social. Facebook, for example, claims to 'help you connect and share with the people in your life'. Nokia's motto is, 'Connecting people'. Cisco, a multinational telecommunications company, brands itself as 'the human network' and claims to be 'bringing people together'. The conceptual leap from electronic connectivity to human and social connections in these corporate taglines appears to be seamless. We are led to understand 'connection' as a fairly straightforward way of referring to social ties, especially ones that are technologically mediated. Connecting to the Internet and connecting to a faraway friend are barely discernible activities.

The fact that 'connection' refers today as easily to social relationships as it does to travelling or to Internet access attests not only to the term's polyvalence, but also to new forms of sociability that revolve less around physically proximate communal relationships and more around geographically-dispersed, mediated and mobile social networks. Bauman (2003) notes that people now refer to their social experiences in terms of connections; connecting and being connected rather than in terms of relating and relationships. Urry (2007: 46) argues that 'all social relationships should be seen as involving diverse "connections" that are more or less "at a distance", more or less fast, more or less intense and more or less involving physical movement'. Because social relations at a distance are never simply fixed or located in place, they must be constituted and maintained through a combination of social, spatial, emotional and technological *connections* (Elliott and Urry 2010). Our ability to talk about our social relations *as* connections relies on a conflation of the digital with the interpersonal that epitomizes the mediated and mobile nature of modern social life.

## The tourist as a metaphor of the mobile world

Interactive travel has a lot to tell us about this changing social world, and especially about the way social life has become wrapped up in technologies of moving and communicating. In many ways, travel, tourism and backpacking are symbolic of this increasingly mobile world (Richards and Wilson 2004a) and, more generally, 'of the problem of "being modern" ' (Minca and Oakes 2006: 1). In this sense, I focus on interactive travel as a set of practices that are embedded in and emblematic of modern life and I look to these practices to reveal the kinds of sociality and togetherness that are possible, or impossible, in an increasingly mobile, mediated and networked world. This book thus extends a long-standing and ongoing agenda in historical and sociological studies of tourism that sees the leisure traveller as a metaphor of the social world.

Scholars have focused on the tourist not only because the tourist is an important figure of the largest industry in the world, but also because the tourist has 'provided a sociological understanding of that world' (Dann 2002: 6). Much of the foundational literature in tourism studies has explored the way changing styles of travel reflect broader social and cultural shifts. For example, Judith Adler's (1989) seminal piece on the history of sightseeing explains how performances of travel shifted over time to reflect changing social values. According to Adler, changes in tourists' ways of seeing and encountering 'scenic' landscapes mirrored broader societal shifts from the Scientific Revolution of the seventeenth century to the Romantic sensibilities of the eighteenth century. By the middle of the twentieth century, tourism practices had shifted yet again, this time toward mass tourism. One of the earliest treatments of tourism in the social sciences, Valene Smith's influential collection *Hosts and Guests* (1989), offers an anthropological critique of this shift. In response to the rise of mass tourism in the 1970s, the studies included in Smith's book described a socioeconomic milieu that made modern tourism an economically viable pursuit for post-war Americans, even as it contributed to the dichotomous and often unequal encounters between travellers and their local hosts in a postcolonial context.

Soon after Smith's collection on the anthropology of tourism appeared, John Urry introduced *The Tourist Gaze* (1990), a sociological exploration of the relationship between mass tourism and modernity. For Urry, the massification of tourism in the mid-twentieth century, with its emphasis on visuality, spectacle and the consumption of place, was emblematic of a shift to a more reflexive and flexible post-Fordist economy. Urry argued that mass tourism in the twentieth century became a crucial element of what it meant to be modern, not only as a marker of status but as a way of coping with the heightened stress and complexity of modern life. In a similar vein, Dean MacCannell (1999[1976]) interpreted the tourist's quest for authenticity as characteristic of the alienating effects of modernity, motivated in part by a desire to escape the strictures and simulacra that define life in the modern world (Rojek 1993).

Out of this literature have emerged some of the key theoretical paradigms scholars use to make sense of tourism as a metaphor of modern social life. The role of place and landscape, the tourist gaze, relations between hosts and guests, the quest for authenticity and the desire to escape are not merely concepts for explaining what tourists do or why they do it; they are frameworks for understanding the complex ways in which travel and tourism are inextricably linked to the broader political, economic, cultural and social composition of the world. These paradigms have also highlighted the complex spatial and social relations involved in tourism, including the way travellers connect to the self, to others, to places and to the world while on the road. The extent to which these connections (and disconnections) are now mobilized, mediated, coordinated and networked through mobile technologies and online media, however, now requires a better understanding of tourism as a socio-technical practice.

Dann (2002) points out that foundational tourism texts like Urry's analysis of the tourist gaze, Smith's collection on hosts and guests and MacCannell's treatise on modernity and authenticity, were all published prior to the arrival of the Internet, mobile phones, blogs or social networking sites. One of my objectives in this book is to reconsider these dominant tourism studies paradigms in light of recent technological innovations. To this end, I devote a chapter to thinking through each of these paradigms. For example, in Chapter 3 I explore the theme of landscape and examine the way mobile technologies shape tourist places and tourists' encounters with urban landscapes. In Chapter 4, I describe the way flashpacking and travel blogging mobilize and mediate the tourist gaze in new ways, resulting in interactive, sociable and hybrid performances of togetherness between travellers and their social networks. A similar theme emerges in Chapter 5, where I consider the paradigm of hospitality and relations between hosts and guests in light of online hospitality exchange sites like *CouchSurfing.org*. I take up the question of authenticity in Chapter 6, where I ask how travellers appeal to a discourse of authenticity to make sense of new socio-technical practices such as travel blogging and CouchSurfing. In Chapter 7, I revisit the notion that tourism constitutes an escape from modernity and ask what it means for travellers to escape or disconnect in a world of ubiquitous computing. I conclude in Chapter 8 by considering the insights that the 'performance turn', a newly emerging paradigm in tourism studies, brings to interactive travel and mobile sociality. Before I move on to these chapters, however, it is important to situate interactive travel and mobile sociality within the broader theoretical debates unfolding around mobility, technology and sociality and to establish the foundation for the questions I ask throughout the book.

## Mobility, technology and the problem of human togetherness

New communication and transportation technologies often enter the public realm on the horns of a familiar dilemma: Will they bring societies together or tear them apart? In other words, will these technologies provide us with new (and better) ways to be social, or will they further isolate an already alienated modern population? During the 1990s and 2000s, the emergence of the Internet, mobile phones and online social media animated this debate along fairly predictable lines. Proponents of these technologies argued that connecting in the digital age held great promise for sociability, insisting that social ties mediated online or via mobile phones could be surprisingly cohesive. Critics argued, however, that online connections were inevitably weak, especially in comparison to the more substantive quality of face-to-face relationships, and were therefore likely to unravel the social fabric. Furthermore, online relationships and virtual communities threatened to replace, or at least distract us from, our 'real' relationships with family, neighbours and friends.

The very same promises of enhanced community and threats of social fragmentation can be traced back to the introduction of the railway, the steamship, the telegraph and the telephone in the nineteenth century. In her historical analysis of the public's reaction to electronic innovations in the late nineteenth century, Carolyn Marvin (1988) explains that new technologies like the telephone and telegraph posed both opportunities and risks to the social order. On the one hand, they heralded a new age of global community, cultural harmony and civilization. New electronic communication technologies promised an era of 'neighborship without propinquity' that would embrace even the most secluded member of society into a tighter community (Marvin 1988: 66). At the personal level, these technologies allowed people to share intimacies from afar in ways that had never been possible before. Marvin recounts stories of telephone operators falling in love over the telephone line and suitors using the telephone to offer proposals of marriage. Not all connections had such happy endings. The introduction of the telephone was also seen as threatening traditional courtship, intruding on the private space of the family, abetting new kinds of crimes, and facilitating the 'wrong' kinds of connections across class and racial boundaries. Advances in transportation met similarly mixed reviews. The railroad, followed by the automobile, was seen as a marvel of technological progress that would unite the far corners of the world in social harmony. At the same time, however, nineteenth century innovations in transportation were met with worries about the socially disruptive and disorienting effects of roads, railways and speed (for a fuller historical account of these tensions, see Kern 1983 and Schivelbusch 1986).

What seems especially salient by contemporary standards is Marvin's (1988: 5) observation that in the nineteenth century, people 'struggled to come to terms with novel ... devices that made possible communication in real time without real presence, so that some people were suddenly too close and others much too far away'. In other words, by enabling communication at a distance, new technologies tightened some social bonds while rendering others more tenuous. What lay at the heart of this public debate, according to Marvin, was the 'ambiguous presence' that electronic communication produced. By divorcing social proximity from embodied co-presence, the telegraph and the telephone threw togetherness into question. In the long run, as we will see, the dichotomy between social cohesion and social fragmentation does not provide a very useful empirical framework, but it does reveal the way a society imagines the parameters and vulnerabilities of its 'togetherness', especially when the terms of that togetherness become uncertain.

Like the telegraph and the telephone in the nineteenth century, contemporary mobile media and communication technologies both transcend and redefine co-presence. Although most of us have by now grown accustomed to communicating at a distance, as well as on the move, we are still a bit uncertain about precisely what kind of togetherness we are doing when we text a friend or update our status on Facebook. Our co-presence remains ambiguous, though in slightly different ways from our nineteenth century counterparts. When I described my encounter with Mark at the beginning of this chapter, I depicted Mark as being both there in the guest house courtyard and yet somehow not there. Recent research on mobile phones, online social networks and interactive communities has tried to pin down this ambiguity of presence. Gergen (2002), for example, uses the term 'absent presence' to refer to the way mobile phones divide one's attention between here and elsewhere. Bauman (2003) would describe Mark's use of the computer as a kind of 'virtual proximity' with his friends back in the United States, but one that also rendered him 'virtually distant' from me and the other backpackers at the guest house. At the time, Mark was able to connect his modem only infrequently, but interactive travellers today are able to stay in almost continuous touch with their extended social networks, a condition Licoppe (2004) has referred to as 'connected presence'. Ito and Okabe (2005), in their study of teenagers' use of mobile phones, call this 'ambient virtual co-presence', suggesting that our social networks are continuously present and available, whether we are actively engaged with them or not. These terms all aim to capture the interplay of connecting and disconnecting, distance and proximity, togetherness and apartness that characterizes social life in technology-saturated societies. The question, then, is not whether new technologies result in more or less cohesive societies, but rather what *kind* of sociality they produce. How do people share with one another, care for each other and integrate themselves into the fabric of each other's everyday lives, even when they are apart?

I am certainly not the first to ask what this togetherness looks like. Among the theories of mobile sociality that have influenced my analysis in this regard are Andreas Wittel's notion of 'network sociality' and Zygmunt Bauman's concept of 'liquid love'. As I describe in the next section, Wittel's and Bauman's accounts of technologically mediated social life provide a provocative, if problematic, departure point for the theoretical direction I take in this book. Bauman and Wittel offer richly-textured accounts of the kind of sociality we might expect from our mediated connections, bringing attention to the tangible ways in which digital connections shape interpersonal relations, but leaving little room for the complex interplay between technological affordances and travellers' desires.

## Network sociality and liquid love

According to Andreas Wittel (2001), the fact that social relationships look and feel different today is unsurprising given that sociality is no longer predicated on spatially proximate communities, but rather on spatially diffuse networks of people and technologies. Mobile social relationships necessarily take on a different texture than those built around place-based community, a point Wittel (2001: 51) makes clear in his definition of 'network sociality':

> Community entails stability, coherence, embeddedness and belonging. It involves strong and long-lasting ties, proximity and a common history or narrative of the collective. . . . Network sociality . . . does not represent belonging but integration and disintegration. . . . Social relations are not 'narrational' but 'informational'; they are not based on mutual experience or common history, but primarily on an exchange of data and on 'catching up'. . . . Network sociality consists of fleeting and transient, yet iterative social relations; of ephemeral but intense encounters.

Network sociality alters the quality not only of online relationships, but of face-to-face ones as well. For instance, Wittel explains, 'in a network sociality, strangers become potential friends', but the very meaning of friendship undergoes a transformation (ibid.: 71). Instead of sharing a common biography or history, friends 'catch up' with quick bits of information. And instead of enduring over time, relations tend 'towards ephemeral but intense, focused, fast and over-loaded social ties' (ibid.: 66).

Wittel offers the example of 'speed dating' as a somewhat extreme example of how social – and potentially romantic – relationships revolve around the quick but intense exchange of information. This example of speed dating also illustrates another feature of network sociality: the tendency to commodify human relationships in both personal and professional realms. Wittel observes that 'connections' are currency in the network society. Quite similar to the kind of network sociality Wittel describes here, the mobile sociality that emerges in interactive travel involves both intense bonding and ephemeral relations. As we will see in the analysis of CouchSurfing and hospitality in Chapter 5, mediated connections can lead to emotionally intense, but ultimately brief and potentially commodified, face-to-face interactions between travellers.

The features Wittel identifies in network sociality are inspired, in large part, by Zygmunt Bauman's notion of 'liquid modernity' (2000). In contrast to the solid modernity of nineteenth century industrialization, Bauman describes contemporary modernity as light, mobile and flexible. In his book *Liquid Love* (2003), he elaborates on the social dimension of this liquid modernity and the consequences of mediated communication for human togetherness. As Bauman (2003: 59) describes it, 'connecting' is both the premise and the effect of mobile sociality:

> Your mobile always rings (or so you hope). One message flashes on the screen in hot pursuit of another. Your fingers are always busy: you squeeze the keys, calling new numbers to answer the calls or composing messages of your own. You *stay connected* – even though you are constantly on the move, and though the invisible senders and recipients of calls and messages move as well, all following their own trajectories. Mobiles are for people on the move.

Bauman's illustration of the nature of relationships in contemporary society focuses in particular on the problem with denoting human interactions *as* connections. The more we perform our sociality on the move and at a distance, Bauman worries, the less we are able to be social without our mobile technologies and the more our social relations take on the character of these 'connections'. Bauman finds this troubling because he sees these mediated connections as frail and fleeting, vulnerable to being 'both substantively and metaphorically, finished with nothing more than the press of a button' (2003: 62). Liquid love may involve connecting, but even more importantly it involves the ability to disconnect; to 'unfriend'; to hit delete. Elliott and Urry (2010: 5) reiterate the clickable nature of mobile life, 'The task of holding self and one's social network together is increasingly reconstituted around instantaneous computer clicks of "search", "erase", "delete", "cut-and-paste", and "cancel".' Bauman explains that 'contacts require less time and effort to be entered and less time and effort to be broken. *Distance is no obstacle to getting in touch – but getting in touch is no obstacle to staying apart*' (2003: 62, emphasis in original).

Digital connections thus make sociality possible, but only by disembedding and distancing human relationships. In this sense, connecting and disconnecting have the effect of respatializing human interactions, as Bauman (2003: 59) explains:

> You would go *nowhere* without your mobile ('nowhere' is, indeed, the space without a mobile, with a mobile out of range, or a mobile with a flat battery). .... It is unimportant which place you are in, who the people are around

you and what you are doing in that place filled with those people. The difference between one place and another, one set of people within your sight and corporeal reach and another, has been cancelled and made null and void.

Bauman argues that human togetherness now revolves around 'virtual proximity' and 'virtual distance', which means that people can be close even while they are far apart, or disconnected even when they are right next to each other. It also means that it does not matter which place you are in, since 'the difference between one place and another . . . has been cancelled and made null and void' (ibid.: 59).

Bauman's critique raises a relevant question: What are the spatial implications of mobile sociality? Will mobile technologies and the virtual spaces of the Internet make space and place redundant? Bauman's observation speaks to anxieties not only about the way technologies transcend spatial distance, but also about a kind of homogenization of places and disconnection *from* place. And yet, places remain vitally central to tourism. The idea that mobile technologies necessarily dilute the distinctiveness of places or detach people from places is a serious matter that I take up in the chapters that follow as I explore the spatial implications, along with the social implications, of mobile technologies and online social media.

According to Bauman, the ease with which we connect and disconnect from people and places also has significant consequences in terms of the *kind* of sociality we perform. Instead of building and cultivating bonds through attachment and engagement, we make and break connections. These connections are short and sweet, instantaneous and disposable, intense yet brief, and frequent but shallow. What results, Bauman argues, is a brittle sociality assembled around connections that are 'too shallow and brief to condense into bonds' (Bauman 2003: 62). In part, Bauman attributes the frailty of this sociality to a consumerist logic that objectifies and trades on human relationships. In this sense, he shares Wittel's concern that the more our sociality revolves around technologically mediated connections, the more complicit it becomes with a market logic that seeks to commodify those connections. Human relationships become resources in themselves that can be used up and consumed. Bauman observes in mediated social relations a 'tendency, inspired by the dominant consumerist life mode, to treat other humans as objects of consumption and to judge them after the pattern of consumer objects by the volume of pleasure they are likely to offer, and in "value for money" terms' (ibid.: 75).

Bauman's cynicism about a sociality of 'connections' stems from the fact that he sees technologically mediated sociality as deeply implicated in a 'market economy'. There is profit to be found in exploiting frail connections. Mobile technologies, and the light and loose ties they facilitate, are the enemy of what Bauman calls the 'moral economy'. In contrast to the market economy, the moral economy revolves around enduring relationships, spatial proximity and shared history. It involves things like 'family sharing of goods and services, neighbourly help, friends' cooperation: all the motives, impulses and acts from which human bonds and lasting commitments are plaited' (Bauman 2003: 69). In a moral economy, Bauman (ibid.: 70) argues, sharing goods, services and help 'without money changing hands' produces a sociality of solidarity, compassion and mutual sympathy rather than frequent, fleeting and frail connections.

I draw attention to Wittel's critique of the commodification of connections and Bauman's distinction between the moral economy and the market economy because these competing impulses appear again and again in the practices of interactive travel that I describe in this book. Whereas Bauman associates mediated communication and frail sociality with the market economy, however, I argue that interactive travellers also use mobile communication technologies to create alternative economies, promote solidarity and fortify connections with other people and with places. For the mobile developers, flashpackers, travel bloggers and CouchSurfers I introduce in this book, mediated communication does not necessarily objectify or commodify social ties; it also facilitates more meaningful and authentic encounters with place, enables sharing and caring at a distance, and underpins non-commercial economies based on generosity and mutual help. Travellers use new technologies to both detach from and attach themselves to the people and places around them, and to participate in but also resist the commercialized nature of global tourism. As we will see, mobile sociality thus involves a negotiation of connection *and* disconnection, of coming together *and* moving apart, that is undoubtedly shaped by, but not reducible to, the technologies involved. To get at this more nuanced interplay between travellers, technology and mobile sociality, I turn to concepts of affordances, aspirations and anxieties, which I describe in the next section.

## Affordances, aspirations, anxieties

The social uses and meanings of new technologies are shaped by relational and contextual factors, and not just by the materiality or functionality of the technology itself. In his study of digital tourist photography, Jonas Larsen (2008a) uses the notion of 'affordances' to make sense of the complex ways in which camera technologies and social practices inform each other in the context of travel and tourism. Coined by Gibson (1979), the term 'affordance' refers to the physical make-up or capacities of the environment. Larsen explains that the material environment, including technologies like the digital camera, may enable or produce certain performances but not others, depending on the place and context. By way of example, Larsen explains that a material space such as a grassy lawn may afford performances like running, walking or lying, whereas performances like diving and swimming are afforded by the deep sea. Technological devices, like environments, also afford certain performances. In the case of digital photography, for example, Larsen describes how the delete function allows for more 'casual and "experimental" ways of photographing', while the display screen ' "affords" new sociabilities for producing and consuming photographs' collaboratively (Larsen 2008a: 148). In neither case, however, does the functionality of the camera itself prescribe these sociabilities. As Larsen notes elsewhere, 'communication technologies afford possibilities but do not determine how people perform them. They are preformed and performed' (Larsen, Urry and Axhausen 2006: 116).

Larsen's use of 'affordance' to study digital photography shapes the approach I take in my analysis of interactive travel. Instead of thinking of mobile sociality as deriving from the technology itself, my analysis asks how certain possibilities for togetherness are opened up or closed down by particular features of the technology, such as interactivity or portability. Like photography, interactive travel is 'a technological complex with specific affordances *and* a set of embodied social practices or performances' (Larsen 2008a: 143). In the first part of the book, I focus on this combination of material affordances and social performances. In my discussion of places and landscapes in Chapter 3, the tourist gaze in Chapter 4, and hospitality in Chapter 5, for example, I describe the way mobile devices and online social media and networking platforms shape a range of possibilities for travellers to connect with places and with other people while they are on the road, but do not necessarily determine the way travellers perform or make sense of this mobile togetherness.

The notion of 'affordance' highlights the realm of physical possibilities for social action, but a range of 'social affordances' can also be observed in the way new communication technologies influence everyday life (Wellman *et al.* 2003; Larsen 2008a). As Larsen points out, these social possibilities are shaped by 'intentions, cultural knowledge and past experiences' (2008a: 146). In other words, technologies also operate within a social and cultural realm of possibilities and their meanings and uses are often constrained and shaped by existing social codes. Interactive travel, and the forms of mobile sociality it makes possible, are thus implicated in a series of ongoing social dramas: what kinds of connections are worth making; what counts as knowledge; when should we break down social distances and when should we shore them up; how should we treat strangers; who may be included and who must be excluded; and what kind of world do we want to make for ourselves?

Marvin (1988: 5) notes in her early history of electrical communication that 'new practices do not so much flow directly from technologies that inspire them as they are improvised out of old practices'. She argues that at the end of the nineteenth century, electrical communication technology 'came to existing groups less as the transformative agent of its own mythology than as a set of concrete opportunities or threats to be weighed and figured into the pursuit of ongoing social objectives' (ibid.: 232). New practices and meanings were grafted onto old ones, revealing in the process the aspirations, anxieties and fantasies that social groups held about themselves, about others and about the world as a whole. 'How new media were expected to loosen or tighten existing social bonds ... reflected what specific groups hoped for and feared from one another' (ibid.: 6). As I described earlier, similar aspirations toward social cohesion and anxieties over social disintegration that greeted nineteenth century innovations in electrical communication continue to shape contemporary public reaction to mobile communications, smartphones, digital photography, new media and online social networking.

As I consider the practices, risks and strategies that emerge alongside these new technologies, I am aware that these technologies are incorporated into an already existing social field of hopes, fears and meanings as well as existing privileges and inequalities. Uncovering and disturbing these social meanings requires a shift in focus away from the technological devices themselves, their engineering or the evolution of their technical capacities and onto the social dramas and fantasies that surround these technologies. In my discussion of authenticity in Chapter 6 and escape in Chapter 7, I follow Marvin's lead by paying attention to the way aspirations and anxieties about representation, global community, the corporatization of social life, modern subjectivity, choice and control are attached to new technologies. As I argue in those chapters, the way travellers embrace, reject and negotiate new technological practices in their pursuit of mobile sociality reveals more about existing social contexts and conflicts than it does about the technology itself.

## Conclusion

My encounter with Mark and his computer in the courtyard of our guest house in Indonesia is emblematic of the way new technologies are given social and spatial significance in particular contexts. Mark may have been making his way through uncharted technological terrain, and even trying to clear a path for other travellers to follow, but he was not doing so in a social or cultural vacuum. Though it is much more heavily travelled today, that path has not been paved in stone. Even as new practices like flashpacking, travel blogging and CouchSurfing become normalized, especially among wealthy travellers from Western societies, the social meanings and embodied performances surrounding these practices remain inchoate and undetermined. In this book, I describe these practices-in-the-making as travellers negotiate a variety of connections, disconnections and missed connections.

# 2 Fieldwork on the move

## Mobile virtual ethnography

From: Jennie Germann Molz
To: Samantha Sayard*
Sent: Mon, January 4, 2010 9:35:24 AM
Subject: academic research on travel blogging

Dear Samantha,

My name is Jennie Germann Molz and I am a sociologist working on a research project about technology and travel. I am emailing you to ask if you would be willing to talk with me about your blog and your experience of blogging while traveling. If you would be willing to take some time to answer my questions, I would sincerely appreciate it. We can arrange a time to Skype, or I can send some questions to you in an email to get started. I know it's not always easy to find time and an internet connection on the road, but I hope you'll participate!

I hope to hear from you soon.
Best wishes for safe travels
and a happy new year,
Jennie

>>> Samantha Sayard 1/7/2010 8:41 AM >>>

Hi there,
Ya sure, send them through. I'm in the middle of nowhere at the moment though so I might not be able to get to it for awhile.

Take care,
Sam

>>> Jennie Germann Molz 2/27/2010 12:26 PM >>>

Dear Sam,
Hi, I'm emailing to check whether you got the email I sent a few weeks ago. I can see from your blog postings that you have been traveling quite a bit and are heading

*The travel blogger's name and identifying details have been changed in this transcript.

back to South America soon. I do hope you'll keep the questions I sent you in the back of your mind while you're traveling. I'll be in touch again soon to see about setting up a time to Skype.

All the best,
Jennie

>>> Jennie Germann Molz 4/18/2010 10:37 AM >>>

Dear Sam,
Hi. I haven't heard back from you, so I'm not sure if you've been able to check this email account. I'm just checking in to see if there's a convenient time to get in touch with you to talk about your experiences with blogging? Maybe we can try to chat on Skype if you're settled in somewhere for a few days? I'll look forward to hearing from you.

Best,
Jennie

## Introduction

Interactive travel emerges out of a set of interdependent mobilities that, according to Urry (2007), produce and shape the contours of mobile social life: the corporeal travel of people; the physical movement of objects; imaginative travel enabled by various media; virtual travel; and communicative travel. Comprised as it is out of these intersecting digital and material mobilities, interactive travel poses a significant challenge to traditional social scientific methods, many of which have relied on somewhat sedentary techniques. How do we study social practices that move, not just in space, but also in between physical and virtual settings? How do we study visible and invisible mobilities? And, how do we do this without destroying the mobile social phenomena we wish to investigate by pinning them down? (Büscher, Urry and Witchger 2010). A repertoire of mobile methods is now beginning to emerge as mobilities researchers grapple with these kinds of methodological questions. In this chapter, I contribute to that repertoire by describing the combination of research techniques I used to explore online, offline and in between instances of interactive travel.

I refer to the combination of techniques I introduce here as a 'mobile virtual ethnography', a phrase inspired by recent efforts to adapt ethnography to the study of mobile and virtual social phenomena. The purpose of this chapter is to introduce the methodological context and describe my efforts to follow and 'move with' interactive travellers across multiple junctures of tourism and technology. As my difficulty connecting with Samantha suggests, these efforts were not always successful. Engaging in an emerging methodological field such as mobile virtual ethnography inevitably involves trial and error. The result in the chapters that follow is an ethnographic narrative that often appears far more coherent than the process of composing it would imply. In this chapter, I attempt to reinsert some of the 'messiness' of social research by reflecting on the ongoing process of trying out new techniques, meeting challenges and adapting strategies throughout the research project. I begin by discussing the ways in which mobile virtual ethnography reconceptualizes the research field and the process of fieldwork. Next, I introduce the interactive travellers who welcomed me into their travel blogs, into their online and offline conversations, and into their homes. Finally, I provide an overview of the three overlapping case studies that constitute this project and describe in more detail the specific methodological techniques I employed in each case.

## Mobilizing the field and following connectivity

Ethnography is an appealing methodological choice for mobilities researchers and Internet researchers alike. Ethnographic techniques such as sustained immersion in communities of practice, ongoing participation, in-depth interviews and detailed observations of corporeal, digital, social and material practices are well suited to understanding lived practice as it occurs. Indeed, many of the methods that are now emerging in mobilities research are adaptations and mobilizations of these ethnographic techniques. In repurposing ethnography to the study of mobile and virtual phenomena, however, researchers have had to rethink what constitutes the field of study and how researchers might engage with that field.

Ethnography originated as an anthropological method for studying distant cultures and communities. Traditional ethnographies tended to be highly localized in their scope, with researchers focusing on interactions within a single bounded community rather than paying attention to the ways in which those communities were connected by travel and communication to the outside world. Although these place-bound methods of ethnography and participant observation were good for producing 'thick descriptions' of everyday life, the problem with this sedentary approach was its tendency to privilege face-to-face relationships, permanent residence and fixed boundaries while overlooking mediated interactions, movements, connections and connectivity (Wittel 2000; Haldrup and Larsen 2010: 29). As James Clifford (1997) observes, such place-based ethnographies tended to be more concerned with 'roots' than with 'routes'. Clifford's efforts to reposition ethnographic fieldwork in terms of 'travel encounters', along with Marcus' (1998) call for 'multi-sited' research that would take 'ethnography through thick and thin', re-envisioned the ethnographic field as mobile, dispersed and reticular rather than static and bounded.

This understanding of the ethnographic field as fluid rather than fixed in place was a boon to Internet researchers as well who, by the mid-1990s, had become intrigued by the possibility that community life could be sustained online in the relatively new realm of cyberspace (e.g. Rheingold 1994; Miller and Slater 2000). Researchers developed concepts like 'virtual ethnography' (Hine 2000) and 'cyberethnography' (Gajjala 2002) to adapt ethnographic techniques to the study of the Internet and computer-mediated social interactions. In the process, they further challenged the notion of the field as a culturally and spatially bounded entity. Instead, online settings were framed as fluid virtual spaces of social interaction. The ethnographer's participation also shifted from immersion in a distant field site to a kind of 'experiential rather than physical displacement' (Hine 2000: 45). In this literature, *connectivity* rather than *place* was proposed as a more useful metaphor for describing the online ethnographic field, a move that also represented a shift from ethnography in the field to an 'ethnography of networks' (Wittel 2000).

Today, mobilities and Internet researchers recognize that mediated social interactions are rarely confined to cyberspace and are instead woven into everyday practices that move continuously between various registers of interaction: from face-to-face to online to on the phone and so on. To account for these interdependent modes of moving, communicating and connecting, especially in the context of travel and tourism, Haldrup and Larsen (2010: 37) propose a research approach that not only mobilizes ethnography, but also extends its scope to include the 'traveling objects' and 'connected communications' that shape tourism performances. They explain that:

> Unlike traditional ethnography, which defines sites as *material* dwelling places, multisited ethnography also deals with *virtual* sites such as databases and blogs, not in an isolated cyberspace, but in relation to physical everyday places such as internet cafés, work places and private living spaces, as virtual worlds and material worlds are not separate entities (Wittel 2000). Multisited ethnography privileges routes rather than roots; connections and networks.
>
> (Haldrup and Larsen 2010: 46)

Foregrounding routes and connections in an ethnography of tourism requires the researcher to 'follow flows', as Haldrup and Larsen suggest. Following flows involves a variety of techniques, including analyzing the circulation of place myths, following the objects tourists carry with them abroad or bring home and travelling *along with* tourists, not only to famous destinations but also to and between ordinary places, including back home. Following flows also entails following the 'communication flows' of digital and virtual travel in order to examine 'what communication technologies travel with tourists and how they are used in practice [to produce] tourists' "connected presence" with people and places at home or elsewhere' (ibid.: 52).

In this study, I conducted a mobile virtual ethnography that shares many qualities with traditional ethnography, but that also entails several distinctive characteristics worth elaborating. First, it is multi-sited, but not just across geographical locations. Instead, mobile virtual ethnography is sited across multiple physical *and* virtual domains, including tourist destinations, urban environments, travellers' homes and my home, along with virtual venues such as travel blogs, twitter feeds and social networking sites. Furthermore, because these physical and virtual domains rarely remain separate, mobile virtual ethnography is often sited in hybrid places, such as the hybrid urban geographies I describe in Chapter 3, where virtual and material places overlap. In addition to envisioning the field as a series of places, however, I also envisioned the field in terms of networks and connections. In a sense, connectivity draws distant places together and produces certain places, such as the virtual space of a travel blog or the physical space of a CouchSurfer's home, as a site of hospitable encounters. However, connectivity also extends beyond place. This means that even though mobile virtual ethnographic techniques must be mobilized across many places, it is not confined to studying interaction *in* places.

Second, in mobile virtual ethnography, participant observation is practiced through the specific techniques of following, moving and communicating. Because mobile virtual ethnography takes place on the move, often occurring in between places while literally and virtually moving, traditional ethnographic techniques like 'immersion' seem too static. 'Following' is much more apt for a mobile virtual ethnography. As a mobile ethnographer, I often found myself following: following mobile guides through the city, following travellers virtually via their online blogs or twitter updates, following travellers' connections to other travellers, and physically following and travelling as a fellow Couch-Surfer. Following was my way of observing interactive travel in practice and being virtually and physically co-present with travellers. Following is not just a mobile method, but also a mode of mobile sociality, as we will see in Chapter 4. Likewise, moving, communicating and networking are crucial and inextricable research methods. While researching mediated walking tours, travel bloggers and CouchSurfing, I moved and communicated as an interactive traveller, networked with other travellers, downloaded applications to my mobile phone, subscribed to blog and twitter feeds, corresponded online, on the phone and in person with other travellers, and participated as a host, a guest and an active researcher in the CouchSurfing network.

Third, mobility may be central to these research practices, but this should not obscure the related immobilities and moorings this method involves. In addition to being virtually and physically mobilized, my research involved moments of stillness, such as sitting behind the computer or sleeping in a CouchSurfer's home. More importantly, the connections and disconnections I explore throughout this book involve both mobilities *and* moorings. Physical and virtual mobilities alike rely on a vast material infrastructure that provides the relatively fixed platform on which bodies and data move – from airports and railways to coaxial cable systems and cellular towers (Hannam, Sheller and Urry 2006; and see Chapter 8). In practice, travel entails constantly relaying between moments of mobility and moments of stillness: being on the road, sleeping in a hostel, walking, stopping, boarding a flight, being stuck in a middle seat, rushing, waiting (Vannini 2009; Bissell and Fuller 2010). Virtual mobilities also reproduce virtual moorings (Paris 2010a). Mobile devices connect travellers back home and travel blogs become a point of stability amidst the motion of travel (Germann Molz 2008). Like Haldrup and Larsen (2010: 50), I recognize that mobile ethnographies must pay special attention to the way tourism performances are 'constructed through routes *and* moorings, connecting home and away as well as physical, object, imaginative, virtual and communicative mobilities'.

Finally, mobile virtual ethnography is reflexive in the sense that mobilities and technologies are not just ways of knowing, but also objects of knowledge (see

Germann Molz 2010). Social media, online networking sites and mobile technologies were the focus of my analysis, but also important tools of the research. The way I connected with travellers or engaged with the field – via the Internet or mobile phone or physical transportation to places – was therefore under just as much scrutiny as the mediated interactions I examined once I was there. Which is not to say that I took 'there' for granted, since the research field itself was constantly on the move.

As I engage it here, mobile virtual ethnography is concerned primarily with understanding the lived practices and social interactions that make up interactive travel. I am also concerned, however, with uncovering the social and cultural meanings, imaginings and understandings that underpin these connections, disconnections, movements and moorings. By following the flows of people, connectivity and communication, I aim to provide a detailed account of mobile sociality as a hybrid phenomenon, afforded not only by the material qualities of mobile technologies but also by the images and discourses through which travellers make sense of these technologies and emerging sociotechnical practices. The interactive travellers we will meet throughout this book are thus situated in complex webs of meaning and practice.

## Connected travellers

The connected travellers I introduce in this book are in a precarious position. On the one hand, they represent the emerging forms of mobile togetherness and separateness that characterize contemporary social life. Travellers, backpackers, and now flashpackers, are particularly salient symbols of the 'new world order of mobility' (Clifford 1997: 1; Richards and Wilson 2004a). On the other hand, to say that interactive travellers are emblematic of modernity and mobility, risks universalizing both tourism and modern subjectivity. In her critique of such broad claims, Kaplan (1996: 63) notes that 'the tourist is as time bound and historically constructed as any other trope' and she advocates against dehistoricizing or romanticizing travel. While the arguments I make in this book are premised on the notion that emerging travel styles are indicative of broader social changes, my intention is not to take the interactive traveller as a figure *par excellence* of modernity, or of the information age. Dann (2002: 12) usefully reminds us that 'not all tourists are identical and hence ... tourists as a metaphor of the social world must be understood as a multiple persona figurative of complex reality'. My goal, therefore, is to describe interactive travel in ethnographic detail, retaining the complexity of people and practices involved while also pointing to the social, historical and technological contingencies that shape these practices.

The people I interviewed and observed in the course of my research – travel bloggers, flashpackers, mobile developers, and CouchSurfers – generally fit the demographic profile identified in other research on tourists, backpackers and interactive travellers (Loker-Murphy and Pearce 1995; Murphy 2001; Sørensen 2003; O'Reilly 2006; Mascheroni 2007; White and White 2007). That is to say, with a few exceptions, the travellers included in my study are white, young, middle-class professionals or students who hold passports from the rich countries of North America and Western Europe. While the relative homogeneity of this group may stem in part from my snowball sampling technique, it more likely speaks to the ways in which race, class and nationality inform the desire to travel the world, enable travellers' access to mobility and shape their communication practices. These travellers may not recognize themselves as part of the global jet-set elite, but they certainly occupy a comfortable corner in the power-geometry of a mobile world (Massey 1993). For the most part, they have control over their own mobility, choosing where to go, when, for how long, and under what circumstances. Their mobility is conditioned by access to material and social resources that inter-active travellers have in ample supply: portable devices, passports, credit cards, and a similarly privileged social network of linked-up friends and family members with whom they can communicate. Furthermore, their ability to be mobile has far-reaching effects for those who are less mobile or whose mobility occurs under more difficult conditions. The 'mobile lives' (Elliott and Urry 2010) of these interactive travellers often relies on the relative immobility or enforced mobility of the people who are resident in – or migrate to work in – the destinations these travellers visit.

As might be expected of individuals with the time and resources to travel for extended periods, the travellers in my study possess high levels of mobility and network capital. If mobility capital refers to the amount of access individuals have to physical and virtual mobility systems, network capital refers to the social currency such mobility generates. Urry (2007: 196) defines network capital as the ability to 'engender and sustain social relations with those people (and to visit specific places) who are mostly not physically proximate, that is, to form and sustain networks'. In other words, Urry continues, 'network capital points to the real and potential social relations that mobilities afford' (ibid.). Urry identifies eight measures of network capital: possession of the appropriate documents (visas, passports, money) that ensure safe movement; friends and acquaintances at a distance who offer invitations and hospitality that make travel possible; the physical capacities to move; access to information anywhere, anytime; communication devices; safe, secure and accessible places to meet; access to multiple mobility and communication systems; and the time and resources to cope with failures of these mobility and communication systems. We might add to this list the element of technological savvy – the know-how required to make mobility and communication systems work to the traveller's advantage.

For the most part, the travellers in my study have ample access to these elements of network capital and, more importantly, are able to maximize their resources in ways that create even more network capital. For example, CouchSurfers with access to the Internet parlay their networking capabilities into invitations and hospitality from other network members to enable extensive travel. Furthermore, the multiple social and digital connections that interactive travellers maintain assume a group of friends, family members and acquaintances who also have high levels of network capital. The forms of togetherness I describe throughout this book rely as well on the privilege of taking these social and digital connections for granted;

travel connections often only become remarkable when they fail. The travellers I profile in this book, therefore, are certainly on the privileged end of global capitalism, possessing not only the material resources needed to travel the world in this way, but also a culturally informed conviction that travelling, connecting, and communicating are desirable and doable practices. As we will see, however, that conviction must be constantly revised and reasserted, especially in light of new technologies whose social uses and implications have yet to be worked out. In this sense, interactive travellers do not just mobilize their network capital in order to travel and connect, but also to define how new habits of travelling and connecting are valued and represented more broadly.

## Between tourism and technology: interactive travel in practice

My objective in this book is not to account for the impacts of technology on tourism, but rather to explore the way togetherness is produced, and precluded, at the fluid intersections between tourism and technology. As I noted in Chapter 1, the empirical context for the project therefore consists of three sites where mobile technologies and online social media become integrated with travel and tourism: (1) mobile mediated urban walking tours; (2) the interrelated practices of travel blogging and flashpacking; and (3) *CouchSurfing.org*, an online hospitality network. I remained committed to examining these three case studies together, even when it meant sacrificing ethnographic depth for breadth, in order to foreground the complexity of practices, discourses, people and technologies that make up interactive travel. One of the benefits of exploring these case studies in tandem is that I have been able to approach questions about 'connecting' from several different perspectives and across different technological registers. As we will see, interactive travellers rarely confine themselves to one technology, one media outlet or one technological practice; instead, they use multiple devices and engage in overlapping practices. For example, many of the travel bloggers I studied are also CouchSurfers; they download travel applications to their mobile phones and take photos with their digital cameras while also using their laptops to upload stories and images to their websites; and they do all of this while on the move with various technologies of transportation.

For nine months during 2009, I conducted intensive fieldwork on these three sites, moving constantly between them. In addition to carrying out an extensive virtual ethnography of the travel blogosphere and doing participant observation as an interactive traveller and CouchSurfer, I also conducted in-depth interviews with forty-nine people, including travel bloggers, CouchSurfers and mobile application developers. In all three cases, my theoretical approach was prompted by the same set of questions about technology, mobility, connectivity and togetherness and my methodological approach was informed by the elements of mobile virtual ethnography I outlined earlier. The particular research techniques I used, however, were specifically suited to the individual case studies and in the following sections, I provide more details about the case study, the respondents, the research design and the methods I applied in each case.

## Mobile mediated walking tours

The first case of interactive travel I examine involves the use of personal portable devices such as iPhones and iPods to deliver mobile mediated urban walking tours in the neighbouring cities of Boston and Cambridge in Massachusetts. With tourism arguably one of the world's largest industries and Internet-enabled mobile phones and personal MP3 devices becoming nearly ubiquitous, it is not surprising that developers and entrepreneurs have sought to capitalize on the travel market for mobile technologies. This move is evident in a recent print advertisement for AT&T and iPhone with a tag line that reads 'Have apps, will travel'. The ad highlights some of the many travel related mobile applications available for iPhone users, including ones for car rental agency Avis, budget airfare finder Kayak, the Zagat restaurant guide, a virtual postcard application called Postman, and Rick Steves' walking tour of Paris. The tours I studied may not have the brand recognition that Rick Steves enjoys, but they are certainly part of a similar innovative impulse to technologically augment tourists' interactions with place. In many ways, these tours and mobile applications overlap with other emerging practices of 'net-locality' (Gordon and de Souza e Silva 2011) both within and beyond tourism. Practices such as geotagging, networked gaming, mobile annotation, location-aware social networking and mobile storytelling are all part of a similar public experiment with the ways technologies can locate users in space, enhance their engagement with places and connect them with one another.

Over the course of six months in 2009, I toured Boston and Cambridge as an interactive traveller. I began this part of the study by travelling regularly into Boston from my home about an hour away. I wandered around the city during the busy spring and summer tourist season. I visited popular tourist areas such as the Freedom Trail, the Boston Common, the North End and Faneuil Hall in Boston, and Harvard Square and the Charles River in Cambridge; that is, until the mediated tours I followed took me off the beaten tourist path, as we will see in the next chapter. Sometimes I travelled on my own; other times I would meet up with a friend, or bring my husband and son along for a family outing. Like the tourists I observed, I took photographs, watched street performers, stopped for coffee, ate lunch in local restaurants and rested under shade trees in the Boston Common. But mostly, I walked. In preparation for my visits to the city, I downloaded tours of Boston and Cambridge to my iPod and my portable GPS device. I also downloaded audio tours onto my BlackBerry, until I switched to an iPhone and was able to download interactive tour applications made available through the App Store. I followed several of these mediated tours, walking around the city for hours at a time. I became intrigued by these tours and the distinct ways in which they sought to position me, as a tourist, in relation to the cityscape.

Several enterprises have emerged in Boston's mobile tour sector and I selected four local companies to study in depth: PocketMetro, Audissey, Untravel Media and Urban Interactive. PocketMetro offers an iPhone application that guides tourists along the Freedom Trail. This application is a virtual edition of the company's popular paperback guidebook, which it sells at a kiosk in the Boston

Common. Audissey offers self-guided narrated tours that travellers can download onto an iPod or smartphone. Untravel Media offers a similar set of audiovisual and interactive tours for phones and iPods that are narrated and scored in a cinematic style. More recently, Untravel Media has also developed location-aware mobile applications to deliver murder mystery and mobile storytelling experiences to pedestrian tourists. Urban Interactive provides location-aware, clue-based adventures that guide tourists through the city. In addition, they offer a mobile platform that allows users to create their own games in the city.

I focused primarily on my own experiences of these tours, engaging methods of 'auto-ethnography' (Butz and Besio 2009) in order to conceptualize my walking practice as both a means and object of knowledge, a point I will return to later. After examining each company's website, I downloaded and followed their tours and mediated adventures on foot. In some cases, I followed the same tour several times to get a sense of the experience and feel out the pace and narrative of the tour. I also recruited a few friends to join me in playing one of Urban Interactive's location-aware urban adventures, 'Guardian of the Relic'. I then analysed each tour and the extensive field notes I kept along the way. Eventually, I conducted in-depth interviews with company executives and mobile developers for three of the companies, PocketMetro, Untravel Media and Urban Interactive. The purpose of these interviews was to understand better how the developers of these tours imagined the possibilities of mobile mediated tourism for connecting tourists to place. With their permission, I use the real names of the companies and these executives in my references to interview and company related data.

Given the centrality of pedestrian movement in this complex interplay of technologies, stories and spatialities, I approached these mediated tours using some of the mobile methods that have been developed around walking. Researchers across disciplines have implemented techniques such as walking interviews (Jones *et al.* 2008), 'walking whilst talking' (Anderson 2004; Moles 2008) and auto-ethnographic walking (Lee and Ingold 2006) to unlock the epistemological potential of walking (Ingold and Vergunst 2008). Ever since the Romantic poets began promoting walking as a reflexive practice (think of Wordsworth wandering through the Lake District lonely as a cloud), walking has been accepted as a way of knowing oneself and encountering the world (Edensor 2000a). Thoughts have a particular pace, according to Solnit, who notes that 'the rhythm of walking generates a kind of rhythm of thinking, and the passage through a landscape echoes or stimulates the passage through a series of thoughts' (Solnit 2001: 5–6). Walking thus spans a series of epistemological possibilities. It can generate thought and prompt self-reflexivity, but it can also provide detailed ethnographic 'insight into the way people and place combine' (Moles 2008: para. 1.1). In fact, Lee and Ingold (2006) have outlined several ways in which walking parallels anthropological fieldwork. They observe that walking requires an attunement to the environment that resonates with ethnographic detail and directness; it allows the ethnographer to engage with the places, 'routes and mobilities of others'; and it is often sociable, producing both a shared rhythm of movement between people and 'an inherently sociable engagement between self and environment' (ibid.: 68). These resonances between walking and fieldwork shaped my walking research as well. I sought to engage with the urban landscape while on the move, alone and with others in an attempt to understand and (re)produce the routes and mobilities of the mediated tours I followed.

In the social sciences, scholars have long understood that walking is more than a way of knowing a place; it is constitutive of space and self (Edensor 2000a; Lorimer 2003; Wylie 2005). The landscape and the walker construct each other. This is certainly the case with urban walking, as de Certeau's work on the practice of everyday life contends. According to de Certeau, walking constitutes the city just as speech acts constitute language; walking is 'a spatial acting-out of the place (just as the speech act is an acoustic acting-out of the language)' (1984: 98). Walking, or 'pedestrian speech acts' as de Certeau puts it, compose the city bringing certain possibilities, but not others, into existence and shaping the way space is traversed and inhabited within the city. Taking de Certeau's point, I observed for example, that face-to-face sociability on the pavement was often precluded by the complicated mix of screens and headphones I was juggling, although these same devices made mediated sociability easier. Which raises an important question: If walking is a way of knowing and producing the city, then what might we make of technologically augmented walking?

In many research accounts, walking only involves portable technologies insofar as they are used to capture the video and soundscapes produced through the walking method. A notable exception is Pink's (2008) method of visual ethnography as a place-making method. In research on the Cittaslow (Slow City) movement in the United Kingdom and related studies, Pink focuses on the way mobility and media practices intersect not only to document people's experiences of place, but to collaboratively produce ethnographic knowledge and visual representations of place. In highlighting the place-making qualities of 'walking with video,' Pink demonstrates how walking, technologies and media can be both means and objects of knowledge. In my study of urban pedestrian tours, 'walking with mobile technologies' enabled me to know the city, but primarily because it was so tightly woven into my performance as an interactive traveller in the city. This doubly mobile method – involving both embodied movement around the city and virtual movement via the mobile devices I carried with me – can best be understood as both capturing *and* creating the hybrid geographies and connections with place that I hoped to investigate. In a very significant sense, I was producing the very phenomena I sought to study.

### Travel blogging and flashpacking

The second case of interactive travel that I explore in the book involves the related practices of flashpacking and travel blogging, two trends that sit squarely at the intersection of tourism and technology. The term 'flashpacking' has two connotations. It refers both to backpackers who travel with ample funds rather than on shoestring budgets and to the tendency for those backpackers to bring digital devices like laptops, digital cameras and mobile phones on their journeys.

A popular practice among flashpackers is to use those electronic gadgets to publish a multimedia travel blog while they are on the road. A travel blog is an online travel journal complete with travel stories, photographs and video that documents travellers' experiences and enables them to share those experiences with friends and family members, other travellers and even strangers they meet online. Even before the term 'blog' had been coined, the first live travel blog, *A Hypertext Journal*, appeared online. Launched in 1996, the website documented the four-week journey of digital artists Nina Pope and Karen Guthrie to the Western Isles of Scotland. Much like travel bloggers today, Pope and Guthrie travelled with a digital camera and a laptop, which they used to share their experiences with an online audience. Those following along, in turn, contributed their own comments and input to the site (Pope and Guthrie 1996). Though the site's layout and navigation feels somewhat cumbersome by today's design standards, that original travel blog contained many of the features that characterize travel blogs today: regularly updated content about the trip, digital photographs, maps, itineraries and interactive features that allowed the travellers and their online audience to communicate with each other throughout the journey.

Since then, however, these elements have become increasingly sophisticated, allowing travellers to post features like location-aware maps and videos. Indeed, in addition to the written text in journal entries, visual images are a vital feature of most travel blogs today (Dann and Parrinello 2007). Many travel bloggers insert photographs and videos into their posts and also provide links to online photo and video sharing sites such as Flickr, YouTube or Vimeo where the online audience can browse extensive albums. In fact, some travel blogs are essentially photo essays, consisting of a series of digital images with brief explanatory captions (and see Nardi, Schiano and Gumbrecht 2004). More and more, these blogs are also converging with other social media formats such as RSS (Really Simple Syndication) feeds, Facebook or Twitter, giving readers several avenues for following the traveller online.

While there are no clear-cut statistics on the number of travel blogs that exist or the number of people who follow them, a few relevant sites provide some sense of the size of the trend. *Travelblog.org*, which claims to be 'one of the most popular travel related web 2.0 sites on the Internet' reports that it has over 200,000 members and hosts over five million photos and more than 600,000 blog entries.[1] *Travelpod.com*, a similar travel blog hosting site, claims that more than 75,000 'travel experiences' from 181 countries are shared on its site in a given week.[2] And *BootsnAll.com*, a website dedicated to budget independent travel, hosts thousands of travel blogs and receives more than three million hits per month.[3] Furthermore, while not all of the travel bloggers in my research sample were willing to share their website statistics with me, those who did indicated staggering audience numbers: hundreds and even thousands of comments posted by readers; thousands of subscribers; and tens of thousands of unique visitors to their sites. Even without quantitative confirmation of the practice of travel blogging as a whole, these statistical snapshots suggest that travel blogging is a significantly popular practice.

Out of this vast travel blogosphere, I selected a sample of forty travel blogs to analyse in depth, focusing primarily on those published by round-the-world travellers. Round-the-world travellers tend to be highly mobile, long-term travellers whose journeys last for several months to a year. Because they are away from home and on the road for an extended period, round-the-world travellers are likely to use mobile technologies and social media to stay in touch with friends and family members back home and elsewhere. In this sense, my sample is not meant to offer a comparison between travellers who use mobile technologies while on the road and those who do not, but rather to offer insight into interactive travellers' strategies and patterns of mobile and mediated togetherness (Mascheroni 2007; White and White 2007).

I used a virtual snowballing technique to compile the research sample (Sanders 2005; Van Den Bos and Nell 2006). This involved following hyperlinks, or the 'blog roll', from one blog to related sites. Starting with *GoBackpacking.com*, a popular blog with a high search engine ranking, I followed links to other round-the-world travel blogs. From there, I continued to follow links from blog to blog until I had compiled a list of hundreds of round-the-world travel blogs. I randomly narrowed the list down to forty travel blogs, some of which documented trips in process and others that were online remainders from recently completed trips. Along with a research assistant, I coded and analysed the content and correspondence from these blogs. The themes from this initial analysis informed the next phase of the research.

From the larger sample, I selected a smaller sample of ten travel blogs documenting current round-the-world journeys. This virtual ethnography involved 'hanging out' online (Kendall 2002), subscribing to blog updates and twitter feeds, following the travel bloggers via their blog postings and online maps, watching videos and browsing photo albums and interacting with the online texts and communities that coalesced around the blogs. In addition, I conducted in-depth interviews with eight of the ten travel bloggers. As the opening vignette to this chapter illustrates, not all of my requests for interviews were successful, nor were my attempts to Skype with travellers. Instead, most of these interviews took place over email or on the phone after the travellers had returned home. With their permission, I use travel bloggers' real names so that interview materials can be associated with their blogs, all of which are online and accessible to the public. However, I have altered or abbreviated identifying characteristics of readers who posted comments on the blogs.

The forty travel blogs in my research sample include seventeen blogs published by solo travellers, eighteen published by friends or couples, and five published by families. In total, these blogs represent seventy-four travellers. The sample represents a diversity of ages (from 4 to mid-50s with an average age of 29) and is evenly split according to gender, but consists overwhelmingly of white, middle-class, Anglophone, middle-class, college-educated travellers. The nationality of travellers is similarly limited, with most bloggers coming from the United States ($n = 64$) and the rest from the United Kingdom ($n = 6$), Canada ($n = 3$) and Australia ($n = 1$). In many ways, the characteristics of my sample are comparable to research on back-packer populations (Sørensen 2003; O'Reilly 2006) and more recent research on flashpackers (Mascheroni 2007; White and White 2007; Paris 2010b). These stud-ies find that, while backpackers are certainly not a homogeneous group, they do tend to share certain demographic features. In line with my sample, the interactive travellers interviewed by Mascheroni (2007) ranged in age from 25–33, had high levels of educational attainment (with many employed as software programmers, webmasters and online journalists) and were evenly split between men and women. These characteristics are reflected in much of the literature on backpackers as well, which reports that backpackers tend to be in their late twenties or early thirties and highly educated. The backpackers in these studies also tend to be Western Euro-pean or North American (though the predominance of US travellers in my sample is uncommon and is likely due to the fact that the source of my snowball sample was a travel blogger from the United States) and 'primarily, though not exclusively, white and middle class' (O'Reilly 2006: 1001).

Flashpackers tend to parallel these backpacker characteristics as well. Hannam and Diekman (2010: 1–2) observe that flashpackers exemplify 'the changing demographics in western societies where older age at marriage, older age hav-ing children, increased affluence and new technological developments, alongside increased holiday and leisure time have all come together'. Sørensen's (2003: 852) description of relatively well-to-do backpackers applies equally well to the flashpackers and travel bloggers in my sample: they are not 'drifters', but rather '(future) pillars of society, on temporary leave from affluence, but with clear and unwavering intentions to return to "normal" life'.

Researchers have documented the difficulties with conducting ethnographies of travellers, and especially backpackers, due to the fluidity of the research field and the ephemeral nature of travel encounters. As Mascheroni (2007: 529) observes, 'backpackers constitute an un-territorialized community characterized by impromptu social interactions'. For Sørensen (2003) and O'Reilly (2006), the lack of a geographically demarcated location or the possibility of ongo-ing, in-depth social interaction with a clearly defined group of individuals defies conventional ethnographic approaches, which rely on continuous observation of a particular community. Studying travel blogs complicates this methodological dilemma in some intriguing ways. On the one hand, as I noted earlier in this chapter, the fluid, ephemeral and dispersed nature of travel encounters is less a methodological obstacle than it is a theoretical focus. It is precisely because trav-ellers do not 'stay put' in any traditional sense that they can be seen as emblematic of shifts in contemporary sociality. On the other hand, travel blogs put an interest-ing spin on the methodological problems Sørensen and O'Reilly identify. Because travellers maintain an online presence via a travel blog, researchers can actually prolong their interaction with a particular group of travellers, similar to the way bloggers can prolong their interactions with one another (Paris 2010a; and see Chapter 4). The travel blog virtually 'moors' travellers, making them available and accessible even while they are on the road.

In addition, travel blogs further extend and complicate the research field. Instead of relying on face-to-face research encounters alone, researchers can now observe travellers in the virtual domains of travel blogs and social media sites. In this sense, the field 'may not be a socially significant physical place at all, but may be more ephemeral', consisting of 'important nodes in the social network' (Howard 2002: 561). As the research field becomes hybrid and fluid, important questions emerge about what kind of data travel blogs are. Travel blogs can be considered from two related perspectives: as diaries and as sites of social interaction. Because blogs take the form of online diaries, researchers can draw on established strategies of diary research to collect narrative data on everyday life. But, blogs are more than narratives or representations; they are interactive stories, social dramas in the making. As Hookway explains, blogs capture a 'tight union between everyday experience and the record of that experience' as it happens, enabling researchers to focus not just on the content of the blog, but also on the immediate and ongoing ' "drama" (Goffman 1959) of everyday interactions, selves and situations' (Hookway 2008: 94). According to Hookway (2008: 96), this focus on the social drama of the blog derives from the notion that, like most diaries, blogs are produced for:

> an implicit, if not explicit, audience. It is this potential presence of an audience and its immediacy to authors that is one of the key ways in which blogs differ from traditional forms of personal diary-keeping – not to mention that blogs enable dialogue and even co-production between authors and readers.

In other words, blogs are not just documentations of daily activities, but rather nodes of social interaction between travellers and their extended social networks in a virtual space.

Indeed, many blog researchers emphasize blogging as a social activity. According to Nardi, Schiano and Gumbrecht (2004: 223), bloggers reach out 'to connect with and insert themselves into the social space of others in their personal social networks'. As they put it, 'blogs create the audience, but the audience also creates the blog ... blogging begets blogging. Or rather, bloggers and readers together beget the social activity of blogging' (ibid.: 224). This happens in several ways:

> Friends urging friends to blog, readers letting bloggers know they were waiting for posts, bloggers crafting posts with their audience in mind, and bloggers continuing discussions with readers in other media outside the blog.... [B]logs [are a] social activity, a form of social communication in which blogger and audience are intimately related through the writing and reading of blogs.
>
> (Nardi, Schiano and Gumbrecht 2004: 224)

From this perspective, travel blogs are not just online diaries, but sites that mediate, mobilize and moor social interactions. Travel blogs are mobile and ephemeral networks constituted by virtual connections and by a series of social relations taking place both explicitly *on* the websites as well as *around* the website. This is the conceptualization of blogs that underpins my analysis of flashpacking and travel blogging. As we will see, I focus less on the narrative or visual content of travel blogs and more on the connections – social and emotional, digital and embodied – that take shape around these sites.

### CouchSurfing

While mobile mediated tours foreground the use of mobile devices in urban tourism, and flashpacking and travel blogging highlight mobile social media practices, my third case of interactive travel, CouchSurfing, reveals the role of online social networking in a travel community. Hospitality exchange networks are online social networking sites that help travellers meet fellow network members willing to host them in their homes for a few nights. The first hospitality network, Servas, was founded in 1949 with the intention of promoting understanding, tolerance and world peace. The Servas network originally consisted of only a few hundred members whose contact details were published regularly in a directory. By the 1990s, once the Internet had made paging through a directory obsolete, several other hospitality organizations began to appear, including CouchSurfing.

*CouchSurfing.org* was originally launched in 2003 by an American web developer named Casey Fenton. Fenton got the idea for the project when he found himself with cheap plane tickets to Reykjavik but with nowhere to stay. Instead of booking a hotel, Fenton used the Internet to spam thousands of students at the University of Iceland hoping one of them would offer him a place to crash for the weekend. Within 24 hours, he had a hundred offers. This experience drew Fenton's attention to the potential of combining social networking with face-to-face hospitality and he soon launched CouchSurfing to help travellers around the world connect with available hosts. The network grew quickly and reached 90,000 members by 2006. But in June of that year, multiple database crashes and the loss of critical data files brought the site down. After failing to revive the system, Fenton sent an email to all of the members informing them that the network would not be rebuilt.[4] What followed was an outpouring of protests from the CouchSurfing community insisting that the website be relaunched. In response, Fenton, along with a handful of other administrators and volunteers, worked around the clock for five days to recover the site (Bialski 2007). Now, CouchSurfing is by far the largest of the online hospitality networks with more than three million members around the world at the time of this writing.

CouchSurfing enables travellers to connect with potential hosts online and, eventually, face-to-face. Through the website, members can search for a host in a particular destination, browse members' profiles to see if what the host has to offer matches what the traveller needs, submit to various security measures intended to maximize the safety of these encounters between strangers, participate in active member discussion boards or join groups based on shared interests. As with other social networking sites, members' profiles are at the heart of the CouchSurfing website. Each member has an online profile with details about their biographical information (age, gender, hometown and education) as well as personal information about their past travel experience, interests and philosophy on life and travel. In addition to describing themselves, members also describe their 'couch' in words and pictures. The 'couch' in CouchSurfing is a metaphor for the hospitality the host is willing to extend. In most cases, this is quite literally a couch in the host's living room where the traveller is welcome to crash for a few nights. Some hosts offer private bedrooms or even access to a guest house, while others may only offer to meet the traveller for coffee or show them around town. The social activities arranged through the site are not limited to hosting travellers. Members of CouchSurfing can join local groups that plan events like happy hours or camping trips where members socialize with their local CouchSurfing community as well as with guests passing through.

A typical CouchSurfing experience involves the traveller searching the website to find a list of available hosts in the destination and then contacting a few hosts with a request to surf with them for a few nights. Hosts and guests can both consult each other's profile pages for more information, and it is common for the traveller and the host to exchange several emails, and maybe even phone calls, as they solidify their plans to meet. Following the visit, both the host and the surfer are expected to log on to the CouchSurfing site again to leave references for each other. The member's profile page displays these references from previous hosts and guests, along with links to the member's friends within the network. References and friend links illustrate how well the member is incorporated into the community and provide further insights into the member's personality. More importantly, these references help to establish an individual's reputation and trustworthiness within the community. As I discuss in more detail in Chapter 5, CouchSurfing is, in effect, a network of strangers and so the technical systems on the website – features that allow members to vouch for one another, to display links to other friends in the network and to publish references for each other – are intended as much to foster security as to facilitate encounters between compatible members.

Although I had been studying the CouchSurfing project since 2005, I did not officially join CouchSurfing until October 2008. This is when my virtual participant observation began. I followed various groups, 'friended' and was 'friended' by people I knew in the network, and corresponded with other members online. Over the course of eight months in 2009, I began actively travelling and hosting as a CouchSurfer. During that time, I had 'ethnographic encounters' with thirty-seven CouchSurfers in Canada, the United States and Italy. In addition, I spoke with a handful of members of another online networking site, Hospitality Club, to understand alternative perspectives on CouchSurfing, some of which were critical of the 'slick' and 'consumerist' layout of CouchSurfing.[5] Many CouchSurfers are identified online by a username and prefer not to share their identifying contact details until they have used the CouchSurfing channels to vet other members. In respect of this fact, the names of the CouchSurfers cited throughout the book have been changed, except where noted in the analysis.

Being an active member of CouchSurfing made it possible to recruit interviewees through the website. I included a brief description of my research on my profile and let potential hosts and guests know that I would be interested in interviewing them. I assembled a convenience sample, beginning with Couch-Surfers I met on a research trip to Montreal and CouchSurfers in my local area in New England. The sample snowballed as many of the local CouchSurfers I interviewed referred me to other CouchSurfers they knew in the area or with whom they had 'surfed' in other states or countries. Throughout that year, as I travelled for personal and professional reasons, I contacted and arranged to meet up with CouchSurfers in each destination. These respondents would also often put me in touch with other local CouchSurfers or network members they had met in other countries. For example, when I travelled to Liguria, Italy, in the summer of 2009, I met up with a CouchSurfer who had also been hosted by a member who hosted me in Montreal.

One of the benefits of constructing my sample by contacting people as I travelled and then branching out into the network from there is that my sample reflects the effects of social networking within the CouchSurfing membership. It is also, for the most part, reflective of the globally privileged position most CouchSurfers occupy. Like me, and like the travel bloggers I interviewed, the people in my CouchSurfing sample tended to be white, educated, middle-class professionals or students from wealthy societies in the global North and West. They also had access to the resources that make leisure mobility possible: passports, credit cards, airline tickets, cars and, of course, the Internet. In this regard, the characteristics of the CouchSurfing community tend to coincide quite closely with the demographics of the travellers I described in the previous section. In many ways, my sample of interviewees is also representative of the broader CouchSurfing membership (see Table 2.1). All of the CouchSurfers I interviewed were from North America or Western Europe, which aligns not only with the trend in backpacker nationalities, but also with the fact that eight of the top ten CouchSurfing countries are in North America and Europe. Though I conducted a handful of interviews in Italian, most of the people I interviewed were Anglophone or Francophone, which also aligns with the fact that more than 90 per cent of CouchSurfers speak English or French as their first language. In other ways, however, my sample diverges from CouchSurfing norms. For example, I interviewed far more women ($n = 25$) than men ($n = 12$), even though there are more men than women subscribed to Couch-Surfing. My sample also included a fairly wide range of ages (from 22 to 62, with an average age of 34), which is considerably higher than the CouchSurfing average age of 28 and contrasts somewhat with the fact that nearly 70 per cent of CouchSurfers are between the ages of 18 and 29.

I use the term 'ethnographic encounter' to describe my exchanges with other CouchSurfers because, although some of the meetings involved fairly formal research interviews, most of them involved being hosted in respondents' homes, hanging out together in restaurants or coffee shops, or taking walking tours of respondents' towns, ranches or farms. The CouchSurfers I contacted often positioned themselves in the role of hosting me, and took it upon themselves to

*Table 2.1* CouchSurfing demographics

| CouchSurfing demographics | Number (%) of CouchSurfers |
|---|---|
| *Top 10 CouchSurfing countries* | |
| United States | 616,474 (20.6) |
| Germany | 283,110 (9.5) |
| France | 258,777 (8.6) |
| Canada | 130,857 (4.4) |
| England | 118,937 (4.0) |
| Italy | 90,245 (3.0) |
| Spain | 89,106 (3.0) |
| Brazil | 81,701 (2.7) |
| Australia | 80,732 (2.7) |
| Poland | 65,819 (2.2) |
| *Most spoken languages* | |
| English | 2,190,590 (73.2) |
| French | 582,946 (19.5) |
| Spanish | 530,386 (17.7) |
| German | 478,375 (16.0) |
| Italian | 156,279 (5.2) |
| *CouchSurfer genders* | |
| Male | 1,491,634 (49.8) |
| Female | 1,280,817 (42.8) |
| Several people | 206,468 (6.9) |
| Unknown | 1 (0.0) |
| *Average age: 28* | |
| Ages 18 to 24 | 1,116,225 (37.3) |
| Ages 25 to 29 | 974,625 (32.5) |
| Ages 30 to 34 | 449,442 (15.0) |
| Ages 35 to 39 | 188,511 (6.3) |
| Ages 40 to 49 | 157,339 (5.3) |
| Ages 50 to 59 | 66,932 (2.2) |
| Ages 60 to 69 | 22,557 (0.8) |
| Ages 70+ | 3,577 (0.1) |

Source: Couchsurfing.org 'Statistics', http://www.couchsurfing.org/statistics.html, site accessed 27 July 2011.

plan local activities or guide me on walks and tours. In this sense, as well, the research process was mobilized and involved quite a bit of 'walking whilst talking' (Anderson 2004). Each meeting was thus a complex hybrid of research and hospitality, a fact that illuminated the extent to which research is often implicated in a similar structure of power as hospitality. The categories of host and guest, researcher and researched, were simultaneously reinscribed and troubled in these encounters.

To a certain extent, the CouchSurfing system itself challenges the dualistic roles of 'host' and 'guest', tending instead toward performances of what Bell (2007, 2011) calls 'hostguesting' or 'guesthosting'. For example, in CouchSurfing, guests often 'host' the host, by preparing meals or helping around the house in exchange for accommodation. Because CouchSurfing operates outside of economic exchange, CouchSurfers are constantly negotiating new terms of exchange, guided primarily by the project's ethos of generosity and mutual support. Where does research fit into an inchoate interpersonal economy such as this, where weighing up what one gives and what one receives from the network is an integral aspect of this sociability? As a researcher, I was simultaneously intrigued and confounded by the ambiguity of this economy, often feeling like an academic 'free-rider' in a network of generosity. I received far more than meals and accommodation out of these encounters, and never quite knew how to repay the material and intellectual hospitality my respondents offered me. Interviewing CouchSurfers, especially in their homes, similarly disrupted the divide between interviewer and interviewee. As I will describe in Chapter 5, CouchSurfing is often an intensely conversational practice, and indeed many meetings that were intended as research interviews unfolded instead as deeply personal conversations, raising ethical considerations about using such intimations as research data.

Not all of these encounters took place in person, however. CouchSurfing is not only a mobile network of travellers, but also a hybrid community that spans both online and offline spaces (Navarette, Huerta and Horan 2008) and an imagined community in which most members will never meet each other, even though they possess a shared sense of membership and destiny (Anderson 1991). As a mobile, hybrid and imagined community, CouchSurfing certainly defies the composition of traditional, place-bound, face-to-face ethnographic communities. Studying it required a combination of the face-to-face and on the move techniques described earlier along with virtual methods. In addition to travelling, surfing, hosting and meeting up with CouchSurfers, therefore, I also spent hours in online participant observation, reading profiles, writing and reading references, linking with friends, interacting with online CouchSurfing groups and forums, and conducting an in-depth analysis of the CouchSurfing website. In this context, mobile virtual ethnography did not just involve following, moving and communicating, but also networking as a way of participating online and in person in the research field. Like the other cases of interactive travel in my study, CouchSurfing poses a challenge to traditional, more sedentary techniques of ethnography. The geographically dispersed, networked and hybrid constitution of the community requires a method that can telescope in to examine localized encounters, but also telescope out to place those encounters in a wider networked context of mobility and online/offline interaction.

## Conclusion

One of the key arguments I make in this book is that mobile technologies and online social media are reconfiguring the central theoretical paradigms in tourism studies. This argument extends to methodological paradigms as well. As technology combines with tourism practices in new ways, tourism researchers must engage mobile methods to follow these emerging patterns of on the move sociability in ways that traditional methods cannot. In this chapter, I have outlined the mobile and virtual ethnographic techniques I used to explore mobile mediated walking tours, flashpacking and travel blogging, and CouchSurfing. Each of these instances of interactive travel requires a new range of methods suited to a research field that is multiple, fluid and hybrid, to communities of travellers that are dispersed and networked, to modes of participant observation that are mediated and mobile, and to the complex interplay of movement and stillness that reflects and produces mobile sociality.

The techniques involved in mobile virtual ethnography are able to account for a research field that is multi-sited, not just across multiple geographic locations, but also across physical and virtual sites. In mobile virtual ethnography, the ethnographic community is similarly imagined as a dispersed, hybrid and, in many cases, imagined community that coalesces around connections and movements rather than around bounded locales. Immersion in these communities of practice thus requires mobilizing techniques of participant observation by following, moving, communicating and networking. At the same time, however, these mobile methods also rely on immobility: immobile infrastructures for transportation and communication; periods of resting with others, not just moving with them; sitting behind a computer or waiting for an email.

Tourism mobilities, mobile technologies and social networking are simultaneously objects of analysis and instruments of research in mobile virtual ethnography. Büscher, Urry and Witchger observe that studying mobilities and mobilizing research techniques is 'not just about how we make knowledge of the world, but how we physically and socially *make the world* through the ways we move and mobilize people, objects, information and ideas' (2010: 14, emphasis added). Mobile virtual ethnography makes visible the way this research 'makes the world' in particular ways. As I moved and communicated with interactive travellers, downloaded mediated tours, hosted CouchSurfers, or followed travel blogs, my research became implicated in the very sociabilities I sought to explore, often in messy and complicated ways. In this sense, mobile virtual ethnography is not just a way of knowing, but constitutes a new empirical realm of social life. This realm of mobile sociality is not confined to interactive travel, but as I will describe throughout this book, interactive travel reveals its defining qualities in both stark and subtle ways. As social life increasingly coalesces around mobility and technology, we will continue to require nimble methods for understanding these emerging patterns of physical, virtual and mediated togetherness.

# 3 Landscape

## Connecting to place, connected places

It is a warm spring afternoon in Boston and I am huddled around a smartphone with two friends. We are secret agents on a mission and the phone is part of the urban adventure game we are playing. The mobile application uses GPS technology to deliver location-specific clues as we race through the city. Our current clue involves the mosaic embedded in the concrete beneath our feet. We are standing in the middle of the pavement on School Street, in front of the historic Boston Latin School and across the street from the famous Omni Parker House Hotel. Commuters, shoppers, school children and other tourists walk briskly past us as we stand there. Our attention is focused on deciphering the clue on our mobile phone so we can move on to the next puzzle and, with any luck, finish the mission ahead of the other teams playing that day. We figure out the puzzle and enter our response into the phone. A few seconds later, our answer is accepted and the next clue is revealed. It leads us toward a statue in the courtyard in front of the school, where we continue the game.

Another clue leads us into a used book shop where we solve a complicated word puzzle and another requires us to stop and study the commemorative brass bricks that dot Winthrop Street, a narrow, cobbled alley in downtown Boston. A guidebook would have pointed out these same landmarks, but the clues buzzing through on our smartphone require us not just to regard these urban elements, but to carefully decipher them and put them in a particular order, all while moving through the city. The information about the city is not on the page, but embedded in the landscape itself and revealed through the location-aware mobile application. Something about the mobile device, the locative media and the real time competition with other teams enables a particular kind of connection, not just with the city, but with each other, with the other teams playing the game, and with the phone itself. Playing the game shapes our embodied performance and paces our mobility through the city in new ways. Instead of prompting us to merely gaze at the city, the game encourages us to puzzle our way through it.

## Introduction

The interactive, location-aware tourist adventure I describe above raises several compelling questions about technology, tourism and place. For example, what is the role of mobile technologies in shaping and mediating the way travellers engage with places? What do these technologically mediated encounters with place entail? And, how are tourists using new technologies to produce places, even as they consume them? To address these questions, I engage in this chapter with one of the key paradigms in tourism studies: landscape. The concept of landscape has been used to make sense of the way travellers envision and embody the places they visit, offering a complex framework for thinking about the overlapping material and symbolic qualities of tourists' connections with place. Spatial metaphors of place and landscape, and the idea that tourism entails the consumption of place, have been central to theories of tourism (Urry 1995; Coleman and Crang 2002). As we will see, landscapes have always been produced and reproduced at the intersection between tourism and technology. Technologies of mobility (such as cars, trains and aeroplanes), technologies of visuality (such as cameras), and, more recently, information and communication technologies (such as mobile phones and social media) enable tourists to access places, but also to produce those places *as* landscapes.

This chapter begins with a description of the historical context in which tourist landscapes emerged, focusing in particular on the relationship between tourists, technologies and places. Next, I describe the blended physical and virtual geographies that interactive travellers move through – and produce. Finally, I present an empirical investigation of the urban adventure game described above, along with three other mobile mediated tourism projects launched in Boston and Cambridge. Electronic guided walking tours delivered on mobile devices enable tourists to move through the physical city and the digital world simultaneously, opening up new ways of navigating, interacting with and learning about the city. As I will describe, these mobile technologies produce a form of 'smart tourism' that enables interactive travellers to connect to places not just as gazing consumers, but also as creative civic subjects.

## From place to landscape

Tourism undeniably revolves around places. It entails moving to, from and between places, and places are in turn shaped and reshaped by flows of tourist mobilities. Questions about where tourists go, why they travel to different places, how places are depicted in glossy brochures or captured in personal photo albums, and how tourist places change over time have inspired a vast literature aimed at making sense of the relationship between tourism and place. Within this literature, the concept of place is both central and contested (see Bærenholdt *et al.* 2004: 4–5). Economic analyses describe tourist places as destinations to be developed, marketed, managed and consumed (Hall and Lew 2009) while environmental approaches see tourist places as fragile eco-systems that simultaneously appeal to tourists' desires to get close to nature and yet must be protected from the impacts of tourism development (McLaren 2003). Social and cultural analyses of place have been less concerned with the economic and environmental impacts of tourism and have focused, instead, on the visual imagery of tourist places, including the markers, sights, discursive texts and tourist mythologies that can be decoded and consumed by tourists (Urry 1990, 1995; Shields 1991; Selwyn 1996; MacCannell 1999[1976]). With its focus on imagery, photography and sightseeing, this approach often privileges the visual over embodied and multi-sensory performances of places. In response to this 'hegemony of vision', another approach to tourist places has recently emerged that turns the emphasis less toward 'seeing' and more toward 'doing' (Bærenholdt *et al.* 2004: 5). This 'performance turn' in tourism studies seeks to understand tourist places neither as static locations nor as cultural imaginaries, but as fluid sites of practice and performance (Edensor 2001; Coleman and Crang 2002; Sheller and Urry 2004; Haldrup and Larsen 2010; and see Chapter 8). In other words, tourist places are not inert containers for tourist activity, but rather fluid, contingent and dynamic 'stages' that are mutually productive of, and constituted by, tourists' embodied performances.

Despite their different ontological assumptions, all of these approaches share my concern with understanding how tourists, technologies and places are interconnected, a concern that many tourism scholars address through the concept of landscape. The conceptual resonance of landscape stems, in part, from the fact that it simultaneously entails both the symbolic and the material qualities of place (Cosgrove 1998; Ingold 2000). In this sense, landscape entails a paradox, one that Minca (2007: 433) describes as its ability 'to refer to both an object and its description; to recall, at once, a tract of land and its image, its representation'. Add to this the fact that landscape often serves as a metaphorical stage for tourist performances, and we begin to see how the concept of landscape captures the complex interplay between tourists and places:

> On the basis of its imageability and tangible, experiential character, landscape constitutes a most significant geographical medium in the analysis of relationships that develop between tourist and visited location. Its easy and ready accessibility, as well as its representational and relational properties, render landscape both a veritable stage for play and recreation and a valuable means and tool of analyzing geographical change through tourism.
>
> (Terkenli 2004: 339)

Thinking of tourist places in terms of this complex metaphor of landscape, many theorists have emphasized the overlapping practices of seeing *and* doing, envisioning *and* inhabiting, and representing *and* performing that are also central to the technologically mediated encounters with place that I describe in this chapter.

Landscapes are as much techno-social accomplishments as they are physical environments. Imagining landscapes, embodying and moving through them, and picturing and reproducing them, almost always involves some kind of technological practice. The very ability to apprehend a tract of land *as* 'scenery' relies on a complex assemblage of bodies and machines. Much of the scholarship to this effect has focused on technologies of mobility and visuality, or what Larsen (2001) refers to as 'mobility machines' and 'vision machines'. Starting with Schivelbusch's (1986) account of the spatial and visual effects of rail travel in the nineteenth century, we see how moving and viewing intersected to produce the landscape and certain ways of seeing it. It is notable that around the same time that trains began speeding across England, the camera obscura was invented, transforming the tourist gaze into a 'photographic gaze' that captured the landscape in new ways (Larsen 2001: 86). Framing the landscape in terms of appropriate views was not new to rail travel and photography; indeed tourists had long used sketchbooks and Claude glasses to create and consume the picturesque (Ousby 1990; Buzard 1993). By the late 1800s, however, moving at speed via rail coupled with photographic techniques to produce new technologically enhanced aesthetics of, and encounters with, landscapes.

Like the camera's lens, the train window, and later the car windscreen, 'facilitate[d] *and* impose[d] distinct technologically mediated and framed ways, even techniques, for seeing the "exterior" world' (Larsen 2001: 88). These techniques for envisioning the landscape marshalled the physical environment into a visually consumable entity while simultaneously producing the tourist as a mobile viewing subject. The technologically mediated relationship between tourists and landscapes that emerged at the turn of the last century was a very specific one. According to Larsen (ibid.: 89), these ways of seeing imputed 'control and possession of a distanced landscape with a detached look' and were powerfully emblematic of 'modern ideas about the subordination of nature as landscape, the privileging of "seeing" over the other senses, and not least the power of the observer over the perceived'. The 'landscape idea', as a way of seeing and inhabiting the material environment, was thus born out of a particular arrangement of mobilities and technologies, cultural production and material practice and human interactions with place (Cosgrove 1998: 2).

From this historical perspective, technologies of mobility (trains and cars) and visual technologies (cameras and windscreens) appear to have mediated the relationship between tourists and places in terms of mastery, detachment and visual consumption rather than in terms of embodying and inhabiting the landscape. The contours of this relationship were shaped not only by new technologies that allowed tourists to move at speed or to capture the scenery in a photograph, but also by a social and cultural climate that included the anxieties of the Romantics over encroaching technologies, and the aspirations of the Futurists who celebrated new machineries of speed. In other words, the possibilities that those new technologies afforded tourists for connecting to, or disconnecting from, the landscape were also socially and culturally shaped. Landscapes are infinitely mutable phenomena, and perhaps one of the reasons landscape has persisted as a key unit of analysis in tourism studies is because the material, symbolic and ideological dimensions of tourist landscapes are such vivid reflections of the social world more broadly. It is important to keep this in mind as we consider how contemporary travellers use mobile communication technologies and online social media to engage with places and landscapes today. How are travellers' encounters with place mediated not only by the portable digital technologies they carry with them, but also by our contemporary hopes and fears about what those technologies do to our sense of place and our orientation to the world around us?

## Tourist landscapes as blended geographies

Although landscapes have always been mediated by techniques of seeing and technologies of mobility and representation, we still know relatively little about how portable digital technologies shape the way tourists move through, imagine and connect to places. In order to understand the way travellers interact with places, it is necessary to consider the ways in which new technologies transform, and in some cases transcend, space and place. In the late 1990s, theorists committed a considerable amount of time and effort to understanding the way new transportation and communication technologies reconfigure the spatial parameters of social life, using concepts like 'time-space compression' and 'deterritorialization' to describe new patterns of sociality. Thanks to relatively cheap and accessible modes of international transportation, and even cheaper and more accessible modes of global communication, social networks stretched across space, friends on opposite corners of the world could be instantly 'together', and distance could be both transcended and redefined. At the end of the twentieth century, the metaphor of a shrinking planet and the idea that social and economic relations were becoming detached from localities captured the *zeitgeist* of a globalizing world. Not only did the world seem to be getting smaller, but common logic also suggested that the more social relations revolved around moving and communicating at a distance, the less places themselves seemed to matter. We are left instead, according to this argument, with a sense of 'placelessness' (Relph 1976), the proliferation of 'non-places' (Augé 1995) and the 'death of distance' (Cairncross 1997).

At the heart of these critiques was an anxious assumption that new technologies would disorient and disconnect us from place. We know now, however, that these proclamations of the death of distance were premature. Even as our social lives have become saturated with mobile communication technologies, distance and place continue to matter. In fact, recent studies of mobile communication technologies suggest that place and location have become more, not less, important in everyday social interactions (Gordon and de Souza e Silva 2011; Sutko and de Souza e Silva 2011). Place does not cease to matter, but it may be the case that it now matters in very different ways. This is equally true in the context of tourism. Even in an age of virtual travel, tourists still desire to encounter places in the flesh, and to encounter one another *in* places. However, tourist places are now more than physical locations. They are networked and hybrid environments that can be encountered simultaneously through bodies-in-places and via mediating technologies like mobile smartphones and social media platforms.

The proliferation in the material world of points of access to virtual and communicative spaces has significant consequences for the way we understand place:

> The wireless world completely changes the relationship between the user's place and the virtual place. Gateways to a virtual place were previously bound to the home or the office, but they can now move around with the individual. To put it another way, the gateway to a virtual place has been made

omnipresent ... and it can be entered anywhere. Given these circumstances, surely people's understanding of 'place' will change.

(Kohiyama 2005)

For Kohiyama, all geographies – not just tourism geographies – are now characterized by this overlap between material and virtual worlds. But what are the sociological implications of this overlap specifically in the context of tourist places and tourism mobilities? For one thing, tourist places are now likely to be hybrid assemblages of physical and virtual environments in which bodies, technologies, virtualities and materialities become entangled with one another. In this chapter, I use the term 'blended geographies' to get at the specific ways in which digitized narratives, sounds, information and images are blended into the material environment in these hybrid spaces. This blending of the digital with the physical entails new possibilities for connection and disconnection, and these are the possibilities I explore in my analysis of the mediated urban walking tours.

As digital and mobile technologies now saturate the cityscape, many artists, scholars, designers and developers have tried to articulate the new possibilities these technologies open up for socializing, inhabiting, touring and knowing in the city. Over the past decade, numerous artists have experimented with digital technologies and locative media in urban spaces. Around 2003, there was a proliferation of performance installations, tourism prototypes and public art projects like the *Yellow Arrow Project* in New York (Kottamasu 2007), *[murmer]* in Toronto (Kottamasu 2007), *Urban Tapestries* in London (Lane 2003; Jungnickel 2004), *History Unwired* in Venice (Epstein, Garcia and dal Fiore 2003) and *Mobile Bristol* (Williams *et al.* 2002; and see Hein, Evans and Jones 2008). These projects all explored how new technologies might enable collaborative knowledge and enhance mobile social interaction in the city. Due, in part, to the constraints posed by the telecommunications infrastructure, particularly in the United States, many of these projects were highly localized and short-lived. More recently, however, the introduction of the iPhone and its user-friendly App Store has fuelled another burst of development in location-based gaming and social networking in urban spaces. This innovation includes tourism applications that utilize the iPhone's location-aware capabilities to guide tourists through the city. Many of these projects have been designed to annotate places in the city with digital stories, sounds or information that can then be accessed by others through mobile devices. At the same time, they help to reconfigure urban geographies into narrative, informational and connected landscapes that seem qualitatively different from the old 'analogue' cityscape. What these projects have been experimenting with, and what urban studies scholars and tourism researchers alike have tried to describe, are the new kinds of geographies, subjectivities and socialities that emerge when digital technologies and locative media intersect with the physical city.

Digital technologies have become so deeply embedded in the urban landscape, and so densely woven into practices of dwelling in and moving through the city, that we apparently now need a new conceptual lexicon to describe the city itself.

De Souza e Silva has written about the city as a 'hybrid space' (2006) while others refer to the 'sentient city' (Shepard 2011), the 'mobile city', the 'network city' or the 'mediapolis' (see de Waal 2007). Aurigi and De Cindio (2008) describe the 'augmented city' and 'augmented urban spaces', referring in part to what others have described as the 'layering' or 'superimposition' of information and media onto the physical environment of the city (Manovich 2006; Allen 2008). What these terms aim to capture is a sense of the city as a simultaneously physical, electronic and interactive entity. As de Souza e Silva (2006: 265) puts it, these terms refer to 'a conceptual space created by the merging of borders between physical and digital spaces … built by the connection of mobility and communication and materialized by social networks developed simultaneously in physical and digital spaces'.

In tourism studies, a similar struggle has been underway to find the words to describe emerging tourism geographies. In the growing body of scholarship on electronic guidebooks, for example, researchers describe how the use of new mobile technologies transforms museum spaces and cultural heritage sites into 'media spaces', 'mixed reality', 'augmented reality' or 'hybrid' environments (Woodruff *et al.* 2001; Aoki *et al.* 2002; Heath *et al.* 2002; Brown *et al.* 2003; Heath and vom Lehn 2010). The concept I introduce here, 'blended geographies', aims to contribute to this terminology a sense that tourist places – including, but not limited to, specific tourist attractions like museums – must be understood as overlapping material and virtual sites. In related tourism contexts, researchers have also described a kind of narrative or fictional space that is produced by mobile technologies (Dow *et al.* 2005; Kjeldskov and Paay 2007; Epstein 2009a). Of particular interest is Epstein's (2009a: 1) neologism 'terratives', which refers to 'stories told on mobile devices in tandem with real places and people'.

Travel journalists have also tried to make sense of this intersection between mobile technologies, locative media and the city. In June 2009, the travel magazine *Condé Nast Traveler* (2009) featured an article titled 'Get Smart?' that followed three travellers as they visited Moscow. Two of the travellers were armed with smartphones – one with an iPhone and the other with a BlackBerry – while a third explored the city with nothing but a guidebook. In January of the following year, the magazine *Budget Travel* published a similar article titled 'The Connected Traveler' (Cohen 2010) which followed one traveller with a BlackBerry and an iPod – but no guide book – as she explored Istanbul. These articles wanted to see what kinds of encounters with the city different technologies might produce. Indeed, it is difficult to pinpoint exactly what makes this urban space unique, especially from a tourism perspective. After all, tour guides and guidebooks have been providing information about places and orienting the tourist gaze for centuries. What makes a tour delivered on an MP3 player or navigated via a smartphone any different? The idea behind these articles was, as the *Budget Travel* article put it, to 'test the limits' of social media and mobile applications 'in a foreign land' (Cohen 2010: 55). The idea that we are in this testing phase suggests that the social and spatial meanings and uses of mobile technologies must still be open to question.

Relevant to new kinds of social and spatial possibilities that are opened up by new technologies is another spatial metaphor in tourism studies, the 'pleasure periphery'. The 'pleasure periphery', introduced in Turner and Ash's 1975 book *The Golden Hordes*, is by now a classic metaphor in tourism studies. As a geographical concept, the pleasure periphery refers to those areas that lie outside the developed tourist belt – peripheral locations with undeveloped transportation routes and few tourist facilities (Turner and Ash 1975: 11). The notion of the 'pleasure periphery' also refers to tourists' seemingly insatiable desire to go beyond where other tourists have already gone – to visit the most remote villages, climb the highest mountains, trek across inhospitable landscapes or perhaps launch into space. Interactive travel redefines the pleasure periphery by shifting what counts as a site of exploration from exclusively physical sites to hybrid sites. The intersection between the material environment and mobile technologies has become a new pleasure periphery for tourists to test and explore. This new frontier is not merely a figment of cyberspace, but rather of the blended virtual-material geography of interactive travel, which is defined not by the limits of Cartesian space or the outposts of tourist facilities, but in terms of coverage and access to virtual and communicative realms. In a world already painstakingly charted and made visible in an era of total surveillance, the thrill of exploration is in navigating old places through new technologies. As Kirschenblatt-Gimblett (1998: 171) notes, we increasingly 'travel to actual destinations to experience virtual places. This is one of several principles that frees tourism to invent infinite new products'. The pleasure periphery is refreshed and the novelty of exploration reinvented as digital worlds combine with the physical one.

Researchers and designers agree that something *is* qualitatively different about inhabiting these blended urban geographies. There is something about the locative, interactive, immediate, immersive and informational potential of these mobile technologies that seems to have fundamental effects. While the vocabulary for describing the effects of mobile technologies in urban tourism spaces remains tentative, these attempts to redefine the city have at least two things in common. First, they all acknowledge that mobile technologies – from digital cameras to smartphones, GPS devices and MP3 players – have shifted our understanding of the city from a physical space to a blended space where the digital and virtual worlds of information, media and narrative are inseparably woven into the physical landscape of the city, resulting in a physical landscape that is dense with layers of information and media. Second, they all suggest that this new urban geography is emerging alongside new forms of subjectivity, identity, sociality, citizenship, knowledge and dwelling in the city. As Aurigi and De Cindio (2008: 1) put it, 'concepts such as public space and "third place," identity and knowledge, citizenship and public participation are all inevitably affected by the shaping of the reconfigured, augmented urban space'. What appears to be at stake, according to these scholars, is our sense of attention to – or detachment from – people and places; our modes of socializing and the potential for new forms of sociality with friends and strangers; our strategies for navigating and moving through the city, from a digital as well as an embodied perspective; the potential for civic action in the city; and our ways of knowing the city. I pick up on some of these themes in the following analysis of mediated urban walking tours and smart tourism. I describe the way mediated tours and tour developers imagine the urban environment not just as a landscape for visual consumption, but as an embodied knowledge landscape and site of civic participation. In this sense, I focus less on the way these applications orient the tourist gaze and more on the embodied performances and tourist epistemologies imagined in these projects. As we will see, smart tourism is a multi-sensuous, intelligent, sociable and, in some cases, potentially more sustainable encounter with the landscape.

## Walking in the augmented city

The four companies I profile in this analysis all offer mobile mediated guides and interactive games on iPods and smartphones for pedestrian tourists in Boston and Cambridge. Both cities are relatively small, pedestrian-friendly destinations. Boston is among the most popular tourist destinations in the United States, welcoming around twenty million visitors per year. Cambridge, just next door and home to Harvard University and the Massachusetts Institute of Technology (MIT), is a hub of technological innovation. These elements converge to make the area an ideal location for small companies to experiment with mobile technologies and walking tourism in the city. My research focused on four companies in the mediated walking tour sector: PocketMetro, Audissey, Untravel Media and Urban Interactive. These companies offer a variety of digital products including digital audio and video guides that tourists can download onto their mobile phones or MP3 players, location-aware tours that use GPS capabilities to deliver location-specific information to a smartphone, and, in the case of Urban Interactive, 'augmented urban adventures' that guide tourists through the city by way of a series of puzzles and clues that users solve and submit via an iPhone. As I noted in Chapter 2, I studied each company's website, followed and analysed their tours, and conducted in-depth interviews with executives from PocketMetro, Untravel Media and Urban Interactive.

There has long been a special relationship between cities and walking. When the city entered the popular imaginary at the turn of the last century as a site for tourism, walking became not just a mode of transit, but also a mode of experiencing, consuming and knowing the city. According to de Certeau (1984), the city and walking are mutually constituted. He argues that walking composes the city, bringing certain possibilities, but not others, into existence thus shaping the way urban space is traversed and inhabited. As I noted in the previous chapter, recent work suggests that walking is constitutive not only of place, but also of self (Edensor 2000a; Lorimer 2003; Ingold 2004; Wylie 2005) and that walking is a way of knowing (Solnit 2001). According to these perspectives, walking enables certain spaces, identities and knowledges to emerge. If walking is a way of producing, consuming and knowing the city, then how might walking, coupled with interactive mobile technologies, produce the urban landscape in particular ways? Starting with PocketMetro, the following sections introduce salient extracts from my field notes and interviews to address this question before I offer some reflection on the wider implications of these projects.

## PocketMetro

PocketMetro offers an iPhone application that allows tourists to access location-specific information about key spots along the historic Freedom Trail in Boston. According to the company website, PocketMetro provides everything pedestrians need 'to explore all of Boston and Cambridge, especially the Freedom Trail and the many shops and restaurants that makes them great cities to explore by foot'.[1] On its website, PocketMetro promises an 'off-the-beaten track' experience and access to 'hidden landmarks, tucked-away architectural sites, and one-of-a-kind shops and restaurants'. It turns out that all of the tours I studied promise a similar experience.

Originally delivered on a proprietary GPS device that tourists could rent while they were in Boston, PocketMetro's Freedom Trail tour is now available as a downloadable iPhone application that tourists can download directly to their own phones. The application provides an interactive version of PocketMetro's popular paper guidebook, *The Walker's Guide to the Freedom Trail*, which retails for US$10 from the company's kiosk in the Boston Common. The route can be followed in a linear manner, or tourists can click links on a map to access informational highlights in an *ad hoc* manner as they wander through the city. I trialled the application shortly after it was released for the iPhone. Users first choose the language they prefer (English, French or Spanish) and then click on a map depicting an outline of the Freedom Trail. Along the trail are numbered points of interest, including Paul Revere's House and the site of the Boston Massacre. Users can click through for a detailed description of each point.

When we met at his Cambridge office, PocketMetro's president and CEO, Simon Dao, explained that he has bigger plans for the application, envisioning PocketMetro's Freedom Trail tour less as a scripted guide and more as a walking companion that uses location-aware technology to highlight other nearby attractions, shops and restaurants. Eventually, the application will also provide interactive links to user reviews of these shops and restaurants that tourists can access as they move through the city. Plans are also underway to allow tourists to buy tickets for harbour cruises and theatre productions through the application (Lamb 2009). The company's original website, which is now defunct, also included links to marketing brochures detailing how the application can help drive foot traffic to local shops and businesses. As such, the product appears to be aimed not just at tourists, but also at local commercial stakeholders. In this sense, PocketMetro's application appeals to commercial ambitions, using the interactive narrative platform to deliver advertisements to consumers and to deliver consumers to nearby restaurants and shops.

## Audissey

Audissey, a Boston-based media company established in 2005, bills itself as 'a new breed of self-guided tours for iPods and Smart Phones' that 'launch travelers off the beaten path – and into the soul of a city'.[2] In addition to Boston, the company provides downloadable walking tours of several other cities, including Houston, Miami, Chicago and Washington, DC. These guides are scripted, narrated excursions that lead the tourist by the ear, so to speak, on a walking tour of the city. The website and the tours themselves emphasize the idea that these tours can provide a local perspective and insider access to the city. In fact, the site promises to reveal 'a side of Boston most tourists never get to see'.

The company's name, a clever combination of 'audio' and 'odyssey', suggests that tourists' experiences of the city are not organized just through gazing, but also through hearing. These tours combine gazing and listening to produce what Bull (2000) refers to as 'auditory looking', a gaze constituted through personalized sound. To experiment with this form of auditory looking, I followed several of Audissey's Boston walking tours, including the downtown Boston tour and a tour of the Boston Public Garden. Audissey also offers tours of Boston Harbour and the Fort Point Channel Neighbourhood, all funded by The Greater Boston Convention & Visitors Bureau and free to download. The company has recently been repositioning itself as a mobile media company. Like PocketMetro, Audissey has plans to integrate location-aware features into a mobile platform that allows tourists to access on-demand content about places and that can use emerging mobile advertising networks to deliver advertisements to tourists' iPhones while they tour the city.

For the downtown Boston tour, I went to the corner of Park and Tremont Streets and turned on my iPod. I was greeted by the narrator, Rob Pyles, who is also Audissey's founder. He introduced himself in a thick Boston accent, 'I live around here and grew up around here. . . . I'm going to take you through my own personal Boston. Down secret alleyways and cobblestone roads . . . You've got a friend that you're travelling with now'. In an interview published online, Pyles explains that he got the idea for Audissey in 2000 while hitchhiking through the Irish countryside (Holt 2007). He ran across a crumbling castle and was eager to know more about the ruin, but he had no way to uncover the castle's story. For Pyles, 'It was frustrating because you knew these places had incredible stories, but you had no way to connect with them' (Holt 2007). He launched Audissey guides to allow tourists to access a city's unique, yet invisible, stories. While making these hidden stories of the city visible to the tourist, Audissey simultaneously claims to make the tourist less visible. The website suggests that with an iPod in my ear rather than a guidebook in my hand, I will be able to camouflage my status as a tourist. Discreet earbuds and a knowing voice in one's ear replace telltale maps and guidebooks, allowing tourists to *look* like tourists without looking *like* tourists. Just as the tour reveals secret or unnoticed aspects of the city, at the same time it helps the tourist move inconspicuously through the city.

Many researchers have noted that travellers are increasingly using portable MP3 players while they travel, which suggests that the auditory sense plays an important role in interactive travellers' experiences of space and place. According to Burns and O'Regan (2008), the use of personal MP3 players may have the effect of disconnecting tourists from their local surroundings or ensconcing them in their own personal soundtracks. Indeed, the original soundtrack and intimacy of the narrator's voice in my ear created an immersive environment that seemed to disconnect me from my surroundings, including the people around me. One journalist blogging about Audissey's Chicago tour even commented that with your iPod and an Audissey tour, you will not need actual friends anymore to show you around the city (Glavinskas 2008). At the same time, however, the tour connected me to the augmented city, revealing stories and histories that would otherwise be unavailable to an unequipped pedestrian. This dialectic of connecting and disconnecting – to places and to people – was a recurring theme in this and the other tours.

The garden tour I followed was also narrated by a local resident, Henry Lee, President of Friends of the Boston Public Garden. In a similar tone to Pyles, he informed me that I would 'hear little known stories' and get 'privileged access into the soul of the Boston Public Garden'. The tour creates this sense of privileged access in part by including commentary from famous locals, such as the late Senator Ted Kennedy and children's author Nancy Schön, and narrating an otherwise invisible history of the park. In my experience, both tours also encouraged an embodied connection to place. The goal is to involve tourists in their surroundings; as Pyles comments, 'It's definitely not a passive experience' (Holt 2007). The narrators constantly oriented my body and gaze: 'Go left. Start walking now.' 'You should now be standing before the pagoda tree.' 'Now look across the street at the building with the flags on it.' 'Climb down those stairs and turn left.' 'Don't get hit crossing the street!' At one point on the Boston Public Garden tour, I was encouraged to literally stop and smell the roses. Like the other tours I will discuss later, the Audissey tours were not meant to be merely digital or virtual experiences. Instead, they aimed at connecting the embodied tourist to the place by encouraging the listener to touch, smell and feel the city.

This embodiment relates to the immersive sensibility that the tours aim to create. According to Audissey's website, 'local narrators, sound effects and original soundtracks make the experience like walking through a virtual movie'. The company's marketing director, Juliet DeVries, commented in an article in the *Boston Business Journal* that the tours are like 'a cinematic experience, where people are walking through scenes. This is so much more emotional than somebody just spewing facts' (Lamb 2009). On its website, Audissey's mission for the garden tour is described like this: '[T]o create an emotional experience that would connect visitors to the Public Garden'. Indeed, one striking aspect of the tour of the Public Garden is its emotional appeal to tourists' civic sensibilities. In the last part of the tour, the soundtrack turns ominous as the narrator claims that, while it may not look like it, this park is actually a battleground. Lee explains how a group of everyday Bostonians, with few resources, fought plans to build skyscrapers adjacent to the park. He encourages me to look up, past the trees, to imagine where the proposed skyscrapers would have been, blocking sunlight to the park (see Figure 3.1).

He continues, 'The darkness, the winds, it would have destroyed this garden. It's quite nearly a biblical image, being cast out of the garden by our own greed and ignorance, a paradise lost'. He concludes by linking this story to a broader

*Figure 3.1* Listening to Audissey's Boston Public Garden tour.

agenda for urban public space, 'Public welfare must triumph over corporate greed. The Boston Public Garden ... belongs to all of us ... it is a part of the collective soul of the people of Boston'. The tour ends with this plea to understand and appreciate the park's vulnerability as a public space and its civic significance to the community, as well as to the cityscape. Similar appeals to 'insider knowledge' and 'civic sensibilities' also feature in the tours offered by Untravel Media.

### Untravel Media

Untravel Media, another Boston-based company offers interactive mobile audio and video tours of Boston and Cambridge. Similar to Audissey, Untravel Media aims to bring spatial stories to life and reveal hidden narrative landscapes of the city. After helping to develop *History Unwired*, a mediated walking tour of Venice, CEO Michael Epstein, a graduate of MIT, launched Untravel Media in Boston in 2006. I met Epstein at the company's small office in a Beacon Hill brownstone building. It was a warm afternoon, so we decided to sit outside in a walled courtyard adjacent to the office. As we talked, Epstein described how he brings his interest in mobile storytelling to bear on the production of Untravel Media tours, using the term 'terratives' (2009a) to describe the way stories are attached to places. Inspired by documentary filmmaking, Epstein seeks ways of prodding people off of their couches and into the urban spaces where these stories unfold. In addition to guided tours around areas of Boston and Cambridge, Untravel Media has developed several other tours, including a tour of the West End called 'The Greatest Neighborhood this Side of Heaven', and a mobile audio guide for visitors to the New England Aquarium. In the autumn of 2009, the company released its first GPS-based iPhone application, 'Walking Cinema: Murder on Beacon Hill', an adaptation of a PBS (Public Broadcasting Service) documentary about an infamous murder that took place in Boston in 1849.

According to the website, the company aims to 'connect people', 'engage people with stories, places, and issues', 'expose people to new things, places and opportunities', and 'provoke reaction and raise awareness about the world'.[3] I followed these mobile stories in two tours, one titled 'Boston's Little Lanes and Passages' and the other titled 'Beyond the Yard' in Cambridge. Using my iPod's video and audio capabilities, I followed the narrator's walking directions, shifting my gaze from the iPod screen to the cityscape around me and back, while simultaneously listening to the accompanying soundtrack.

Echoing the cinematic aesthetic of the Audissey tours, the Untravel Media tours were immersive audiovisual experiences of the city. As in a movie theatre, I felt myself caught up in the stories unfolding in my ear. For example, I stood in the doorway of Christ Church in Cambridge as the church archivist described an angry mob gathering outside in 1778. Sounds of gunshots and people yelling accompanied her story. Then, inside the quiet and empty church, the voice of the church's organist directed me to notice the organ at the front of the church. As I looked at it, organ music filled not the air, but my ear. Toward the end of the tour, back near Harvard Square, the narrator described the myriad of local people, shops, culture and perspectives with the sound of chattering and traffic in the background. Losing myself in the audio environment of the tour disconnected me to some extent from the urban soundscapes around me. At one point, I had to pull out my earbuds to determine whether the sirens I heard were real or part of the soundtrack.

Epstein is fully aware of this effect. He comments in his blog that 'we struggle with the isolating effect of our tours because they just demand headphones. Sure it's our aim to make stuff that blends, enhances, and gets you more into your surroundings, but the headphones cut you off from stuff' (Epstein 2009b). He worries that the design of the mobile device – smartphones or MP3 players that require individual headphones – puts travellers in a bubble and undermines Untravel Media's vision of 'insider' and 'sensitive' experiences of the city (see Bull 2004). Possible solutions to this disconnect, he notes, include building breaks into the narrative or requiring users to take off the headphones at various points on the tour. He has implemented some of these solutions into the 'Murder on Beacon Hill' application where travel companions are required to collaborate with one another and with shopkeepers and hotel concierges along the route.

In both Untravel Media tours, I found myself directed to something hidden, invisible, or seemingly inaccessible. For example, in Christ Church, the narrator told me where to find some bullet holes from that night in 1778 hidden behind a door. I searched for and touched the place in the wall where the bullet holes remain today. The Cambridge tour also took me through a secret garden path behind the Repertory Theatre and in Boston, the 'Little Lanes' tour encouraged me to walk behind buildings and down narrow alleys that, under normal circumstances, I would have actively avoided. Epstein explained in our interview that one of the goals of his tours is to 'get people, in their own ways, to look differently at the environment around them'. This can re-animate the pleasure periphery by layering it with otherwise unknown stories, histories and information, or it can involve leading tourists off the beaten path altogether.

As the titles of the tours – 'Beyond the Yard' and 'Little Lanes and Passages' – suggest, the routes are designed to guide walkers away from densely touristed spots like Faneuil Hall or the Boston Common. In fact, during our interview Epstein explained that redirecting the flow of pedestrian traffic was one of the key objectives of the mediated walking tour he helped develop for Venice, 'You've got environmental stress in Venice that comes from a groove that's been carved out between the Rialto Bridge and St. Mark's Square, where most of the tourism concentrates. So if you can disperse that tourism, you can relieve some of the stress on a somewhat fragile structure of the city'. Redistributing the flow of tourist pedestrian traffic helps ease the burden of tourism in more famous areas, like St. Mark's Square in Venice or Harvard Square in Cambridge, and brings attention to less-well-known sights and spaces in the city. Epstein imagines technology's potential to veer tourists away from well-trodden routes, reveal hidden places and recount forgotten stories. Dispersing tourists throughout a city may solve some problems, but it raises others. The more widely and unpredictably tourists move through the city, the more local residents may find their everyday routines disrupted or their private spaces breached by curious tourists.

The vision Epstein holds for Untravel Media's urban tours also involves the possibility of raising awareness and promoting civic action. He explained:

> I think ultimately what we want to do more and more with our story telling is allow people to dig into the issues of places; the key issues that are sometimes pretty harsh and sometimes uncomfortable, and allow them in some way – through conversation, or donations or physical activities – to help with those problems.
>
> (Interview transcript)

This civic sensibility underpins a tour of Boston's West End that Untravel Media developed. The tour, titled 'The Greatest Neighborhood this Side of Heaven', walks tourists through a neighbourhood transformed by urban renewal policies. The tour tells the story of the forced displacement of 12,000 Boston residents from the culturally rich West End in the late 1950s to make room for skyscrapers. Former residents, along with historians, architects and government officials, help to tell the story. Epstein explains that the story of this urban planning disaster could be told in documentary film form, but that it is far more effective to use mobile devices to bring this story to life in the place where it occurred. You could sit on your couch and watch the documentary, he says, or:

> You could walk it and actually see for yourself ... [Y]ou could walk through these high rise suburbs that they tried to create there, and then *meet* some of the people ... at the West End museum [one of the stops on the tour]. So you can walk in and then some of the voices that you've been hearing are all of a

sudden in front of you. And that juxtaposition is very powerful. And that's a way to do documentary story telling that's extremely effective.

(Interview transcript)

With this form of mobile mediated storytelling-in-places, Epstein explicitly imagines the potential for tourists, equipped with MP3 players or smartphones, to become civically engaged in the cities they are exploring.

### *Urban Interactive*

Urban Interactive offers 'augmented reality' urban adventures in the style of *The Amazing Race* or *Mission Impossible*.[4] Depending on their level of technological know-how, users can either create their own urban clue-based games on the Urban Sleuth platform, or they can play one of the scripted games created by the Urban Interactive team. Allowing users to write and coordinate their own spatial narratives is an intriguing aspect of the company's offerings. The developers clearly imagine their customers as producers of the urban cityscape. However, although Urban Interactive was initially intended to provide content writers with a user-friendly platform on which to deliver location-aware tours in the city, few customers have actually used the back-end platform. Instead, tourists and corporate clients have tended to make up the bulk of users.

I met with Nicholas Tommarello, CEO of Urban Interactive, and Richard Paik, who writes the content for the urban adventures, in the bright conference room of their shared office space in Cambridge. During our interview, I asked them to comment in more detail on some of the phrases posted on their website, especially the term 'augmented reality' and the company's slogan, 'Connecting the Digital World with Physical Spaces'. Both Tommarello and Paik found it somewhat difficult to express what they meant by these phrases, as Tommarello explained:

When I started this thing in 2003, the words did not exist. It was very hard to tell someone what you were doing . . . when it hasn't been done before and no one knows what you're talking about. . . . My first stab at it was 'augmented reality'. No one knows what the hell that means.

(Interview transcript)

As I mentioned earlier, developers, like academics, have struggled to articulate the emerging spatial implications of using mobile digital technologies to engage with the urban environment. But when I pressed Tommarello to explain, he said, 'It means you have this cell phone which can take your reality and display stuff on top of that . . . any kind of virtual information on top of your physical surroundings. It's your reality, your physical surroundings, augmented with more information'.

Tommarello and Paik both acknowledged that their terminology was meant to emphasize that their adventures are not *substitutes* for being in the city. Their adventures use location-aware technology and require tourists to input location-specific information in order to advance through the adventure, which means that

*Figure 3.2*  Urban Interactive kiosk in the Boston Common.

travellers have to actually be in the city. Paik explained that their games 'require you to get out there. ... You have to actually go to places'. Being in the physical space is just as important as accessing the digital world. Technically, tourists could watch video iPod tours from Audissey or Untravel Media at home, though when I posed this possibility to Untravel Media's Michael Epstein he insisted that this would defeat the purpose of the tour. For all of the developers I spoke with, being in the physical space is just as important as accessing the digital world.

So, along with three teammates, I played one of Urban Interactive's iPhone adventures, 'The Guardian of the Relic'. We met at the Urban Interactive kiosk in Boston Common, where the adventure began (see Figure 3.2). The tour led us via an iPhone through a 'secret agent mission' around Boston's Downtown Crossing, Beacon Hill, the State House and Boston Common. As described at the beginning of the chapter, we were prompted to use information embedded in the urban environment to solve messages and find our way to the next clue. Once we discovered an answer, we would key it into the iPhone and send it off for confirmation. The iPhone application used location-aware technology to track our progress and reveal location-specific puzzles along the way. In this sense, the adventure positioned us not as tourists, but as sleuths with the city as a puzzle to be deciphered as we moved through it.

Whereas the Audissey and Untravel Media tours felt like very individualized, immersive experiences, the Urban Interactive adventure had a converse effect. My teammates and I had to cooperate and interact intensively throughout the adventure in order to think through the puzzles and examine the urban landscape for answers to the clues. Urban Interactive also involves live actors positioned along the adventure route, and we had to interact with these actors to get additional clues. In this sense, the adventures were highly social experiences. On the other hand, as one of my teammates commented, the pace of the adventure meant that we raced through the city, engaging with it in an instrumental way (trying to answer clues) rather than soaking in the city in a leisurely way. In my teammate's case, our sociable connecting was offset by somehow disconnecting from the city.

In our interview, Tommarello and Paik explained to me how they try to make these adventures fun, but at the same time information-rich and intellectually challenging. They explained that they have no intention to promote civic action, like Untravel Media for example, but at the same time, throughout the interview, they expressed what I would consider a social agenda. They spoke about their desire to get people off their couches, away from their computers and out into the city. They critiqued 'canned tourism', like bus tours and even Boston's famous Duck Tours, for putting a bus window between tourists and the city. Urban Interactive may have replaced the tour bus window with an iPod screen, but its aim was to insert tourists into the urban action, not detach them from it. Along these lines, Tommarello asked me if I had ever heard of another local mobile company that creates GPS-based scavenger hunts around the city. The company had recently received a large investment from a local venture capital firm. I replied that I had heard of the company, but that I did not realize it was aimed at the tourist market. Paik nodded, explaining that the company's product did not involve anything like the level of narrative and intellectual engagement that the Urban Interactive adventures provided. Tommarello responded, 'Yeah, but it's going to do better than we do, because it's very low end – there's really just no thinking involved. It's just pop trivia questions … It's much more dumbed down'. Paik added, 'I'm sure they're going to be richer than we are'. Tommarello agreed, 'Yeah, they're going to be richer than we are' but 'I wouldn't want to do that with my life, basically'. Paik then explained that he liked the fact that their adventures are built around a complex narrative, 'Maybe that's just being indulgent. … I guess it is. Otherwise, we'd just go for the money, I suppose'.

Tommarello and Paik see themselves as resisting the pressure to 'sell out' or 'dumb down' their tours. Their desire to create smart, intellectually challenging, narrative-based experiences of the city rubs up against the commodifying logic of the market economy. Untravel Media has found a way around this: most of their projects are funded by public grants. PocketMetro and Audissey, however, are necessarily exploring the commercial potential of mobile technologies. In either case, however, these developers seem to be trying to create intelligent, meaningful and sustainable encounters with the city that are not dictated by the bottom line.

## Blended geographies as knowledge landscapes

In the tours I have described, the urban landscape emerges as an assemblage of digital devices, material environments, information and stories, tourist bodies and practices of walking. These tours overlay audio and visual media onto tourists' physical reality and link locations in the city with information and narratives, as well as with people and places elsewhere. At the same time, though, these tours assume that the city is not self-evident. Walking the city is important, but just walking is not a sufficient way of knowing the city. Tourists who wander through the city without mobile devices are likely to find themselves falling into the grooves worn by tourists before them, looking at sights or buildings without understanding their historical significance, or perhaps looking at the place where no building exists, and not understanding the significance of its absence. According to the logic of these mobile mediated tours, tourists must be equipped with the digital devices that allow them to get off the beaten path, to access local knowledge about the place, to unlock and reveal the city's secret spaces, to puzzle through the cryptic stories hidden in the city's architecture, or to make visible and audible the contested terrains of public space, urban planning and collective voices.

In part, mobile mediated tours can be understood through the paradigm of consumption Urry describes in *Consuming Places* (1995) and elsewhere in relation to *flânerie*. To the extent that the *flâneur* 'seeks the essence of a place while at the same time consuming it' (Urry 2000: 54), interactive tourists might be considered digital *flâneurs* in this augmented cityscape, visually and kinaesthetically consuming the city as they traverse it. In a literal sense, PocketMetro's initiative to guide tourists to local businesses, and Audissey's plan to enable location-aware advertising on their mobile platform, both imagine the tourist quite clearly as a consumer. However, even the mobile practices of the *flâneur* are not fully captured by the consumption paradigm. In her distinction between the leisurely walking of the *flâneur* and the purposeful march of the urban commuter, Game (1991: 150) suggests that 'scrutinising, detective work, and dreaming set the *flâneur* apart from the rush-hour crowd'. The idea of the *flâneur* as a detective, and not merely a consumer, seems to align with the way Urban Interactive positions the tourist as a sleuth, with the cinematic aesthetic of Audissey's and Untravel Media's tours and with the way Untravel Media aims to get people to see their environment in a new way. This produces the city as a narrative terrain, or, as Epstein (2009a) puts it, a 'terrative', in which the spatial stories of the city unfold as tourists move through and tap into these stories through their mobile devices. Following de Certeau, we might consider the way these terratives 'traverse and organize places; they select and link them together, they make sentences and itineraries out of them' (1984: 115). In these tours, connecting to the city using mobile digital technologies constructs the cityscape as an informational, narrative, enigmatic and contested public space and, in turn, the tourist as a protagonist, a sleuth or a citizen.

These multiple ways of framing the urban landscape and the tourists who engage with it emerge at the intersection of tourism and technology in the city. Reflecting on the relationship between walking and the city, de Certeau (1984: 98) writes:

> If it is true that a spatial order organizes an ensemble of possibilities (e.g., by a place in which one can move) and interdictions (e.g., by a wall that prevents

one from going further), then the walker actualizes some of these possibilities. In that way, he makes them exist as well as emerge.

The mobile digital technologies that tourists carry with them are part of the city's ensemble of possibilities and interdictions, affording and foreclosing certain practices and interactions within the urban landscape. In this sense, this study of mobile mediated walking tours is as much about the way tour developers imagine a range of possibilities for mobile digital technologies as it is an account of empirical practices.

As we have seen, these developers envision using mobile digital technologies to promote intelligent encounters with the city, to foster sociable connections between tourists and locals, and to engage tourists not just as spectators and consumers but also as civic participants. These possibilities coalesce around an emerging trend of 'smart tourism', a practice that foreshadows several qualities of the mobile social relations I uncover in this book. Therefore, I conclude this chapter by outlining some of the key features of smart tourism and discussing how these features relate to the broader contours of mobile sociality.

## Smart tourism and contested landscapes of mobile sociality

Smart tourism has several defining characteristics that we see evidenced in the tours profiled throughout this chapter. First, smart tourism is connected. It involves mobile and Internet-enabled 'smart' devices with spatially organized interfaces and locative capabilities (i.e. built-in GPS or Google Earth). Not only do these devices make new modes of wayfinding possible, but they also enable new forms of inhabiting the city. Location-aware applications orient tourists in place and to place, revealing otherwise invisible place-based information and underpinning location-based social networking between people.

Second, smart tourism appeals to tourists as intelligent and creative producers of place. For example, Urban Interactive's Tommarello and Paik commented that, even though it is not always successful with the mass market, their aim is to create complex and sophisticated puzzles that challenge tourists intellectually. Ideally, they would like to develop open-ended adventures that allow tourists to create their own narrative trajectory through the city. 'Intelligent tourism' refers to a travel ethos that combines respect for the local destination and culture with travel savvy (Epstein, Garcia and dal Fiore 2003). Epstein and Vergani (2006) have also explored ways of promoting creative tourism through applications and platforms that help tourists become active co-producers of their experiences in a place. These approaches position tourism primarily as a project of knowing and creating rather than just as a form of consuming.

Third, smart tourism is multi-sensuous; it embodies the interface between the physical urban space and the digital realm. Smart tourism is not intended to be a simulated experience or virtual tour of a place. Instead, the technology aids, enhances or augments tourists' embodied encounters with the urban landscape. It opens up possibilities of touching, smelling, feeling, tasting and gazing as tourists inhabit and move through the city. Significantly, the developers I spoke with were insistent that tourists not be mere spectators, imagining their mobile products as an antidote to touring via the television, the computer screen or even the tour bus window. They sought to encourage embodied immersion in the physical environment of the city and in the informational or narrative landscape created by the mobile application.

Fourth, smart tourism is sociable. Even if we acknowledge that the use of mobile digital technologies always involves a process of connecting *and* disconnecting, there are ways of designing moments and possibilities for social interactions between people. Although Epstein worries about the disconnecting effect of the headphones (as mentioned earlier), elsewhere he notes that mobile media can become a means for creating interactions between tourists and locals (Epstein and Vergani 2006). The 'Greatest Neighborhood this Side of Heaven', for example, encourages tourists to visit the West End Museum to talk and interact with local residents there. Mobile digital technologies can also become a means for creating both asynchronous and real time interactions between tourists within the city. Urban Interactive is exploring this possibility in a new initiative called uSonar, a mobile platform that alerts tourists when other tourists are nearby and helps facilitate a meeting between them.

Finally, smart tourism is intended to be more sustainable, with the potential to promote both social and environmental sustainability. It uses technology to relieve environmental stress on the urban infrastructure and to promote civic engagement in the city. All of the tours I studied promised to re-route tourists off the beaten path. Getting off the beaten path has long been a key marketing claim in tourism, a desire MacCannell (1999[1976]) describes as a quest for the 'backstage' of a culture or destination (see Chapter 6). The emphasis in these tours on providing local, insider knowledge is related to this desire as well. The potential in smart tourism, however, is that mobile digital technologies can make other routes accessible to tourists, enabling them to produce new, even unique, tourist geographies of the city. Of course, diverting tourists away from congested areas or encouraging them to traipse into more remote places is not necessarily a sustainable solution, and may in fact create more stress for local people and places than it alleviates. But, smart tourism also tries to appeal to tourists as civic actors by raising awareness about urban issues, soliciting donations for civic projects or involving tourists in activities to help the city. Epstein, Garcia and dal Fiore (2003: 9) argue that tourists should be seen as 'dynamic citizens'. They suggest that mobile digital technologies can 'offer tourists ways of getting civically involved, even after they leave the city' and that 'tourists move from being mere economic units in the civic registry to knowledge-units'. Again, this approach to smart tourism positions tourists not just as consumers but also as civic actors and as knowing subjects.

As these features of smart tourism illustrate, the kinds of social and spatial connections that become possible in blended tourism geographies are imagined around a series of tensions, for example between mobility and stasis, connection and disconnection, and consuming and knowing. One tension that is especially evident in smart tourism revolves around competing civic and commercial imperatives. Tour developers imagine using digital technologies to drive consumer traffic and deliver advertisements, but also to fortify social relations between people and to create meaningful and responsible connections to place. Perhaps what is at stake is Bauman's (2003) dialectic between the market economy and the moral economy, which I discussed in Chapter 1. Bauman suggests that a sociality of technologically mediated 'connections' is complicit with a market logic in which those connections become commodities to be used up and consumed in great quantities. Bauman presents the 'moral economy' as a corrective to the 'market economy' and its frail sociality of connections. He argues that when people create forms of togetherness outside of monetary exchange – that is, in the moral economy – they produce a sociality based on 'mutual care and help, living *for* the other, weaving the tissue of human commitments, fastening and servicing interhuman bonds, translating rights into obligations, sharing responsibility for everyone's fortune and welfare' (ibid.: 74). Bauman clearly associates mobile technologies with a sociality of connecting rather than committing, and with a cancellation of place rather than a deeper connection to place. The material I have presented in this chapter suggests that alternatives exist and that mobile technologies and forms of mobile sociality might operate within the moral economy as well.

As we will see in the chapters that follow, this tension between consumerist tendencies and civic aspirations emerges in other facets of interactive travel as well, including travel blogging and CouchSurfing. My intention is not to pose these commercial and civic imperatives as mutually exclusive – indeed, they are in many ways logically inseparable. Instead, my intention is to explore how mobile sociality – the way we connect to people and places on the move – is shaped around these two intertwined if contradictory impulses. For example, Untravel Media's Michael Epstein points out that using location-aware technologies to drive foot traffic to local shops might represent a form of consumerism, but it can also be a way of re-generating a neighbourhood that has been left out of tourist circuits. Observations like this can be fruitful points of departure in understanding the contours of mobile sociality, not least because they remind us that technological devices do not produce their own effects. The way we design, develop, use and negotiate new technologies may be shaped by the limits of the device or by the communications infrastructure, but our use of technology always reflects as much on our shared histories, contested social values and cultural anxieties and aspirations as they do on the device or technology itself.

## Conclusion

In this chapter, I have considered the role of mobile technologies in shaping the way travellers imagine and engage with places, and explored what happens when networked and portable communication technologies become integrated into travellers' engagement with landscape. Historical accounts suggest that tourist landscapes have always been blended geographies. They emerge in the coming-together of travelling bodies with physical environments and material machinery. At the dawn of the last century, that machinery included trains and analogue cameras, with cars and commercial aeroplanes following soon after. At the beginning of this century, portable communication technologies, locative media, networked smartphones, digital cameras and virtual spaces are blending with embodied mobilities and physical environments to produce new kinds of tourist landscapes and new possibilities for tourists to engage with places – and with each other – while on the move. Mobile mediated walking tours enable tourists to navigate, inhabit and know the city in ways that connect interactive travellers to places not just as gazing consumers, but also as creative civic subjects. Nevertheless, the tourist gaze remains a powerful organizing logic in the performance of interactive travel and in the next chapter, I explore the way mobile and social media technologies reframe the tourist gaze.

# 4 Gaze

## Mobilizing and mediating the tourist gaze

Outside my office window in central Massachusetts, an early winter storm is tapering off, leaving the ground, the trees and the roads covered in several inches of snow. A pale sun hangs low in the sky as the last few flurries swirl past my window. Inside, I am looking at a different kind of window. I have opened several browser windows on my computer screen, each displaying a travel blog published by one of the flashpackers I have been studying. The panes cascade to fill my monitor: India, Argentina, China, Fiji. An image of a white sandy beach, aquamarine water and palm trees in one of the browser windows seems a cruel contrast to the wintry scene unfolding outside. I scroll through another post displaying vibrant photos of the Yangtze River and read the accompanying descriptions and comments posted by readers. 'Your photos are insanely beautiful,' they gush. On another blog, I click on a video link and watch as two travellers wish their families a happy Thanksgiving from a beach in the South Pacific. A post from Argentina appears in yet another blog, illustrated with photographs of Magellanic penguins. At the bottom of the post, an icon pinpoints the travellers' exact location on a Google map. I click on the map and zoom out to see how much distance these travellers have covered since their last post from Tierra del Fuego a few weeks ago.

The websites on my monitor constitute a rich combination of movement and technology. The text and images that fill my screen document the travellers' corporeal mobility around the world and, in turn, virtually mobilize readers, like me, who follow along. 'We are travelling vicariously through you!' the comments declare. The photos, stories and comments that appear on this particular morning are instantiations of how these travellers stay in touch with friends, family members and other travellers. From a sociological perspective, there are many ways to make sense of what is happening on my computer screen this morning, but the one that seems most striking to me as I literally stare at my monitor is the 'tourist gaze'.

## Introduction

The tourist gaze, as defined and refined by John Urry (1990) in *The Tourist Gaze*, calls to mind a particular way of seeing, of course, but it is more than that. It involves a set of social discourses and mobile practices that organize relations between tourists and places and between tourists and other people. These relations often coalesce around practices of looking and being looked at, but the tourist gaze, as a theoretical paradigm, also refers to a broader social framework in which certain ways of relating to people and places are organized, normalized and performed. In this chapter, I explore the way mobile communication technologies and social media platforms mediate and mobilize the tourist gaze, enable new ways of seeing and being seen, and orchestrate connections and disconnections across distance and on the move.

The tourist gaze, much like tourist landscapes, has always been a technological achievement. Visual technologies from the camera obscura to Claude glasses to digital photography have framed the tourist gaze in particular ways and with particular consequences. Now, technologies of visualization are converging with technologies of communication to produce new ways of seeing and staying in touch with travellers while they are on the road. The gaze has become more mobile and sociable, narrative and mediated, virtual and vicarious. Portable laptops, digital cameras, mobile phones and other devices, along with related social media practices like blogging, are redefining what the tourist gaze means and how it operates.

Bringing the tourist gaze to bear on the way travellers are using mobile technologies and social media opens up new areas of exploration, many of which I address in this chapter. By appealing to the concept of the tourist gaze to make sense of the convergence between communication and visualization practices, I am not just interested in the visual images that travellers post online, but also in the social effects of those images. For example, how might we engage the tourist gaze to understand new patterns of embodied and mediated sociality – including both co-present and 'face-to-place' (Larsen 2009) interactions, *and* on-the-move and at-a-distance social relations – between travellers and their friends, family members, other travellers and even strangers? In particular, how does 'gazing' upon the traveller on the computer screen become a way for distant loved ones to stay in touch, for the unacquainted to get to know each other and for bloggers to engage in a mobile community of travellers?

In the discussion that follows, I begin by describing the tourist gaze in greater detail, introducing some of the critiques of Urry's original formulation of the concept and some of the theoretical alternatives that have been proposed. I then situate the tourist gaze within broader debates about mobile technologies, social media and travel in order to highlight the sociological issues that are at stake when travellers use these new interactive technologies not only to gaze upon the world and each other, but also to make themselves visible and present online. Drawing on research material from my virtual ethnography of flashpackers and travel blogging, I then describe what happens when the gaze becomes mediated, mobilized and interactive. I propose that within this context, the gaze is implicated in new forms of mobile and at-a-distance sociality, such as sharing and caring at a distance, 'travelling with' virtually and vicariously, following and collaborating with mobile communities of travellers.

## The tourist gaze revisited

It is difficult to overestimate the impact of John Urry's concept of the tourist gaze within tourism studies over the past two decades. It has served as a powerful paradigm for understanding the sociological and historical significance of the tourism industry, individual and collective tourist practices and the structuring of social relations in the context of modern tourism. In his analysis of modern tourism, Urry (1990, 2002; Urry and Larsen 2011) observes that tourists desire to gaze upon views and scenery that are unique, unusual and, above all, different from the tourist's everyday life. A modern urbanite, for example, may wish to gaze at rural landscapes or at quaint villages, whereas a rural dweller may yearn for the bright lights of the cityscape. In turn, tourist destinations construct themselves as distinct and appealing 'sights' to be 'seen'. It is through this dialectic between normal, everyday society and its contrasts, Urry argues, that the gaze 'organize[s] the encounters of visitors with the "other"' (2002: 145), including other people and other places.

In order to understand the tourist gaze as a social framework, it is important to remember that Urry's initial emphasis on the visual dimension of tourism was informed by Foucault's (1970, 1976) notion of the gaze. For Foucault, power, knowledge and discourse intersect in the gaze to produce certain objects as 'knowable' and to deem certain ways of seeing and knowing as valid and proper. Certain institutional settings, such as the medical clinic or the prison, legitimize an expert gaze that regulates the conduct of others, for example patients or prisoners, by framing them as objects of surveillance and knowledge. The study of tourism, with its emphasis on fun and pleasure, seems far removed from the clinic or the prison, but Urry argues that the tourist gaze is, nevertheless, as 'socially organized and systematized' as the medical gaze (Urry 2002: 1). Like the medical gaze, the tourist gaze is embedded in certain social structures and discursive strategies that organize and regulate where tourists go, what they do and how they interact with each other and with local people. Gazing is never an innocent practice of looking at a 'simple pre-existing reality', but rather is a learned skill that 'orders, shapes and classifies, rather than reflects, the world' (Larsen 2006: 245). In other words, the tourist gaze refers not to individual practices of looking, but to 'scopic regimes' that systematize and govern ways of seeing the world.

Urry's concept of the tourist gaze also builds on MacCannell's (1999 [1976]) analysis of sightseeing. MacCannell argues that sightseeing is a form of social structure that organizes behaviour and objects in public places. Tourist 'sights' do not emerge naturally or inevitably. Instead, they are the product of very specific practices that mark out objects or views as meaningful, and establish how such sights *should* be appreciated by tourists. In other words, sightseeing and the tourist gaze refer to socially structured and systematized practices that imbue sights with particular meanings. For MacCannell, a particularly powerful collective discourse that makes certain tourist sights meaningful is authenticity, a concept I will return to in Chapter 6.

Given its prevailing influence, it is not surprising that Urry's concept of the tourist gaze has been subjected to intense critique by tourism scholars. Many of these critiques target the disembodied and somewhat static character of the tourist gaze. Feminist critics, in particular, argue that 'the tourist gaze' elides embodied differences and quietly implies a relation in which men gaze and women are part of the spectacle (Veijola and Jokinen 1994; Swain 1995; Jokinen and Veijola 1997; Veijola and Valtonen 2007; Jordan and Aitchison 2008). Some critics have questioned the assumption that tourists are the ones doing all the gazing. They describe, instead, instances in which the gaze is reciprocated between tourists and hosts in a 'mutual gaze' (Gillespie 2006; Maoz 2006), returned as a form of resistance against the power of the gaze to define one's being (Sheller 2004), or deployed as a 'local gaze' by local males who gaze upon female tourists as sexualized and embodied 'others' (Jordan and Aitchison 2008). We can think of tourists not just as gazers but also as objects of the gaze. This is especially true when travellers publish their photographs and stories online, making themselves visible for a distant and dispersed online audience.

Despite the fact that Urry acknowledges tourism to be a multi-sensory practice, his concept of the tourist gaze has also been criticized for over-emphasizing the sense of sight to the exclusion of other embodied senses. In contrast, Veijola and Jokinen (1994) remind us of the phenomenological status of the fatigued, queasy, sunburned and sandy body on holiday and on the move. Many researchers have since demonstrated the importance of other senses in tourism practices, describing how smell (Urry 1999; Dann and Jacobsen 2003), taste (Germann Molz 2007a; Everett 2008), hearing (Waitt and Duffy 2010), touch (Markwell 2001) and physical activity (Perkins and Thorns 2001; Crouch and Desforges 2003; Arellano 2004) shape tourist experiences and performances of place. In some ways, the mediated tourist gaze may seem even more disembodied, an abstraction of pixilated representations. As we will see, however, the mediated tourist gaze also makes the tourist's body accessible as an object of care from afar, and mobilizes the body as a site of visceral experience.

Finally, theorists have countered that the tourist gaze is enacted by bodies on the move, not fixed in place. Larsen (2001) argues that the tourist body senses landscapes as it moves through them, constituting a mobile 'travel glance' rather than a static 'tourist gaze'. Perhaps the most systematic effort to (re)embody and mobilize the tourist gaze can be found in the 'performance turn' in tourism studies, which I introduced in the previous chapter. Researchers have described how tourists physically perform places, for example, by walking around the Taj Majal (Edensor 1998), building sand castles on the beach (Bærenholdt et al. 2004) or bungee jumping in New Zealand (Bell and Lyall 2002). This perspective sees tourism not just as a detached way of seeing, but as a multi-sensory, mobile and embodied 'way of being in the world, encountering, looking at it and making sense' (Bærenholdt et al. 2004: 2). If the tourist gaze is concerned primarily with perceptions and representations, the performance turn is concerned primarily with doing and acting. Interactive travel involves these kinds of embodied performances, but as I will illustrate below, in practices of travel blogging and flashpacking the gaze remains a vitally important element of these performances.

This brief review of the tourist gaze and its critiques is meant to underscore the extent to which the gaze refers to a social structure rather than to personal motivations or individual practices of looking. Tracing its genealogy through Foucault's notion of the gaze and MacCannell's structural analysis of sightseeing reveals that the tourist gaze in fact refers to historically specific practices, structured not just by individual desires to see certain landmarks or landscapes, but also by broader discourses surrounding visuality as a practice of classifying, appreciating or interacting with the world. As Urry (2002: 145) explains, 'gazes implicate both the gaz*er* and the gaz*ee* in an ongoing and systematic set of social and physical relations'. The gaze thus refers to a combination of embodied practices, representational technologies and social discourses that choreograph, regulate, authorize and enable particular relations between people. It is an organizing logic around which certain social and spatial relations are patterned. This is the meaning of the gaze that I carry into my analysis of flashpacking and travel blogging as I consider, in particular, how the *mediated* tourist gaze enables new patterns of mobile sociality between travellers and dispersed social networks of friends, family members, other travellers and strangers. Before I move on to that analysis, however, it is important to consider the relationship between the gaze and new technologies of communication and visualization.

## Mediating the tourist gaze

I have a feeling that if Toot traveled today, there'd be no more postcards. He'd be blogging his way around the world. And Puddle would enjoy it all the more.

(Blog entry posted on *TheWideWideWorld.com*)

Despite a robust and growing literature on how the tourist gaze is mediated via the big screen (cinema) and the small screen (television) (see inter alia Acland 1998; Riley, Baker and Van Doren 1998; Beeton 2005; Couldry 2005; Gibson 2006; Tzanelli 2007), relatively little has been said about how telephone displays and computer screens are reshaping the tourist gaze (see Figure 4.1). Indeed, a theory of the mediated tourist gaze seems incomplete without a discussion of the social and spatial implications of online and mobile media, particularly blogs.

In order to make sense of what happens when mobile technologies and social media meet the tourist gaze, it is necessary to understand the social and spatial implications of these technologies more generally. As I noted in Chapter 1, we are witnessing a fundamental shift in the spatial and temporal parameters of social life as mobile phones, iPods and the Internet enable users to be both here and elsewhere, absent and present. Individuals can enjoy 'virtual proximity' online with friends who are far away, but they can also create a kind of 'virtual distance' by plugging into mobile phones or laptop computers to detach themselves from the people or places around them (Arnold 2003; Bauman 2003; Bull 2004). As social networks become mobile and stretch across space, sociality increasingly revolves around a new kind of 'anytime, anywhere availability' that requires 'perpetual contact' (Katz and Aakhus 2002) on the move. This 'perpetual contact' not only reconfigures the spatial and temporal distinctions that have previously shaped social life, but also points to the issues of self-presentation (Fortunati 2005), surveillance and control (Green 2002; Qiu 2007) and nomadic or digital intimacy

*Figure 4.1* Gazing at/from my computer screen.

(Fortunati 2002; Thompson 2008) that are at stake when people 'do togetherness' while on the move and at a distance.

Flashpacking and travel blogging reflect these shifting social practices. Now more than ever, leisure travellers are likely to use mobile digital devices to stay in touch with a geographically dispersed group of friends and family members while they are on the road. Thanks to the 'digital immediacy' of camera phones and the Internet, snapshots and travel stories that would have been shared after the journey can now be shared in interactive formats *while* the traveller is experiencing them. Travel mottos like 'I was here!' or 'Wish you were here!' seem obsolete in an age of 'I am here right now and you are (virtually) here with me!' (see Bell and Lyall 2005: 136). By making themselves visible to a mediated gaze, travellers today are able to make and maintain ongoing, often instantaneous, and multiple social connections in order to forge a sense of community and sociality both online and on the road.

The fundamentally mobile and sociable qualities of the mediated tourist gaze often inform travellers' decisions to become flashpackers or to blog in the first place. As I explained in previous chapters, flashpackers are independent travellers who are backpacking, but not necessarily on a shoestring. These travellers, often mid-career professionals in their late twenties and early thirties, are known for bringing electronic gadgets with them on their travels and using those devices to stay in touch while on the road. Commonly, flashpackers will publish an interactive travel blog to document their trip and interact with their social networks. Blogs, including travel blogs, are a cornerstone of the so-called 'Web 2.0' evolution in online practices. Along with social networking sites, wikis, and video and photo sharing websites, blogs represent a shift toward interactive uses of web-based platforms that emphasize collective information sharing, decentralized user-centred design, user-generated content and online collaboration (O'Reilly 2005; xtine 2008). Far from merely consuming the picturesque, travel bloggers actively participate in reproducing – and often starring in – travel imagery.

The visual and multimedia elements of travel blogs constitute a mediated tourist gaze that has specific social implications. Of particular interest is the way these new media formats place travellers themselves at the centre of the gaze. In their analysis of personal blogs, Nardi, Schiano and Gumbrecht (2004: 222) ask a key question, 'Why would so many people post their diaries – perhaps the most intimate form of personal musing – on the most public communication medium in human history, the Internet?' A similar question might be posed about travel bloggers: Why do they post personal photos and videos in such a public arena? Bloggers' motivations are, of course, multiple and complex. For some, it is the desire to participate in new forms of creative self expression or dispersed collaboration, but critics also see these formats as emblematic of the postmodern obsession with the self (see Giddens 1991; Rifkin 2010). The mediated tourist gaze is certainly implicated in this tension between collaboration and narcissistic 'ego-enhancement' (Dann and Parrinello 2007: 23). As Crouch, Jackson and Thompson (2005: 8) explain, 'the very accessibility and immediacy of digital media production allows the tourist to become central to the theatrical drama of their own lives'. In detailing the minutiae of their daily lives and publishing photos and videos of themselves online, are travellers participating in a form of public exhibitionism or new modes of togetherness?

Much of the current research on blogging emphasizes its creative and sociable nature, noting that even when personal blogs revolve around presentations of the self and intense self-reflexivity, these displays and disclosures of the self ultimately underpin sociable interaction and community-building (Blood 2004; Herring *et al.* 2005; Sevick Bortree 2005; Hadley and Caines 2009). For Nardi, Schiano and Gumbrecht (2004: 224), displaying personal musings in the public forum of the Internet is less about a narcissistic display of self than it is about enacting new forms of social activity and social communication 'in which blogger and audience are intimately related through the writing and reading of blogs'. Presentations of self are thus not merely exhibitionist or narcissistic, but primarily intersubjective and social. In the context of travel blogs, then, the mediated tourist gaze enables travellers to show and tell what they are seeing and doing *and* to put themselves on display as well, primarily as a mode for socializing with a distant and mobile social network. This means that the tourist gaze is mediated not merely through visual images, but also through the stories that accompany those images.

Travel blogs fit fairly easily into the legacy of photography and storytelling that has long characterized tourism practices and communication. Tourism and photography are 'modern twins', emerging together around 1840 with the coincident invention of the camera by Louis Daguerre and Fox Talbot and the organization of the first 'packaged tours' by Thomas Cook (Urry 2002; Larsen 2006). From 1840 on, Urry (2002: 149) argues, 'tourism and photography came to be welded together'. Likewise, writing and narration have long been defining elements of travel and tourism experiences. From the earliest explorers and pilgrims, the Grand Tourists of the eighteenth century, to the twentieth century's mass tourists and backpackers, travellers have kept logs, journals and diaries – some held privately, others published for mass consumption – to document their experiences on the road. Furthermore, storytelling and photography have themselves been intricately fused, both within and beyond tourism. Storytelling is often anchored in personal photographs (Chalfen 1987; Balabanović *et al.* 2000; Langford 2006). Especially in the context of tourism, photographs are used to illustrate written travel narratives or as 'catalysts' and 'mnemonic devices' for oral storytelling (Yeh 2009).

The mediated tourist gaze extends an already robust relationship between seeing and telling. Travellers and tourists are often among the first to play with the new possibilities that technologies of visualization and communication technologies afford for capturing and sharing experiences with others while on the move. Löfgren (2002: 74) observes that tourism generates:

> a range of artistic creativity that in other situations would be unthinkable. Here is an arena where nonartists and nonauthors do not hesitate to try their hand at producing a watercolor, a photo narrative, a travel diary, a video documentary, or a collage of shells or dried flowers. Here you may become your own director, scriptwriter, or scenographer.

The immediate, interactive, mobile and distributive possibilities of creative pursuits like digital photography and digital storytelling expand travellers' socialities in significant ways.

My analysis of the sociability of the mediated tourist gaze is indebted to Larsen's (2005, 2008a; Haldrup and Larsen 2003) compelling descriptions of the way analogue and digital photography practices are social performances and performances of sociality. Larsen characterizes tourism photography as a complex 'social drama' that revolves around embodied choreographing, technological experimenting and social interacting. He argues that it is less concerned with consuming places than with performing social relationships, such as family togetherness, tenderness and intimacy. At the same time, wireless-enabled laptops and mobile camera phones, online photo sharing sites, and social media allow for a speed and scale of image sharing that has not been possible before. He explains:

> Photography's convergence with mobiles and the Internet means that the technical possibilities of photography expand dramatically: tourists can consume their photographs instantaneously on the screen; continuously delete and retake unsatisfactory images; send live postcards by mobiles; email photographs

to their network back home; and update blogs with their latest photographs so that people can travel along with them.

(Larsen 2008a: 152)

Digital photography entails an assemblage of portable devices, technological infrastructures and social networks that enable people to make, store and share images in new ways, which in turn underpins new sociabilities and new ways of 'being together' among travellers.

For Larsen, digital photography's technical and social mechanisms afford several new ways of relating on the move and at a distance. First, the ability to instantly make, display and distribute images engenders a sense of immediacy and 'ongoingness'. Images are not just produced for a future audience, but to be shared right now with fellow travellers or with a dispersed social network (Bell and Lyall 2005; Larsen 2008a). Second, the enormous storage capacity of most digital cameras and online sharing sites coupled with the ease of deleting unwanted pictures mean that travellers can take and erase as many photos as they desire. This lowers the stakes of the photographic moment and encourages travellers to experiment more, to take more photographs or to focus the lens on the everyday and mundane, not just the special and extraordinary (see Okabe and Ito 2006; Larsen 2008a). Third, the digital camera's display screen affords 'new sociabilities for producing and consuming photographs' by making photographing a 'social and collaborative event' (Larsen 2008a: 148). Onlookers can monitor the screen as the photo is being taken, and people in the photos can instantly see the results and delete or reframe the photo. Camera phones, in particular, are not just a personal technology, but 'also a collective technology, a resource for "face-to-face" sociality' (Scifo 2005: 367, cited in Larsen 2008a: 148). Finally, the digital camera is woven into broader social and technological networks that make it possible to share images not just with co-present others, but quickly and widely with a distant social group.

In travel blogs, photographs and videos are almost always presented alongside stories. Travellers' journal entries, commentaries and photo captions embed shared images, many of which feature the travellers themselves, within a narrative arc. While digital storytelling online has, in general, been associated with similar forms of self-creation and sociability both with co-present and geographically dispersed social networks (Couldry 2008; Lundby 2008; Hartley and McWilliam 2009), its use in the specific context of travel and tourism has not been considered in as much detail as digital photography. In the analysis that follows, I show how digital storytelling *along with* digital photography make the traveller 'visible' online in ways that mediate and mobilize the tourist gaze.

## New sociabilities of the mediated tourist gaze

In the past, tourism photography studies have tended to be preoccupied with representation, focusing primarily on the inert images that tourists or the tourist industry have already produced: photographs, albums, print advertisement and brochures

(Larsen 2006, 2008a). More recently, theorists have paid attention to the embodied performances and creative practices of photography (Crang 1999; Larsen 2006), paving the way for my focus here on the 'doing' of travel blogging and the 'sharing' of stories and images (see Cohen 2005). This approach also brings attention to digital photography and digital storytelling as creative and productive practices that position travellers and tourists not just as consumers, viewers or audiences, but as producers of experiences and media. When travellers make and upload photographs and compose and edit stories, they participate in a kind of 'vernacular creativity' (Burgess 2006; Davies 2006) that has come to characterize the interactive ethos of current online practices more generally. To this end, the discussion that follows focuses less on the content of the photographs and narratives travellers post online and more on the clues these images and stories provide to new forms of social interaction in online and offline spaces. I consider the way blog entries and uploaded photographs become objects of commentary and connections to other online spaces, and I try to uncover the forms of virtual and face-to-face 'togetherness' that these blogs enable (and in some cases preclude). In this sense, I see digital photography and digital storytelling as integral elements in a broader hybrid performance of mobile sociality. Encounters on the move and across distances are organized around a mobile and mediated gaze that makes the traveller visible and available to share, care and collaborate with distant others.

In the following sections, I introduce a set of new metaphors to explore how this sociality plays out in round-the-world travel blogs. I start by describing how digital imagery and online narratives become a way for travellers and their dispersed social networks to share at a distance, and then describe how this affective sociality plays out in terms of caring, following and collaborating. Along the way, I consider the various new problems this virtual closeness poses for travellers and describe some of the strategies they use to cope with the implications of constant surveillance and control at a distance. The themes I address here emerged out of my ethnographic analysis of a sample of forty round-the-world travel blogs (see Chapter 2). However, the data I present below is drawn from four blogs that I have chosen to profile in detail: *TheWorldEffect.com*, *TheWideWideWorld.com*, *FollowourFootsteps.com*, and *IShouldLogOff.com*.

### Sharing at a distance

> Thanks for taking me to all these amazing places. The photography is so beautiful. I'm visiting one place at a time with you so I get to travel somewhere every few days. Thank you so much for sharing your adventures!

> Just found your blog recently and I LOVE it! Thanks for sharing the amazing journey you are on.
>
> (Reader comments posted on *TheWorldEffect.com*)

These two reader comments were posted on a website titled *The World Effect*, published by Beau and Meggan, a married couple in their thirties from Colorado. The first comment, in response to Beau and Meggan's post about Casablanca, and the second about their visit to Machu Picchu in Peru, reveal the way a rhetoric of 'sharing' infuses travel blogs. On travel blogs, as elsewhere on the Internet, 'sharing' has become shorthand for 'virtual togetherness', conflating several connotations of the word: talking about one's thoughts, feelings and experiences; experiencing or enjoying something with others; having something in common. Social networking sites like Facebook, for example, encourage users to 'share' everything from web links and status updates, thoughts and feelings to photos and videos as a way of connecting with a dispersed network of friends.

In travel blogs, photos and stories are the main currency of this sharing. As photography and storytelling have become increasingly embedded in technological infrastructures that allow for the quick, easy and interactive distribution of images and narratives, these practices have undergone a profound social shift. Photographs are now less about sharing memories than they are about sharing experiences (Van Dijck 2007: 112). In digital photography and online sharing platforms, the key is '*sharing . . . both virtually and materially, close by and at-a-distance*' (Larsen 2008a: 150, italics in original). Digital images and online narratives are not merely documenting the travellers' experiences to be recounted at some later date; instead, photos and stories become hubs of real-time sociability and mediated co-presence through which the journey is shared *as it happens*. Digital cameras and online blogs thus support a sense of 'social presence' amongst a dispersed and mobile social network (Counts and Fellheimer 2004). In this sense, travellers and their friends and family members can experience what Southern (2011) refers to as 'comobility' – a sense of being mobile with distant others thanks to communication and locative media technologies.

The way travel blogs comobilize an extended social network through sharing becomes clear in the comments posted on *The Wide Wide World*, a blog documenting the round-the-world journey of a family of four from Maryland: Craig and Dani and their 13-year-old daughter and 11-year-old son. The following comments posted by readers in response to the family's final 'homecoming' post reveal the extent to which people understood their online interactions during the family's journey as a form of travelling with them:

> Welcome home! Your trip was a real inspiration for all of us families who spent the past year living vicariously through you. . . . We hope to, one day, follow in your footsteps!!!

> I want to thank you all for your wonderful stories, beautiful pictures and the videos that made me laugh out loud and the ones that made me cry. I am not sure how I feel about the end of your posts. They have become a big part of my day and I will miss them.

> Many thanks for all you did to include us in your grand adventure. You did not go alone and we never felt left out. Though the beginning of this journey implied an end, I do feel the loss of this contact with you.

> Thank you for sharing. I will miss stalking you from my laptop.
>
> (Reader comments posted on *TheWideWideWorld.com*)

The relationship expressed here is quite different from conventional notions of the traveller telling stories or showing photos after returning home. The real-time, ongoing character of the travel blog elicits a sense of actively 'travelling with' rather than listening to stories or looking at photos after the fact.

What is also striking in these travel blogs is the extent to which travellers post photos and stories to share the mundane moments of their journeys rather than, say, images of famous landmarks. The ease with which travellers can take, store and upload photos means that they can afford to include photographs of the less-than-extraordinary aspects of their journeys. Many of the travel bloggers in my sample include descriptions and images of their backpacks, their hostel bunks or budget bungalows, their sandals, plates of food, or the insides of their campervans. Images like these provide insight into the everyday, embodied experiences of long-haul travel. For example, in their blog post about a cruise on the Yangtze River, Beau and Meggan include panoramic shots of the river and images of the impressive locks at the Three Gorges Dam. But, they also include photos of their modest stateroom with its twin beds, a close-up of a jumble of colourful drinking straws in the dining room, a smoke-belching factory on the river banks, a man smoking a cigarette, and that same man on the boat's deck doing push-ups on his thumbs. These somewhat banal snapshots of 'life on the boat' are not conventional holiday photography, but rather photos of personal, everyday moments.

Okabe and Ito (2003) suggest that the intimate and ubiquitous presence of camera phones and digital photography 'invite sharing that is more immediate, ad hoc and ongoing'. The banal photos that travellers post online are not necessarily memorializing a particular experience, but rather sharing and communicating it in the moment. The quantity and 'ongoingness' of these kinds of mundane images and stories help to create what Ito and Okabe (2005) call an 'ambient virtual co-presence' or a 'distributed co-presence' among geographically dispersed groups. In other words, these kinds of images help travellers and their friends and family members feel closer together.

Connecting with an absent, distant or mobile social network sometimes involves *dis*connecting from localized experiences. There are competing perspectives on the effects of photography practices in this regard. Some scholars argue that practices of photographing encourage co-present socialization between families or between tourists and other strangers in the same place. For example, families gather together in intimate poses (Larsen 2005) or tourists use photography as an excuse for chatting with people around them (Yeh 2009). On the other hand, the compulsion to photograph places and events for a distant audience may take precedence over the embodied experience of those local places and events (Van Dijck 2007). In their blog, Meggan and Beau describe both of these effects. They use their digital cameras to communicate with people they meet locally (for example, by taking pictures of children and then showing them the photos in the camera's display), but they also describe how taking photos for the blog sometimes has a distancing effect. Like most of the other travel bloggers in my sample, Beau and Meggan describe occasionally shutting themselves away in their hostel or in an Internet café for hours on end to write, edit and publish their blog. In one instance, when they visited a gorilla refuge in Rwanda, Beau and Meggan described being focused more on shooting photos and video for the blog than on paying attention to the gorillas. They eventually put their cameras away so they could 'just [take] it all in and really experience the situation' (interview transcript).

### Caring at a distance

In addition to sharing experiences, travellers' blogs also serve as a resource for social networks to express a sense of caring at a distance. Travellers will often post entries about their emotional and physical status, noting when they are ill, injured, homesick, anxious or euphoric, to which the blog community responds with timely notes of sympathy, encouragement and sometimes jealousy. For instance, when Beau and Meggan undertook a four-day hike along the Inca Trail in Peru, they posted a series of videos of their trek. In the videos, it is clear that Meggan is struggling to cope with the altitude of the mountain pass. Words of encouragement poured in from readers after these videos were posted, 'You can do it Meggan!', 'WAY TO DO IT MEG!' and 'way to go Meg ... WAY TO GO!'

Similar expressions of encouragement and empathy from readers appeared on *The Wide Wide World*. *The Wide Wide World* included stories of personal reflection and soul-searching which, as the blog's author Craig explained, was a key purpose of the blog:

> For me, the blog was about 'storytelling'. I wanted, in words and pictures, to tell a story about both the outer and inner journey of one family going RTW.
> (Interview transcript)

In sharing both the inner journey and the outer journey, Craig and his family opened themselves up to be 'cared for' from a distance. When they posted about their anxieties or frustrations on the road, members of their social network would respond with humour or words of comfort. The blog enabled a distant social group to exchange encouraging and caring remarks – such as, 'God I miss you guys' or 'I feel like my heart and mind are with you' – easily and often throughout the journey.

Not all of the emotions expressed in readers' comments were necessarily supportive; some readers expressed criticism and jealousy as well. By the same token, not all of the travellers in my sample used their blogs to reveal deeply personal information. However, the autobiographical bent of travel blogs, in particular, and blogging more generally, seems to lend itself to moments of self-disclosure in which travellers make their private thoughts and feelings public. In other words, the travellers themselves become the object of a mediated tourist gaze in ways that allow others to share with them and care about them while they are on the move. While some theorists focus on the risk of vulnerability entailed in these kinds of public online confessions (Viégas 2005; Qian and Scott 2007), others highlight the role self-disclosure plays in constructing social relationships (Van House 2004; Sevick Bortree 2005) and underpinning a sense of intimacy at a distance (Hadley and Caines 2009). The blog often operates as a place where family members and friends back home, as well as other travellers and strangers who follow the blog, can keep a caring eye on travellers and engage them in 'caring dialogue' (Dann and Parrinello 2007).

Sharing and caring at a distance entails a kind of affective mobility on the part of both travellers and their readers, but it also entails being viscerally moved. In the comments left on travellers' blogs, readers describe feeling exhausted or having sweaty palms or pounding hearts when they read stories of the travellers hiking the Inca Trail in Peru or watch adrenaline-inducing video footage of the traveller bungee jumping in New Zealand, for example. In this sense, the mediated tourist gaze is not disembodied; it coalesces around the traveller's corporeal mobility on the road and around readers' visceral responses to the visual images and narratives posted online. As well, it would be a mistake to assume that these 'armchair travellers' are a static audience, literally ensconced in their armchairs or fixed in place back home. Many of the people following these travel blogs are other travellers who are currently on the road, who are planning to take a round-the-world trip or who have previously travelled. Gaz*ers* and gaz*ees* are thus mobilized and (inter)connected in complex ways. These practices of sharing and caring at a distance correlate to another form of being together with the traveller on the move: 'following'.

### Following

The term 'following', which we have already seen used in the excerpts cited earlier, relates travel blogs to a broader shift in which interactions within new social media platforms are increasingly patterned around status updating and interpersonal monitoring. The steady stream of status updates posted on blogs, social networking sites like Facebook and microblogging sites like Twitter reproduce sociality in terms of 'following'. These brief but constant updates become a 'continuous background presence' of 'ongoing yet diffuse engagement' through which friends and acquaintances can keep tabs on each other (Crawford 2009: 526; see Paris 2010b on the 'statusphere'). On Twitter, subscribers are literally referred to as 'followers' and this terminology now pervades the social media space as a way of describing how people interact with each other online and on the move. In fact, some commentators argue that 'following' and 'sharing' are far more accurate descriptions than 'friending' for the kind of sociality that occurs in these social media spaces (Vander Wal 2007).

The social implications of this concept are evident in a travel blog, appropriately titled *Follow Our Footsteps*, authored by Greg and Ashley, a couple in their twenties from Chicago. Greg and Ashley launched their round-the-world trip in September 2009. Their fourteen-month itinerary included South America, Fiji, New Zealand, Australia, Southeast Asia, India, Japan, China, Eastern Europe, Africa and the Middle East. Ashley writes in the introduction to the blog, 'Greg and I will be using this blog as a way to communicate about experiences abroad. We will post often to keep you updated on our whereabouts and what we have been doing. So please follow!' With more than sixty-five page visits per day and 500 fans on their linked Facebook page, it is clear that many people took them up on their invitation to follow along.

Throughout the blog, comments posted by readers reiterate this emphasis on following. For example, in response to Greg and Ashley's blog entries about hiking the Inca Trail, two of the readers comment:

> We are so enjoying following your travels! Gets us so excited to get on the road. Ashley – Sorry to hear your stomach got the best of you. Hope that turns around soon. . . . In the meantime, we are looking forward to a glorious reunion together in Buenos Aires :) We arrive Oct. 20. Keep us posted on your plans.

> I want to know what happens next and I don't like waiting . . . Did Greg make it to Machu Picchu? Did Ashley make it safely with Hernan and the horse? Did Ashley get better? Stay tuned tomorrow??????? Love you both!!!'
> (Reader comments posted on *FollowOurFootsteps.com*)

Following can create a sense of intimacy at a distance as readers keep up with the day-to-day details of the traveller's journey, which often include topics as mundane as a stomach bug. It also creates a sense of eager anticipation through which readers become invested in the journey. The blog's reverse chronology gives it a serialized, open-ended and addictive quality and according to Dann and Parrinello (2007: 23) the 'in-built future orientation' of this narrative organization gives the travel blog a sense of immediacy that draws readers actively into the storyline. Following is a way for readers to participate in the drama of the journey.

The notion of following via the blog (and via other platforms that interlink with the blog) places the traveller at the centre of the mediated tourist gaze, which Greg and Ashley acknowledged when I interviewed them about their blog:

> To us, to 'follow' does not mean do what we are doing. It is more for people to keep track of our adventures. . . . We like that it is a one stop shop for updating our friends and family. We don't have to send out multiple emails and make multiple phone calls. Also it is more visual for them and in a way, puts them there with us. . . . They [are] able to keep up with what we are doing and . . . to live the experience through Greg's words and our pictures. It keeps them from missing [us] and . . . worrying about us.
> (Interview transcript)

As Greg and Ashley point out, following is a visual mode of sociality, inflected by the serialized and chronological patterning of blogging and social networking. Following is a specific form of sociality that relates to 'keeping track', 'updating', and 'keeping up' as a way of being 'there with us' so as to not 'miss' or 'worry' about the travellers. In other words, affective connections at a distance are interwoven with techniques of constant tracking and monitoring online through words and pictures. In this sense following also ties in to various techniques of monitoring travellers as they move around the world.

The matter-of-fact tone with which the term follow is invoked in popular discourse surrounding social media like blogs, Facebook and Twitter belies the nuances of social connection and power that following suggests. At stake here are new patterns of sociality, intimacy, togetherness and control. With social media practices still in their infancy, the broader social implications of following are only now beginning to be addressed. Two frameworks for making sense of how following operates as a form of mobile sociality have been suggested in relation to mobile phones and Twitter. The first sees following as a form of 'interpersonal surveillance' and the second sees following as a form of 'social listening'. Both of these frameworks help to reveal the texture and quality of 'togetherness-on-the-move' encapsulated in the concept of following.

To begin with, following revolves around a framework of social surveillance. Instead of states and institutions monitoring populations, individuals 'are "surveilling" themselves and each other through new, mobile technologies in the course of intimate and interpersonal everyday relations' (Green 2002: 33). Social life – especially social life on the move and at a distance – is increasingly saturated by a logic of surveillance, underpinned by the ability to remain in 'perpetual contact' (Katz and Aakhus 2002) with a dispersed social network. Following, watching and monitoring online or on the phone overlap almost seamlessly with making and maintaining social relations between distant individuals, including practices of sharing and caring at a distance that I described earlier.

The tourist gaze is complicated when the gazing tourist is also the object of the observing gaze. By making themselves visible online, travellers insert themselves into surveillance relationships with a dispersed network of friends, family members, other travellers and strangers. And they do this willingly, literally inviting others to 'watch' and 'follow' them as they move around the world. In fact, for many travellers, being monitored by a geographically dispersed online audience and managing to stay in touch from ever more remote places is part of the fun and excitement of interactive travel (Germann Molz 2006). Following and being followed involve the benefits of intimacy and sociability while on the move, but they are also an opportunity to play with new devices and online features. New technologies for locating and visualizing the traveller – from portable GPS devices to online mapping features like BlogLoc (a piece of software that broadcasts the blogger's live location) – contribute to the reshaping of social relations around concepts of surveillance. Like most of the travel bloggers in my sample, Greg and Ashley provide a link on their blog to a Google map that displays their itinerary and current location. Other travellers have road-tested geotagging features that automatically link their photos to an online map, mapping features that update their location when they log on to their blog, and GPS devices that transmit their location to a specified group of people.

In an ironic twist, many of the mapping and locative features travellers inserted on their blogs turned out to be unreliable or inaccurate. In many cases, travellers abandoned automatic features mid-trip because they did not operate properly.

These technological failures remind us that the social practices surrounding these technologies, and the technologies supporting certain social desires to follow and be followed, remain underdetermined. Beyond unintentional technological 'failures', however, travellers engage other strategies to manage the kind of surveillance that following entails. Some travellers edit identifying information on their blogs or deliberately delay posting blog entries so that the online audience never knows precisely where they are. These failures and strategies reveal the extent to which travellers negotiate the capacities and limitations of following.

Surveillance generally operates within a visual paradigm of watching or gazing upon the traveller, but following has also been interpreted within an aural paradigm, especially by theorists who liken blogging to radio. As Nardi, Schiano and Gumbrecht (2004: 231) suggest, blogging is 'as much about reading as writing, as much about listening as talking'. In her analysis of the social networking and microblogging site, Twitter, Crawford (2009) compares following in social media contexts to practices of 'paying attention' or 'listening'. She argues that listening is a vital form of online attention that gives shape to the intersubjective potentialities and qualities of being that emerge in online spaces. In social media spaces like Facebook and Twitter, practices of 'listening' and 'following' contribute to a sense of 'ambient intimacy' by providing 'access to the details of someone's everyday life, as prosaic as they often are' (ibid.: 527). From this perspective, 'following', constitutes 'a significant practice of intimacy, connection, obligation and participation online' (ibid.: 527).

In the context of travel blogs, then, following is not just instrumental, but affective. It constitutes a way for the traveller's social network – including strangers – to connect with them emotionally, to care about them at a distance and to 'travel with' them. Consider, for example, a comment posted on *The Wide Wide World* in response to a blog entry Dani posted at the end of their trip. In the blog posting, Dani reflects thoughtfully on the strangeness of being at home, the challenge of fitting back in to her daily life in Washington, DC, and the inadequacy of the word 'amazing' to describe the journey. The emotions Dani expresses in this story prompt one of the blog's readers, a fellow round-the-world traveller, to post her first public comment:

I'm sitting in a hostel in China and checking in on your family via your blog as I do a few times a week. . . . This particular post compelled me to write on this blog after being an anonymous viewer into your families [sic] daily travel life. . . . I also wholeheartedly echo your sentiment about returning home. What do people want to hear when they ask 'How was it?' They don't want descriptions of the delicious foreign foods, the quiet everyday event of riding public transportation with people who speak a different language, the changing landscapes or friendly faces you encountered. You say something like 'Amazing' and they are satiated but you have so much more to tell, but it's impossible. Regardless, I hope you all continue to check in with your faithful followers and know that I thoroughly enjoyed your journey.

(Reader comment posted on *TheWideWideWorld.com*)

Even though this reader commented only once, at the very end of the family's trip, it is evident that she felt emotionally connected to Dani and to the family's experiences throughout the course of their journey. The people who follow these travel blogs are not *just* listening, of course. In many instances, they are contributing their own words and content and participating in dialogues with the traveller and with each other on the blog. Even when they are not explicitly contributing in these ways, by merely following the blog, they contribute by 'acting as a gathered audience' (Crawford 2009: 527) that pays attention to the traveller on the road.

The constant availability made possible by mobile phones and social media platforms can help to develop emotionally supportive relationships amongst a geographically dispersed social network, providing travellers with a sense of familiarity, intimacy, community and ontological security in the midst of mobility (Mascheroni 2007; White and White 2008; Crawford 2009). On the other hand, this constant availability can feel oppressive, giving travellers the sense that they can never escape or hide from the constant contact and implied observation. Because travellers can always be contacted and are always at least virtually present online, the audience back home comes to expect that the traveller will be 'there' (Crawford 2009; Green 2002). Ashley and Greg express the pressure they feel around this expectation:

> Once people start following our blog there is a constant expectation for fresh content. This is something we dislike as it is very difficult to find the time to constantly update our blog.
>
> (Interview transcript)

As Crawford (2009: 528) observes, the 'intimacy of social media contexts is not always pleasant or positive; it can generate discomfort, confusion and claustrophobia'. Being the object of a mediated tourist gaze can just as easily feel like a leash as a lifeline (Qiu 2007). Whether understood as 'interpersonal surveillance' or as 'social listening', the social relations involved in following present both positive and negative repercussions that travellers must negotiate along the way.

### Collaborating

In detailing the way togetherness and intimacy are performed in these online social media spaces and through a mediated tourist gaze, I have aimed to uncover some of the nuanced qualities of mobile sociality. One of the things this analysis indicates is that most travellers do not see their journey as a solitary endeavour, but rather as a collective experience. In this sense, the mediated tourist gaze is a collaborative project. The term 'collaboration' has been infused with technological resonance by the ideological discourse surrounding Web 2.0. Along with buzzwords like 'distributed intelligence' and 'crowd-sourcing', collaboration has come to represent the potential for geographically dispersed but technologically-connected groups to interact and work together in computer-mediated environments (Rheingold 2002; Howe 2006). Travel blogs are an interesting example of collaborative interaction because they assemble travellers' social networks around two related projects: the virtual project of the blog and the physical project of the journey.

This sense of collaboration is evident in an entry posted on *I Should Log Off*, a blog authored by Jillian and Danny, a married couple in their twenties from Washington, DC. In this entry, titled 'We're not the only crazy ones', Jillian and Danny describe exchanging advice and information with other travel bloggers – online and face-to-face – about travelling and blogging:

> Other travelers are an invaluable source of information on the road- be it from a hostel or hotel recommendation to a bus company to avoid to advice on a 'must-see' that isn't really so. . . . In Panama we had the good fortune to skype [sic] with Andy at hobotravler.com. A world traveler for the last 11 years, Andy was full of invaluable information for us regarding improvements on the website and tips for entertaining our readers. He helped us focus the mission of our website and gave us plenty to think about regarding travel in general.
>
> Last month in Bogota we had the honor of eating dinner and drinking beer with Dave from gobackpacking[.com] on his last night before returning to the States. One of the first website[s] we came across while planning our trip, Dave and his website were an invaluable resource as we planned and prepared for our trip. Meeting for him the last night of his trip, and four months into ours, we talked about the high and the low points of his trip and ours so far. Funny enough he's from the DC area, so maybe we'll meet up again someday.
>
> (Blog entry posted on *IShouldLogOff.com*)

During their trip, Danny and Jillian communicate via Skype with Andy, another blogger who gives them technical advice about their website, and they meet up in Bogotá with Dave, whose *GoBacking.com* website had been a source of inspiration and information when they were planning their own trip. Elsewhere on their blog, they solicit advice about rearranging their itinerary and, throughout the journey, they receive comments from readers offering tips on where to go and what to do in various places.

In addition to connecting travellers to friends and family back home, travel blogs are also an arena where travellers can see and be seen by other travellers within a broadly defined travel community that revolves around online and offline interaction. Flashpacking and travel blogging are thus significantly reconfiguring the way travellers interact with other travellers on the road. Tourism researchers have observed for decades that *ad hoc* backpacker communities coalesce, at least intermittently, around the exchange of travel stories and advice, for example when backpackers meet each other in hostels (Loker-Murphy and Pearce 1995; Murphy 2001; O'Reilly 2006). These studies have noted that backpackers tend to meet by chance, spend a brief but intense time together, during which they exchange travel information, and then disperse to travel along their separate itineraries. Indeed, among the key motivations backpackers cite for interacting with other backpackers on the road is the exchange of up-to-date stories and information on destinations and travel routes (Anderskov 2002).

In recent years, researchers have begun to observe that mobile technologies, social networking sites and social media offer new tools for the exchange of such travel information, and at the same time reshape the very contours of these travel communities, both online and offline (Axup and Viller 2005; Olson 2008; Hofstaetter and Egger 2009; Paris 2009; Germann Molz 2010). So in addition to using their travel blogs as sites of caring and intimate interactions with distant loved ones, the travellers in my research sample also use their blogs to insert themselves in a broader travel community that emerges around the circulation of stories, information and advice about travelling and blogging. The social experience of backpacking continues to involve coincidental meetings, but social media bring new efficiencies to the way travellers assemble and communicate. For one thing, the intense, but unplanned and brief friendships that have long characterized backpacker's social relations (Riley 1988) can now be intentional and ongoing, prolonged through email and the use of online social networking sites. Mobile phones, online social networking and email make it possible for backpackers to make flexible arrangements to meet up with friends (new and old) while they are travelling, without having to leave these meetings to chance or coordinate them far in advance. Online spaces such as blogs and discussion forums also provide an *ad hoc* and mobile community of travellers with material support and a sense of belonging to a group with shared interests and practices.

At the same time, this ability to stay in touch makes it more difficult for travellers to leave behind friendships that should have remained temporary or avoid connections with people they do not really want to meet. In an interview, one female traveller described avoiding meeting up in person with another traveller who left suggestive and awkward comments on her blog; another described having her follow-up emails ignored by a traveller with whom she had connected deeply, or so she had thought. Travellers also use different social media spaces to negotiate different levels of intimacy and access. Several of the travel bloggers I interviewed described shifting their more intimate relationships onto Facebook or email while using Twitter and their blogs for more public social interactions. New mediums for communicating and prolonging relationships across time and distance make it easier for travellers to meet like-minded wanderers, but also require new strategies for returning each other to arm's length if and when those relations fade or misfire (see Chapter 5).

In general, though, the kind of online presence and interaction made possible through blogs and other social media helps to establish a group awareness among the travel community. This is illustrated by Danny and Jillian's observation that:

> Each blogger we meet or chat with puts us in touch with more travelers. There's a core group of people that we email and 'chat' with regularly and they have become like travel buddies to us. ... It helps to have someone to commiserate with or touch base with, exchanging advice, travel anecdotes and even recommendations. We might never meet them ... but its [sic] nice

to know that they're there, just an email away whenever you need a reminder that you aren't alone.

(Blog entry posted on *IShouldLogOff.com*)

As Danny and Jillian describe it, social media technologies are a key tool in 'imagining' this hybrid, collaborative and mobile community of travellers and feeling a sense of co-presence, whether physical or mediated.

This community also coalesces in other social networking contexts, as we will see in the next chapter when I discuss the practice of CouchSurfing. Like many of the travel bloggers in my research sample, Danny and Jillian are active members of *CouchSurfing.org* and before departing on their round-the-world journey, they frequently hosted CouchSurfers at their home in Washington, DC. While on the road, they arranged to stay with members of the network in Europe and South America. This more structured network intersects with the *ad hoc* community of travel bloggers that Danny and Jillian describe. In this case, the community is not entirely virtual, but neither is it entirely co-present. Sometimes face-to-face meetings are an end in themselves (as is often the case in CouchSurfing), but sometimes they are the foundation for an ongoing online relationship. In either case, the Internet serves as a somewhat fluid anchor around which this mobile and dispersed network of travellers – with its often shifting membership (as some travellers return home and new travellers depart) – finds some structure.

Unlike hybrid communities which are organized around a specific geographical locality that then convene online (see Gaved and Mulholland 2005; Navarette, Huerta and Horan 2008), this hybrid travel community is fundamentally mobile and de-located, or rather re-located in combinations of intermittent online and face-to-face interactions. As Mascheroni (2007: 527) argues, 'personal communities become a mobile phenomenon, relocalized in a plurality of online and offline social spaces'. Travellers may meet up intermittently, but rarely in the same place twice. Social interaction within this community is premised on a shared interest and active participation in blogging and travelling, which revolves around the intersection of virtual and physical mobilities and electronic and social connections. The hybrid and mobile travel community that these bloggers form and perform, and in which many of them find a sense of belonging, is founded on this complex intersection of virtual and face-to-face collaboration. In this sense, the mediated tourist gaze helps to choreograph a hybrid and mobile community of travellers, enabling them to keep an eye on one another.

## Conclusion

Travel blogging entails a complex assemblage of visual and narrative practices: ways of looking, showing, telling, seeing and being seen. Of course, the tourist gaze has always been mediated by lenses and screens. And it has always reflected not only the object of the tourist's gaze, but the everyday social structures that shape and authorize particular ways of seeing and particular ways of being together. However, as technologies of visualization increasingly converge with technologies of communication, these ways of seeing and being together are undergoing a fundamental transformation. In this chapter, I have described how mobile technologies and social media are implicated in emerging patterns of 'togetherness' and qualities of sociability on the move and at a distance. These technologies and the way travellers use them relate to what theorists have observed as a more general reconfiguration of proximity and distance, absence and presence, physical and virtual co-presence in the age of digital communication. In the context of backpacking, in particular, the possibility of being in constant touch with parents or friends back home transforms the travel experience and requires travellers to develop new social skills. For example, backpackers must find new ways to manage their digital availability, engage new communication practices for letting distant friends and family members know they are thinking of them and negotiate new forms of interpersonal surveillance.

This chapter has also revealed that as much as flashpacking and travel blogging are about connecting, they are also about disconnecting. Travellers develop strategies to manage the constant availability and new forms of surveillance and control implicit in these emerging sociotechnical practices. In addition to staying in touch with friends and family and performing a sense of community with other travellers on the road, therefore, travellers also develop techniques for maintaining distance. At the same time, travellers are able to play with new creative possibilities for sharing their experiences digitally as they happen. This 'real time' sharing of experiences has the effect of making individual travel experiences more collective in the moment, but it also 'often replaces face-to-face narrative once back home' (Mascheroni 2007: 538). In this sense, new mobile communication practices also rearticulate the distinctions between home and away, near and far, or alone and together that have traditionally underpinned the backpacking experience. Complex new configurations that blend home with away and the near with the far are not unique to the realm of tourism, but rather reflect broader social shifts in the way we perform mobile, mediated and networked sociality at a distance.

As this analysis suggests, 'perpetual contact' (Katz and Aakhus 2002) is now a characteristic of travellers' everyday lives, with significant consequences for the way travellers socialize with other travellers on the road and stay in touch with friends and family members back home. By making themselves available to be gazed upon by a dispersed social network, travellers prompt new possibilities for socializing with other travellers and participating in geographically dispersed travel communities while on the road. The intense, but brief friendships that have long characterized backpacker's social relations with the travellers they meet on the road can now be prolonged through communication technologies, which also make it possible for backpackers to make flexible arrangements to meet up with each other while they are travelling. In the next chapter, we will see how these online resources make it possible for travellers to connect not just with friends, but with a global community of strangers in the context of CouchSurfing.

# 5 Hospitality

## The mobile conviviality of CouchSurfing

My plane touches down in Montreal on a damp afternoon in late spring. When the immigration officer asks the purpose of my visit to Canada, I tell her I am visiting friends. What I do not tell her is that I do not actually know anyone in Montreal – yet. My flight is late, so I ask the taxi driver to hurry to my destination: a street corner where I have arranged to meet Noelle. I arrive a few minutes before the agreed time and wait on a bench, wrapping my coat tightly around me. Soon, a petite and vivacious young woman approaches me. 'Jennie?' We recognize each other from the photographs on our CouchSurfing profiles. 'Noelle?' We both smile and shake hands and then I follow her around the corner and down the street to her apartment. She welcomes me in and gives me a quick tour of her tiny home. She invites me to prepare meals in her kitchen, indicating where I can find saucepans and plates, and shows me where she has hung towels for me in the small bathroom. She then points at her bed and informs me that is where I will be sleeping; she will sleep in the living room. I object, reminding her that I am the one who should be sleeping on the couch. 'It's not negotiable!' she replies, and then takes me out again to collect her bed linens at the laundromat a few blocks away.

Back at her apartment, we pull the fresh sheets onto the bed and then talk while she gets ready to go out. She has tickets to a friend's performance and so I will be on my own for the evening. While Noelle makes herself a small dinner and then gets dressed, we talk about Montreal, local restaurants and our shared interests in tourism and urban mobilities. I give her a small book as a gift and she protests, 'You know you don't have to bring a gift! That's the beauty of it. But thank you!' I know from the CouchSurfing website that gifts are not required, but that it is a good idea to help with the washing up and tidy after yourself. 'Oh, these cats!' she laments as she pulls on her black coat, which is covered in cat hair. She grabs a lint brush and runs it over her sleeves. She then hands it to me to run over her back, which I do. The intimate gesture is one I might share with a friend or my sister. I hand the brush back to her and tell her to have fun. She gives me a key and tells me to enjoy myself. I stay with her for three nights. Over the course of the weekend, we share several meals and spend hours laughing and talking about our families, childhood experiences, travel stories, love, research and food.

One day, while Noelle is studying, I meet up with another CouchSurfer named Marise. I had contacted Marise weeks earlier about staying at her house, but since she had already agreed to host some other CouchSurfers that weekend, she could not accommodate me. Instead, she had offered to show me around the city. I meet her downtown, along with her guests, two CouchSurfers from France. Again, we recognize each other from our online profile photos. Despite the pouring rain, Marise leads us on a walking tour around Montreal, narrating her city in French and then in English for my benefit. In the afternoon, we find ourselves at the Jean Talon market where we purchase ingredients for the typical Quebecois supper Marise will prepare for us that night. Marise confides to me that she is annoyed that her guests from France, an older couple who have never CouchSurfed before, have not offered to help cook or pay for any of the ingredients; she suspects that they do not really understand CouchSurfing and see her instead as a free 'bed-and-breakfast'. She is unfailingly polite to them, but quietly tells me she will be relieved when they move on to their next destination. Later that night, two more CouchSurfers join us at Marise's home for the impromptu dinner party and we all eat, drink and converse late into the night. The next day, I fly back to Boston. This time, when the US immigration officer asks me what the purpose of my visit had been I again reply 'visiting friends', still unsure of what I mean by that.

## Introduction

In this chapter, I ask how tourism and technology intersect in hospitality encounters such as the ones described above. Hospitality, like the concepts of landscape and the tourist gaze that I discussed in the previous two chapters, is a key paradigm through which tourism researchers have sought to understand the way tourists relate to people and places while on the move. So far, I have argued that mobile technologies and online social media have reshaped these paradigms, requiring us to pay attention to the way tourists connect to, and disconnect from, the blended geographies of urban landscapes or dispersed social networks of friends and family members. Here, I ask how online social networking technologies enable new configurations of togetherness on the move in the context of hospitality. In a world where mobile devices linked to online social media and social networking sites are nearly ubiquitous, individuals lead increasingly hybrid lives. It is the blending of the material and the digital, not the distinction between them, that has become the backdrop of contemporary social life. As I have argued, mobile sociality is fundamentally hybrid, emerging precisely out of the blurred boundaries between embodied and electronic (dis)connections. The question at stake, then, is not whether online social networks are distinct from face-to-face ones, but rather how we live with and through this medium. In other words, what *kinds* of sociabilities and lived experiences of togetherness do social networking sites afford?

To address this question, this chapter examines a third case study: *Couch-Surfing.org*. CouchSurfing is an online hospitality exchange network that helps travellers locate other members who might be willing to host them in their homes for a few days. As I described in Chapter 2, the network has more than three million members worldwide and facilitates thousands of face-to-face introductions per day. CouchSurfing epitomizes the hybrid togetherness of mobile sociality, spanning as it does the virtual and embodied, online and offline character of such interactions. CouchSurfing involves a similar kind of navigation through hybrid sociality that all social networking sites entail. It is, in many ways, organized like other social networking sites: members post profiles and photographs, leave messages for each other online, and link themselves to friends in the network. Unlike in most social networking sites, however, CouchSurfers join the network with the intention of parlaying online interactions into face-to-face encounters in hosts' homes, and they join not to interact with pre-existing acquaintances, but in order to connect to strangers (Rosen, Lafontaine and Hendrickson 2011). The vignette that opens this chapter previews some of the qualities of this togetherness and prompts the themes I address in this chapter: virtual and embodied encounters; the negotiation of risk and trust online; the use of technology to engage in informal economies of reciprocity; and the interplay between moving, talking and instant intimacy in hospitality encounters.

In the previous chapter, I argued that modern social life entails forms of mobile and mediated togetherness that enable friends and family members to stay in touch. However, many theorists argue that one of the conditions of modernity is that we are increasingly together and on the move with people who are strangers to us. If this is the case, then a theory of mobile sociality must also account for the way travellers interact with strangers while on the move. Therefore, I begin by considering how sociologists have theorized interactions between strangers and how the concept of hospitality has been used, especially in tourism studies, to make sense of such interactions. What tends to emerge in these studies is a picture of the stranger either as a figure to be mistrusted and avoided or as a figuration of exotic otherness to be consumed by the tourist. My experiences in Montreal and the CouchSurfing stories I will share later in the chapter are perhaps best understood against a backdrop of these two competing narratives about strangers and mobility. In some ways, CouchSurfing reiterates discourses of suspicion and consumption in relation to strangers. In other ways, however, the emotionally intense and non-commercial nature of these hospitality encounters gestures toward an alternative conceptualization of relations among strangers. I spend the rest of the chapter describing the way the paradoxical desire to get close to and yet remain detached from the stranger is renegotiated in the networked hospitality of CouchSurfing. I examine the way CouchSurfers use technical systems to establish trust with strangers both online and offline. Next, I describe how social networking technologies like CouchSurfing underpin an informal economy of generosity and reciprocity among strangers. Finally, I describe the unique kind of togetherness – which I refer to as 'mobile conviviality' – that characterizes many of these hospitality encounters.

## Hospitality in a world of strangers

Long before CouchSurfers began showing up at each other's doorsteps, kind strangers have offered refuge to wanderers, pilgrims, travelling merchants and vagabonds (Bialski 2007). In the context of CouchSurfing, however, social networking technologies, tourism mobilities and hospitality practices converge in new ways. Since the first member-based hospitality network, Servas, was established in 1949, hospitality networks have evolved into online networks that bring the tools of social networking to bear on the practice of hospitality, reorganizing and redefining the social relations between strangers in the process. As technical connections forged online are translated into face-to-face connections, new forms of sociality, as well as new forms of exclusion, become possible. Couch-Surfing thus raises questions of risk, trust, identity and belonging – all-important dimensions not only of hospitality, but also of new forms of mediated social relations.

In the context of CouchSurfing, where people meet each other online in order to meet each other face-to-face, how travellers establish trust with strangers, how they encounter strangers and even what they mean by 'stranger', are all open to reinterpretation. The implications of online hospitality networks are only now being analysed in depth by researchers interested in overlapping questions of trust, intimacy, friendship, identity, technology, mobility and power (Bialski 2006, 2007, 2009; xtine 2008; Lauterbach *et al.* 2009; Pultar and Raubal 2009). The questions I pose in this chapter about risk and trust, for example, and the analysis of mobile conviviality that I offer below coincide to some extent with these investigations. Like Bialski (2007), for example, I am curious about the technical mechanisms that enable 'complete strangers' to share intimate physical and emotional spaces in the context of mobility.

For many sociologists, the stranger is the figure par excellence of modernity. If modern society is essentially a 'world of strangers' (Månsson 2008: 160), then it is worth asking what kind of sociality is at stake between strangers. In order to understand the kind of togetherness made possible through a social networking site like CouchSurfing, it is necessary to reach back a bit further for clues about modernity, social life and strangers. For this, I turn to the work of sociologists Georg Simmel and Erving Goffman, and more recently Zygmunt Bauman, to make sense of the way the fabric of modern social life is woven out of interactions between strangers in public places.

According to Simmel, the stranger is an ambivalent figure that epitomizes the shifting relationship between remoteness and proximity that lies at the heart of modernity. In his description of the stranger as a type of person who is simultaneously inside and outside of society, Simmel aims to capture the various dimensions of nearness, distance, connection and separation that characterize human interactions in modern society. The stranger is both spatially and socially ambiguous; both mobile and still, included and excluded. This translates into certain patterns of sociality with the stranger. As Simmel explains, the stranger's position 'involves being both outside [the group] and confronting it' and 'elements which increase distance and repel, in the relations of and with the stranger, produce a pattern of coordination and consistent interaction' (1950: 402–3).

To Simmel, modern social life is a stimulating and disorienting melee. Faced daily with a torrent of strangers, the urban dweller must mobilize 'a defensive disposition to insulate himself against the sensual shocks of the modern city' (Edensor 2006: 41). To maintain eye contact and engage in meaningful conversations with the hundreds or even thousands of strangers an urbanite encounters each day would be completely exhausting, if not impossible. Among the defensive strategies Simmel observes, then, are a variety of systems that serve to distance individuals from each other. For example, he describes how the credit system abstracts trust from personal relations and enables it to circulate within society in a rational and objective manner. Placing trust in currency rather than in one another, for example, allows strangers to interact while remaining detached from each other (Allen 2000: 66).

In addition to participating in extensive systems like the credit economy, individuals also deploy interpersonal strategies for coping with strangers. Goffman's (1959, 1963) observations of public social life reveal that individuals engage a multitude of small techniques, gestures and postures in order to cope with the daily barrage of interactions with strangers. One such technique is the practice of 'civil inattention', an embodied strategy that entails making space for the stranger in public while avoiding eye contact, or as Goffman puts it, 'dimming the lights' (1963: 84). Social order, Goffman argues, relies on both a working consensus among strangers of the social situation (for example, the shared pavement) and a mutual agreement to ignore each another (dimming the lights).

Like Goffman, Bauman (1995) acknowledges that living with strangers is an inevitable feature of modern life, requiring both extensive and everyday management strategies. Among the mundane strategies for coping with this togetherness between strangers is a technique Bauman calls 'mis-meeting'. Mis-meeting, much like civil inattention, refers to a way of managing encounters with strangers in order to avoid any close relation or responsibility for the stranger's plight. This is the strategy that Bauman alludes to when he describes the kind of 'mobile togetherness' strangers perform in the city:

> There is a *mobile* togetherness of the busy street or the shopping mall. A site of passing by, of momentary closeness and instant parting. ... In the street-style togetherness, the stranger is an obstacle; encounter is a nuisance and a delay. In the street, being *aside* each other cannot be escaped. But one tries hard not to be *with* each other.
>
> (Bauman 1995: 44, emphasis in original)

The same is true of sharing a railway carriage or an aircraft cabin where passengers do what they can to avoid their fellow strangers, ' "Anything but invite encounter; anything but get involved." All this to keep "the stranger at arm's length" ' (ibid.: 45).

Goffman's concept of civil inattention and Bauman's notion of mis-meeting highlight the delicate balance strangers strike, often unconsciously, between recognizing and ignoring each other when they come into contact on the street, on the train, or in other public and mobile places (see Bissell 2010). But sometimes, as Simmel also points out, the stranger elicits quite the opposite reaction. Sometimes the stranger is pulled in quite close. For Simmel (1950: 404), the stranger's indeterminate social position both inside and outside the group means that they are seen as occupying a dispassionate perspective since 'the proportion of nearness and remoteness ... gives the stranger the character of objectivity'. This in turn means that the stranger is often made privy to 'the most surprising openness – confidences which sometimes have the character of a confessional and which would be carefully withheld from a more closely related person' (ibid.). As we will see, this connotation of the stranger resonates with the emotionally intense and often deeply intimate exchanges CouchSurfers share with one another in the context of their hospitality encounters. It is important to note, however, that even though Simmel sees the stranger as evoking a surprisingly intimate degree of sharing, it is only because the stranger is seen as somehow objectively detached – that is, *not* implicated in the mutual responsibilities of group life – that such intimacies become possible. As Simmel explains, the stranger remains uncommitted to the group, maintaining a freedom 'which allows the stranger to experience and treat even his close relationships as though from a bird's-eye view' (ibid: 405).

The consensus among these three sociologists seems to be that social relations between strangers are generally detached, objective and dispassionate. Their observations suggest that strangers keep each other at arm's length, beyond the sphere of commitment and responsibility. After all, it is the danger of becoming embroiled in mutual obligation – as much as the threat of violence – that makes encounters with strangers such risky affairs. But, this aloofness toward the stranger is upended in the context of CouchSurfing. Rather than ignoring or distrusting strangers, CouchSurfers seek to 'connect' with them. As Bialski (2007: 16) describes it, CouchSurfing hospitality encounters are 'quite exciting, intense connections with complete strangers'. In this sense, CouchSurfing may be understood in the context of tourism where the fear of commitment is superseded by the charm of the exotic, the temptation to peek behind the curtain at the stranger's 'backstage' (MacCannell 1999[1976]), or the desire to 'consume the other' (Hooks 1992; Ahmed 2000). Instead of repelling strangers, these desires work to draw strangers closer together. It is precisely this pleasurable frisson of risk associated with getting close to strangers that often motivates tourists to travel, that shapes the practices they engage in while travelling and that is evident especially in the context of tourism and hospitality.

Since the publication in the late 1970s of Valene Smith's collection *Hosts and Guests*, the paradigm of hospitality has provided tourism researchers with an important framework for analyzing the way strangers connect to each other in the context of leisure mobilities. With many of the chapters in the book examining the complex ways in which guests consume the culture, places and bodies of their hosts, Smith's influential collection played a crucial role in shifting the focus of tourism studies away from an emphasis on tourists, and toward a critical concern with tourism's unequal social relations and the impact of tourism on local populations and environments. As McNaughton (2006: 3) notes, the metaphor of hospitality provides a 'simple (but not unproblematic) way of conceptualizing social relations and social interaction in tourism'. For one thing, tourism encounters are embedded within hierarchies of power that often work to normalize tourists and their cultures as ordinary, and to exoticize and commoditize the local host populations and their cultures as extraordinary and 'other'. The strangers involved in these encounters are thus not 'strange' in the same way. As Ahmed notes, not all strangers are mobile or displaced under similar conditions. Therefore, the act of naming anyone a stranger 'works to conceal differences' and permits us to 'avoid dealing with the political processes whereby some others are designated as *stranger than other others*' (Ahmed 2000: 5–6, emphasis in original). While the openness of the CouchSurfing network and the emotional intimacy found in CouchSurfing encounters challenge the assumption that strangers must be greeted with suspicion and kept at arm's length, we will see that the way Couch-Surfers negotiate risk and trust online implicitly suggests that not all strangers are equal or equally welcomed.

Over the years, many scholars have sought to revise and refine the hospitality paradigm to make room for more fluid definitions of the host and the guest, and for practices of hosting and guesting (Sherlock 2001; Duval 2003; Bell 2007, 2009, 2011). Oppositions between the categories of host and guest rarely hold up in practice. For example, cases of diasporic migrants revisiting their 'homeland' as tourists (Duval 2003, 2004); second-home owners (O'Reilly 2003; Hall and Müller 2004); migratory labourers working in the hospitality industry (Choi, Woods and Murrmann 2000); or travellers employed on working holiday programmes (Clarke 2004; Heuman 2005) all call into question who is the host and who is the guest. The distinction between hosts and guests is also dissolved in the making of hospitable spaces, where guests often work to accommodate each other or to establish a welcoming ambience (Laurier and Philo 2006; Cuthill 2007; Lugosi 2007). This is certainly the case in CouchSurfing, where members perform both hosting and guesting within the network and within specific encounters.

Another critique of the hospitality paradigm stems from its close association with commodified forms of mass tourism, in which it is often reduced to the provision of food, drink and accommodation (Lynch *et al.* 2011). According to Aramberri (2001: 746), the 'old covenant' of hospitality presumed an offer of generosity based not on the exchange of money and services, but on mutual rights and duties that bound both host and guest. Commodified forms of hospitality so faintly resemble that 'old covenant' that Aramberri argues that the 'host' and 'guest' should 'get lost' and be replaced with terms like 'consumer' and 'service provider'. This critique underscores the tension between proximity and distance, framed here in terms of monetary exchange, that characterizes all hospitality encounters. In its commodified form, hospitality ostensibly brings strangers together, even as the impersonal exchange of money keeps the host and guest at a safe distance. As we will see, CouchSurfing replaces monetary exchange with more informal economies of trust and generosity, a move that seeks to reassert mutual obligation between and among strangers in the network.

The concept of hospitality remains a powerful metaphor, not least of all in its ability to bring meaning to certain social arrangements between strangers, both within the commercial sphere and beyond it. Set against these narratives of detachment and commodification, CouchSurfing can be understood as an alternative form of mobility and sociability. In the sections that follow, I outline some of the salient features of this new kind of togetherness among strangers, especially as they relate to the use of social networking technologies while on the move. Because trust is crucial to the somewhat counterintuitive way strangers relate to one another in the context of CouchSurfing, I begin in the next section with questions of risk and trust before discussing the informal economies and mobile conviviality that shape these relations.

## Trusting strangers in a risk society

As I was planning my CouchSurfing visit to Montreal, two stories dominated the news. The first was the story of a Boston medical student who had allegedly murdered a woman he met through Craigslist, an online marketplace; the second was the global spread of H1N1 influenza, otherwise known as 'swine flu', illustrated with images of travellers wearing facemasks in an airport. These news stories seemed to be timely reminders of the way the Internet and travel are both implicated in discourses of risk, especially the kinds of risks posed when strangers get physically close to one another. Risk is an increasingly significant factor in modern social life. According to Beck (1992), modernization produces new kinds of hazards, such as pollution and crime, which modern society then seeks to calculate, minimize or prevent. In other words, modern society is organized around a logic of making and mitigating risk. In the accounts by Simmel, Goffman and Bauman, we see how modernity brings urban strangers into unexpected, and often unwanted, daily interactions, and how individuals organize their social behaviours to minimize the risks of commitment, imposition or mutual responsibility posed by these interactions.

CouchSurfing is implicated in the modern risk society in several ways. Not only is it notoriously difficult to establish trust in virtual settings like online social networks, but in the context of hospitality between strangers, issues of risk and trust become especially complex. The term *hostis*, from which the word hospitality derives, can be understood as either 'guest' or 'enemy', 'favourable stranger' or 'hostile stranger' (Benveniste 1973: 75). Hospitality is thus fraught with the anxiety that the stranger who appears at the doorstep may not be a friend, but rather a hostile enemy. The online interactions and face-to-face hospitality encounters arranged through CouchSurfing are potentially quite risky but CouchSurfers are not interested in mitigating risk by keeping strangers at arm's length. If anything, CouchSurfers seek to bring distant strangers physically and emotionally closer. And yet, the CouchSurfing website and CouchSurfers themselves state that risk and security are foremost concerns, especially given the mutual vulnerability involved in sleeping on a stranger's couch. Beyond the threat of violence, however, hospitality entails other risks: the possibility that the guest may take too much, stay too long or otherwise take advantage of the host's generosity. So how do CouchSurfers come to trust each other?

The CouchSurfers I interviewed described two related strategies to establish trust online with people they had never met before. First, they use the technical security systems instituted on the site – features like references, vouching and verification – to make themselves appear trustworthy and to determine the trust-worthiness of potential hosts and guests. Second, they appeal to a discourse of 'like-mindedness' to describe the CouchSurfing network itself as a trustworthy community. Both of these strategies have the potential effect of creating a sense of cohesion and shared responsibility within the community, which in turn elevates levels of trust across the network (Lauterbach *et al.* 2009). At the same time, as we will see, these strategies can also be exclusive, with the potential effect of framing some strangers as stranger than others.

### *Online security systems: reputation, friends and vouching*

CouchSurfing operates a variety of security systems to establish an individual's reputation as a 'trustworthy' member of the network. In order to join the site, new members must complete a fairly extensive questionnaire that is then published on their profile. In addition to these questionnaires, 'References', 'Friend Links', 'Verification' and 'Vouching' are all technical resources that, according to the CouchSurfing site, help members 'keep each other safe'. As I explained in Chapter 2, references are comments members leave about each other on their profile pages after they have met each other. Friend links show associations between members. With friend links, travellers can connect themselves with other reputable travellers, demonstrating themselves to be trustworthy by association. Membership in CouchSurfing is technically free, but for a fee of US$25 charged to a credit card, members can also get 'verified'. Verification, which is indicated by a green checkmark on the member's profile, confirms that the member's name and address matches the information on the credit card. Finally, members can be 'vouched' for, which is described on the website as 'a very serious form of showing trust in another person'. A member cannot vouch for others unless they have been vouched for by at least three other trusted members of the network. Friend links and references posted by other members along with icons indicating a member's 'vouched' or 'verified' status are made public on each member's profile and constitute the member's reputation within the network.

The CouchSurfers I interviewed use these security systems to varying degrees. Steve, a Peace Corps volunteer in his twenties who had hosted dozens of Couch-Surfers while living in Africa, noted that he would often accept a CouchSurfer's request without checking their profiles or references. This was partly because he had limited access to the Internet from his home in Africa and so found it hard to monitor guests' profiles, but also because he 'invariably trusted people, even if only because they were from the CouchSurfing website'. Other respondents used the reference, verification and vouching systems far more judiciously. Vera, a retired flight attendant from Oregon, told me that she and her husband:

> Read thoroughly through people's profiles and I even send them notes of reprimand if I am sure they are safe guests but don't have a fully filled out profile or are requesting a stay in an unsafe manner ... Everyone worries that we are going to get some weird person. Our response is that we thoroughly check out

their profile before we even say yes and that CouchSurfing itself monitors the people through references, vouching, etc.

(Interview transcript)

For Vera, the technical security systems are reliable, but only work if members use them properly. Like many of the CouchSurfers I spoke with, she sees it as her responsibility to help police the use of the system.

Therese, a student in her twenties from Canada, also takes the reference system very seriously. She told me that although her CouchSurfing experiences have been almost entirely positive, she experienced an uncomfortable incident in which one of her hosts in Europe, a single man, made sexual innuendoes during her stay. Initially, because her host had made no physical advances, Therese left a positive reference for him. Later, after seeing a discussion on the CouchSurfing website about a CouchSurfer in London being raped, she decided to revise her reference for the sake of the community's overall safety:

> I realized that ... I avoided being honest. It was an uncomfortable situation, because this individual didn't ever harm me or even touch me, but because he kept choosing to focus on sexual topics. ... I chose [to leave a] positive [reference] ... I wanted to acknowledge that he put me up last minute and made me a nice breakfast. [Y]et it was nagging me ... I don't think it was appropriate the way he acted and I wouldn't want another girl to stay with him alone like I did. ... So I went back and I left neutral ... [and] I explained in detail why it was neutral.

(Interview transcript)

Therese's comments underscore the public way in which threats are aired and trust is negotiated in this online setting. It is worth noting in light of Therese's comments that, of the CouchSurfers I spoke with, women more than men paid assiduous attention to potential hosts' or guests' profiles and references. This suggests that in CouchSurfing, as in society more generally, risks are often unevenly distributed according to gender.

Rather than transcending or resisting the risk society, then, networking technologies implicate CouchSurfing in it in complex ways. CouchSurfers who use references and the 'verified' or 'vouched' status to determine a member's trustworthiness place their trust in the security systems rather than in people. The 'leap of faith' from online to offline interaction in hybrid communities like CouchSurfing requires both individual-to-individual trust and trust in technology (Tan 2010). According to Simmel, in highly differentiated and complex societies, people are less directly familiar with each other, and therefore unable to verify personally every piece of social information or premise of social action. In this situation, instead of trusting in individuals, they trust in the abstract capacity of systems. As I noted earlier, Simmel understood the credit economy as precisely this kind of system. In the credit economy, trust does not need to be established through personal relations because it can be abstracted into systems like currency (Allen

2000: 66). In the absence of 'traditional' factors that foster trust – such as embodied interactions like eye contact and handshakes, a shared history or the prospect of ongoing social interactions – trust between strangers can be established at a distance via these systems.

Determining trust in the 'traditional' way involves getting close to the stranger first. In external trust systems, these determinations can be made from a much safer distance. In other words, externalized systems – such as Simmel's credit economy or online reputation systems – are modern solutions for the complex relations of proximity and distance in social life (see Resnick *et al.* 2000). Technology is thus both the source of and the solution to risky encounters. The technical security systems on CouchSurfing reproduce hospitality and online interaction as inherently risky, but suggest that these risks can be mitigated and contained through online systems and diligent self-regulation – and that they are risks worth taking. Practices of self-regulation include Vera's and Therese's efforts to regulate their own and others' use of the technical systems, but they also involve a discourse of 'like-mindedness' that generalizes trust across the CouchSurfing community.

### Generalized trust: a community of like-minded people

During my interviews with CouchSurfers, I was intrigued by how often discussions of risk, trust and technology were embedded in a discourse of shared values and desires. Time and again, my respondents explained away their concerns about risk and safety by describing other CouchSurfers as 'like-minded'. In my interview with Dierdre and Santosh, the term came up yet again. Dierdre, an international student advisor, and Santosh, a graduate student from Nepal, are a young couple who live in Massachusetts and have hosted several CouchSurfers at their home there. As Dierdre explained the way she and Santosh use the reference and vouching system to vet potential guests, she used the term 'like-minded':

> You can't be 100% certain when you're [checking references]. But I feel like the kind of people who would use this website are a like-minded community of people anyway, and you kind of self-select out bad people. Maybe I'm being a bit too optimistic, but I feel like the people who are on that website tend to be safe people anyway.
>
> (Interview transcript)

When I asked her to say more about what she meant by 'like-minded', she and Santosh both expanded on this idea:

> DIERDRE: I think that there's a certain kind of person who is open to having those types of social interactions and I guess that's what I mean by like-minded.
>
> SANTOSH: It's sort of a tight group and you wouldn't be on that website unless you loved traveling.

DIERDRE: If you were a person who had a lot of strict personal rules and you didn't like to interact with people and you were really big on privacy, it wouldn't make sense for you to have a profile.

SANTOSH: If you're outgoing, kind of flexible with stuff, and open to crashing anywhere, then you would be on that website. But yeah, I mean for the security at least, I mean the reviews ... the profiles, the comments that other people leave, the amount of information that the person has given, like their photographs, all that stuff helps to give you an idea of what the person is like, at least.

(Interview transcript)

In this exchange, Dierdre and Santosh overlay their use of the technical systems with a sense that the community is, in general, trustworthy primarily because it attracts a like-minded community of strangers who are similarly outgoing, flexible and open-minded. The website itself is seen as a clearinghouse of kindred spirits.

This is the thing about online social networks. The people they are connecting us to are not, as many CouchSurfers put it, 'complete strangers', but rather strangers *like* us. Discovering other individuals who share our interests or philosophy of life and finding a shared space to interact with them – beyond the confines of geographical location or physical proximity – is precisely the promise of online communities (Chayko 2008). In this sense, the Internet plays into the modern freedom to choose our social networks on the basis of shared interests rather than face-to-face proximity. The ability to form communities 'out there' and online puts CouchSurfing in a somewhat paradoxical spot. The website and its networking technology operate to connect a global community of like-minded strangers, who might not otherwise meet, but they do so by filtering out strangers whose values or circumstances do not align with the project's mission. Elsewhere, I have pointed out that, despite an overriding rhetoric of inclusion, tolerance for difference and global community, these trust systems are actually premised on including the 'right' kind of strangers by excluding the 'wrong' kind of strangers (Germann Molz 2007b: 78).

While CouchSurfing is free and open for anyone to join, it is clear that inclusion in the community is subject to certain prerequisites. Membership, verification and vouching, for example, require access to the Internet, possession of a credit card and social capital in the form of already-existing friendships with other members. Participation in the community assumes that members have not only the financial capital required to travel and to host other travellers, even under modest conditions, but also access to documentation like passports and visas. Clearly, these resources are more readily available to some members of the global community than to others. The discourse of 'like-mindedness' also suggests that membership is subject to intangible criteria – qualities like 'flexibility' and 'open-mindedness' – that include *some* strangers while excluding others.

Given the demographics of the CouchSurfing population, which is reflected in my own research sample as well, we can see that this 'like-minded' community is made up primarily of white, North American and Western European, Anglophone university students and young professionals. 'Like-mindedness' may make sense to a global community like this one, which imagines the world in its own image, but not necessarily to members with contrasting values, expectations or understandings of hospitality. For example, Chen (2011) and Buchberger (2011) both describe how difficult it is for local members in Taiwan or Morocco, respectively, to participate fully in the CouchSurfing community due to language barriers, cultural stereotypes and conflicting social mores. These findings remind us of Ahmed's (2000) observation that not all strangers are strange in the same way.

### *The transformative potential of trusting strangers*

Despite this often unacknowledged paradox, many of the CouchSurfers I spoke with saw their willingness to trust strangers in the context of hospitality as a radically new way of doing social life. Consider the following comment from Mary, a medical student living in Massachusetts, who has been a member of CouchSurfing since 2008:

> [CouchSurfing] really refreshes my faith in humanity. It's kind of an uplifting thing to participate in the world, to know that people who are strangers ... can provide a lot of kindness and generosity to each other. I feel like that just reinforces the idea that people are good. And for me that's really an important thing to remember in the world. You hear so much about the bad things that happen and the negativity and I feel like things like CouchSurfing are really good to keep that in check and remember that no, you don't have to be scared of everybody all the time and people are actually pretty good.
>
> (Interview transcript)

Like Mary, many CouchSurfers see themselves as performing a unique kind of trust between strangers, one that we almost never see represented in the western (especially American) media or sanctioned by broader cultural discourses.

Critics of CouchSurfing, on the other hand, suggest that online security systems do not extend an ethos of openness and faith in the goodness others. On the contrary, they belie a particularly 'American' paranoia about strangers. This was the view of some of the members of Hospitality Club, an exchange network similar to CouchSurfing, whom I also interviewed. Like CouchSurfing, Hospitality Club also employs a profile and reference system to help hosts and guests connect with one another, but according to its members, the system is less centralized and less stringently applied than on CouchSurfing. According to Isabelle, a Canadian graduate student living in Boston, there is an impression among Hospitality Club members that CouchSurfing's approach to security is about fear rather than faith in strangers. In explaining why she decided to join Hospitality Club and not CouchSurfing, Isabelle explains:

> Because the way I understood it was that [CouchSurfing] was by and for Americans. ... [T]he general understanding was that CouchSurfing was

created by Americans ... to be sort of a slick, better-run, American version of ... Hospitality Club. ... And also the fact that they, before you can join, they ask you all these questions. It's a much more vetted process than Hospitality Club. And I think the feeling about that is that it's these paranoid Americans who don't believe in just the good of people. ... Whether this is true or not, this is kind of the impression.

(Interview transcript)

To travellers like Isabelle, then, CouchSurfing's use of technology to produce a 'slicker' and 'better-run' system of vetting members undermines the discourse of trust in the goodness of strangers that characterizes hospitality exchange projects more generally.

Keeping in mind the uneasy power relations described above and the limits that critics ascribe to CouchSurfing's 'openness', I want to explore how it is that CouchSurfers see this networking technology as fundamentally transforming the potential for, and performance of, togetherness with strangers. In this section, I have shown how CouchSurfing's networking technology – online profiles, reference and reputation systems, and the public negotiation of individual and community like-mindedness – enables trust to circulate among strangers. These systems implicitly exclude some strangers, but they also underpin new ways of connecting to and being together with others. For example, as I describe in the next section, they enable informal economies of exchange between strangers that resist the distancing effects of the commercial market.

## Technology and the informal economies of hospitality

Thanks to new networking technologies, travellers are able to engage each other in radically new economies of exchange that shift hospitality out of the commercial arena of hostels and hotels and into the private realm of the host's home. One of the key tenets of CouchSurfing is that surfers do not pay for accommodation, nor do hosts expect monetary compensation. To some extent, CouchSurfing recuperates the 'old covenant' of hospitality (Aramberri 2001), relying primarily on an exchange of generosity and goodwill rather than an exchange of money. In this sense, it bypasses the credit economy that Simmel saw as insulating strangers from each other, and relies, instead, on what Bauman (2003) refers to as the 'moral economy'. As I described in previous chapters, the moral economy produces an entirely different kind of sociality from the market economy, one based on solidarity, compassion and mutual sympathy rather than distant, impersonal connections. This is what makes it so distinct from the forms of commercial hospitality we generally associate with tourism, from staying in a four-star hotel or bed-and-breakfast to arranging a paid homestay with a local host.

CouchSurfing revolves around reciprocal exchange between the host and the guest and across the community as a whole. Guests may bring small gifts or bottles of wine, buy groceries or wash the dishes. Hosts offer a place to sleep or provide a guided tour or a home-cooked meal. There is also an implicit reciprocity in the social relation itself: hosts and guests anticipate conversing with each other, learning from one another and generally experiencing an enjoyable interaction. In terms of the community as a whole, members are not necessarily expected to exchange hospitality directly, but rather to 'pay it forward' by hosting someone else who needs a couch in the future. Most of the members of CouchSurfing have been, are currently or soon will be travellers in need of a bed; likewise, members are expected to offer hospitality in their own homes at some point. This arrangement thus challenges any fixed notion of the 'host' and 'guest' category; at some point, anyone who is a guest will be a host, and vice-versa.

By framing hospitality as an equitable exchange of resources and generosity, CouchSurfing creates an environment in which members must trust each other to not take too much or give too little. This 'generalized reciprocity' inserts a sense of empathy into each hospitality encounter, which helps to promote trust among members and impose a sense of cohesion across the group (Lauterbach *et al.* 2009). Of course, there are exceptions. Many of the CouchSurfers I spoke with told stories of guests who did not contribute sufficiently or who overstayed their welcome. For example, as I noted at the beginning of this chapter, one of my hosts in Montreal felt that her CouchSurfing guests were taking advantage of her generosity. In her view, they had mistaken CouchSurfing for a commercial form of hospitality – a bed-and-breakfast – and therefore failed to reciprocate properly by contributing to the communal dinner. CouchSurfers often find themselves negotiating somewhat messy terms of exchange like these which require strangers to involve themselves with one another, as opposed to the more distanced and commodified forms of hospitality based on the straightforward exchange of money.

For a few of my respondents, CouchSurfing's status as a non-profit organization and its ability to facilitate a non-commercial form of exchange between strangers represented a resistance to the corporatization of social life in general. This was particularly important to Nico, an artist I met in Italy. When I contacted Nico about an interview, he invited me to spend an afternoon with him in the village where he lives. The village is more or less a ruin, having been destroyed by a massive earthquake in the 1950s. In the 1960s, artists moved into what remained of the village, renovating small spaces into living areas and studios. The village is now a thriving artists' colony and a fairly popular tourist destination. One summer afternoon, I joined Nico, his girlfriend Maria-Eve, both of whom asked me to use their real names in my account, and two of their friends. We sat outside around a large wooden table and talked for several hours about CouchSurfing, the Internet, the revolutionary potential of networks and the evils of the market economy:

NICO: The beauty of these Internet sites and programmes, in my opinion, is that they all serve a huge revolution. The revolution to no longer use money. This is the real aspect of the revolution that is embedded in these networks, social networks.

MARIA-EVE: Yes, you escape the capitalist consumer system.

> NICO: These websites make possible something more beautiful: to travel the world without money.
>
> (Interview transcript)

Nico described several other websites he and his friends use to travel cheaply, or free, such as ride-sharing or hitchhiking websites. He said of travelling for free and sleeping on someone's couch, 'This is the revolution'. For Nico, CouchSurfing represents the revolutionary potential of the Internet precisely because it facilitates an economy of sharing, mutual help and generosity that operates outside of the market economy.

Nico, along with several of the other CouchSurfers I encountered during my fieldwork, saw CouchSurfing as tool for living beyond the corporate grid. Along with CouchSurfing, they participate in non-commercial exchanges such as WWOOFing (a network that links volunteers with work on organic farms), free-ganism, bartering and hitchhiking to coordinate their material and social lives. Through websites like CouchSurfing, the Internet is mobilized in support of these alternative lifestyles, a point Beth, an educator who lives in New Mexico, noted in our interview:

> [T]hroughout human history ... there's been oppression of the migratory-ness of people. It seems to me like most people I know who are travelers ... live more of a bohemian kind of lifestyle and are kind of looked down on by family members. Or people question their choices, like, 'Why don't you have a steady job? Why don't you have a home?' ... It seems to me that something like CouchSurfing is creating a support network for people like that, which I think is really great. And also kind of legitimizing that way of being, whether it's for a few days, a few weeks, or your whole life.
>
> (Interview transcript)

One member posted a comment on the website stating that CouchSurfing 'subverts the evils of late-capitalism ... by utilizing the greater capital of generosity'. Instead of abstracting relations between strangers into monetary exchange, as Simmel describes, CouchSurfing embeds relations between strangers in an exchange of a different order where generosity and mutual support, offered online and face-to-face, serve to commit strangers to one another, if even for a few hours or days. Furthermore, the non-commercial nature of these interpersonal interactions is seen, to some extent, as particularly genuine and authentic, a point I will discuss in detail in the next chapter.

Of course, this does not mean that CouchSurfing operates entirely outside of the capitalist economy. One of the critiques levied against CouchSurfing has to do with its veneer of commodification. For example, according to Isabelle, the Hospitality Club member I cited earlier, Hospitality Club is true to its non-commercial objectives whereas CouchSurfing is:

> Really all the glossy stuff that Americans like so much. All the superficial stuff. ... Just how Hollywood will take a really great European movie and

they'll doll it all up, gloss it all up, and re-release it and make millions and millions of dollars, that that's sort of what CouchSurfing was trying to do.

(Interview transcript)

Even proponents of CouchSurfing recognize that the networking imperative within CouchSurfing has a tendency to commodify human relationships in terms of 'choice'. Some members describe it from a networking logic as a never-ending supply of potential new contacts and as a way to 'collect' friends. According to some critics, this frames friendships as commodities (Bialski 2007). Even the most vocal critics, like Nico, find themselves hamstrung by the capitalist economy. At one point in our interview, Nico acknowledged that during the high tourist season, he rents out his spare bedroom to paying guests, which means he cannot host CouchSurfers for free during this time. After telling me this, he asked, 'Are you disappointed?' I was not disappointed. I could see that he was struggling to negotiate between the intrusion of the market tourist economy into this small village, and a desire to create and participate in an alternative moral economy, one based on mutual help, care and support with no expectation of monetary exchange.

When viewed as a way of collecting contacts, CouchSurfing's brief encounters between strangers appear to be somewhat cold and utilitarian. The idea that there is always another CouchSurfer to meet and add to one's collection relates to Bauman's critique that consumer life constitutes human relations as light and ephemeral. In this context, connections are frequent and plentiful, but lack any sense of deep commitment or ongoing intimacy. After meeting up, the host and guest float to the outer edges of each other's social orbits. But, does this necessarily mean that the quality of this encounter is lacking in depth or shared intimacy? Indeed, hospitality encounters can often be quite emotionally intense. Like Bialski (2007: 72), I question the assumption that links intimacy with long-term commitments or brief encounters with a lack of emotional depth. Many of the CouchSurfers I interviewed, or who have posted testimonials on the Couch-Surfing website, describe these brief moments as life-changing encounters. If we step back and fit a single hospitality encounter into the broader constellation of the CouchSurfing network, we begin to see how these millions of brief but intense interactions constitute a resilient and flexible network of strangers. Instead of creating a frail sociality that isolates people from each other, CouchSurfing potentially creates an economy of mutual help, solidarity and a sense of belonging within a wider network.

The Internet is fundamental to this informal economy both in terms of technical connection and in terms of a technological fantasy. For Nico, using the Internet to facilitate non-commercial exchanges of any kind – such as hospitality and car sharing – recuperates the original intention of the Internet. Indeed, hospitality exchange sites like CouchSurfing and Hospitality Club hark back to the early principles of non-commercial, grassroots, democratic peer-to-peer communication and community. In describing its non-profit status, the CouchSurfing website reiterates 'The goal of CouchSurfing has never been about money … It's all about helping to reach our vision of a better world'. By rejecting profit models and commercial exchange, CouchSurfing reasserts the 'true' intentions of the Internet: to create a global village of strangers meeting strangers. Every time CouchSurfing members exchange generosity rather than money, they are participating in broader claims against corporate cultural governance. This non-commercial ethos reiterates some of the rhetoric surrounding the Internet and the virtual communities that were forming on bulletin boards and multi-user domains in the early 1990s (Rheingold 1994; Stone 1996). Utopian thinkers at the time suggested that not only could virtual communities replace the sense of belonging that was missing in modern social life, but they could also form better, more democratic and all-inclusive communities.

CouchSurfing appeals to this original utopian promise of the Internet to unite strangers across geographical and cultural divides and to form a truly global community. As Nico argues, websites like CouchSurfing and social networking sites in particular, will eventually 'demonstrate that we're all one family. One big family'. In the case of CouchSurfing, this 'family' of strangers may connect online, but it coalesces offline.

In this sense, CouchSurfing is not *just* a virtual or imagined community. It is, as I described in the previous chapter, a mobile hybrid community where members interact intermittently online, face-to-face and on the move. According to media artist and theorist xtine (2008), CouchSurfing offers a good example of a new kind of Internet-mediated activism that 'relies on participation both online and offline' to resist the 'lifestyles promoted by corporate campaigns' (xtine 2008: para. 10). What xtine recognizes in CouchSurfing is a new social practice that promotes alternative lifestyle solutions through both online and offline participation.

The way face-to-face togetherness is arranged and performed in the CouchSurfing network is an important example of how technical or electronic connections translate into embodied and emotional connections. By establishing trust online, members feel comfortable inviting each other into the intimate spaces of their homes where strangers come together in embodied ways. But, what does togetherness with strangers actually look and feel like in the hybrid context of an online/offline social network like CouchSurfing? So far, I have described how the technical and networking systems of CouchSurfing enable people to establish trust with one another and exchange resources in ways that defy normative understandings of strangers as a threat to be kept at a distance. I have also suggested that the reason these systems work to connect some strangers is because they implicitly exclude other strangers; strangers whose lack of access, cultural capital or resources represents the 'wrong' kind of difference to a cosmopolitan global community like CouchSurfing. In critiquing its limits, however, I do not want to lose sight of its potential to generate new ways of thinking about and living with strangers. Therefore, in the next section, I explore the unique kinds of embodied and mediated togetherness that CouchSurfing makes possible.

## Mobile conviviality: living with strangers

Jack is an artist who decided a few years ago to start a small organic farm in New Mexico. On his CouchSurfing profile, he describes his farm as a place 'where friends and strangers come and work and live in tee-pees and a yurt'. Intrigued by this reference to 'friends and strangers', I contacted Jack about an interview. He told me that he had a few CouchSurfers staying with him and invited me to join them all for a meal. I arrived in the late afternoon so that Jack could take me on a tour of the farm before dinner. He pointed out the yurt mentioned on his profile and several built structures, including a shared kitchen. As we walked around the farm, I met two CouchSurfers doing a few chores: Dylan, a graduate student from New York who was working in a local art gallery for the summer, and Viv, a student midwife from Oregon. In the kitchen, I met Kurt, a building apprentice from Massachusetts, who was mixing up a sesame tahini and lemon dressing for the organic salad that would be our dinner. A cherry pie was baking in the oven, filling the kitchen with a sweet aroma. The lettuce in the salad and the cherries in the pie had all been harvested from the farm earlier that day. Bottles of beer and glasses of homemade apple wine completed the meal. Just as we were filling our bowls with salad, Jack's friend, Maddie, also a member of CouchSurfing, arrived and the six of us arranged ourselves in lawn chairs around an outdoor fire pit, balancing our plates on our knees.

Even though the interview quickly turned into a group conversation with everyone asking questions, making jokes and telling stories, the CouchSurfers did their best to stay focused on the questions I asked them about hosting and guesting. For example, Viv described her experiences hosting CouchSurfers in her hometown in Oregon. She explained that her guests were:

> Constantly going out and doing things that you wouldn't know about if you were just staying in a hotel, like going to pot lucks and going to concerts and going blueberry picking in the summer with my roommate. . . . You get kind of that local view, or these connections, which is why I like . . . sharing that with people who come and stay with me. . . . [Y]ou should really see what this town is really about. Or what community is like in our town. That's more interesting than seeing the sights. Or can be a lovely embellishment to seeing the sites.
>
> (Interview transcript)

At which point Dylan added:

> And you're experiencing it *with* people. The community aspect, I think, is so crucial. That sharing. Because things are always more fun when they're shared over laughing and connecting and bonding than reading a plaque, you know! . . . I mean, it's community, it's connecting.
>
> (Interview transcript)

Dylan then reflected on CouchSurfing at Jack's organic farm:

> [W]hat's so cool about Jack's place is . . . that different CouchSurfers are interacting. . . . We're experiencing Jack's space, but we're also experiencing each

other. And we all have our own stories and our own backgrounds, so it's almost like a quickening of the whole thing because you're not just interacting with one person, you're interacting with multiple. And that, for me, is totally awesome. Just to . . . drop into this little community.

(Interview transcript)

The amiable setting of this interview, along with Viv's and Dylan's comments, illustrate the extent to which CouchSurfing encounters are temporary but richly heterogeneous forms of living together. These connections are shaped primarily by shared meals, shared space, shared activities and shared conversation. Indeed, the word that comes to mind is 'convivial'. But, the contours of these encounters are quite unlike the kind of conviviality we have been told to expect between strangers.

In their study of the way strangers interact in urban cafés, Laurier and Philo (2006) use the term 'conviviality' to refer to the collective life of the city in which strangers make queues together, hold doors open for one another or share seats on a bus, but rarely speak to one another. They argue that this kind of conviviality is usually interpreted as strangers merely abiding each other's presence, though they read it as evidence of sociability between strangers (Laurier and Philo 2006: 4; and see Bell 2011). For Simmel, Goffman and Bauman, conviviality with strangers usually falls short of emotionally meaningful sociability. However, a closer look at the provenance of the term 'conviviality', which literally means 'living with', reveals that the word derives from the Latin terms *convivium*, meaning 'feast', and *convivere*, meaning 'to carouse together'. This suggests an embodied, dynamic and fun connotation of conviviality, the possibility that being with strangers is an enjoyable end in itself, not a togetherness to be endured. In this section, I explore some of the key features of this CouchSurfing conviviality in order to flesh out the lived experience of togetherness in a hybrid community of strangers. What kind of face-to-face sociality does online social networking make possible?

The CouchSurfing conviviality that I observed and that CouchSurfers described to me is, amongst other defining qualities, mobile, embodied, ephemeral and conversational. To begin with, CouchSurfing encounters entail a complex combination of stillness and mobility. The point of hospitality, of course, is to offer travellers a meal and a place to sleep (often the eponymous couch). And yet, CouchSurfing encounters are perpetually on the move. As Viv put it earlier, CouchSurfers are 'constantly going out and doing things'. When we were not eating, the CouchSurfers I interviewed took me on guided walking tours of their towns and cities, invited me on hikes, or showed me around their ranches and farms while we talked. For example, Giancarlo and Vittoria, two CouchSurfers I met up with in Italy, both took me on long, meandering walking tours, pointing out the personally significant attributes of their respective villages (see Figure 5.1). As we walked and talked, CouchSurfers described their other hospitality encounters as similarly mobile experiences.

When I interviewed Therese, an undergraduate student from Canada whom I cited earlier, she emphasized the extent to which CouchSurfing involves mobile

*Figure 5.1* Walking and talking with a CouchSurfer in Italy.

hospitality and helped to illustrate the nature of this mobility. Therese is a very active CouchSurfer. She has been a member of CouchSurfing since 2005, during which time she has CouchSurfed more than forty times and has hosted dozens of travellers. When I asked her to describe a typical CouchSurfing experience, she told me the following story about her most recent trip to a folk festival in Canada:

> I found this CouchSurfer who was a few years older than me, a single guy, living alone, a high school teacher. ... I asked ... if I could stay with him the night before the festival was going to start and he said, 'Yeah that'd be great.' ... [S]o we exchanged quite a few emails before we ever met and then we met and it was great. He lives in this small, small town in Canada ... and we probably spent several hours just walking through the town and he told me story after story about the town. ... I [felt] like I was getting this incredible insight into the typical Canadian town.

> So he spent all of that time and that energy to really give me a sense of the town. You might be travelling through a town or a city anywhere, and wouldn't you love it if someone devotes two hours of their afternoon to give you a walking tour with all of their personal anecdotes and just conversing with you and interacting with you at the same time? Not just mechanically giving you a tour but treating you as a person and just sharing? ... [W]e talked about travel and places he'd like to go, like New Zealand, and it was just back and forth ideas. ... Overall it was extremely positive and prior to

CouchSurfing we never would have met. ... [But with CouchSurfing] that's the way things work. It's no problem that you spent this time to really show me a city because we exchanged ideas and we talked and we talked and who can say who benefited? It's about the exchange.

(Interview transcript)

Therese's story raises several points, including the idea that CouchSurfing encounters are more personal than the 'mechanical' provision of hospitality in commodified settings. The exchange is in itself rewarding for both host and guest. But more importantly for the point I want to make here, her story also suggests that hospitality is a mobile and fluid encounter that revolves around networking and walking and talking.

Not all CouchSurfing hosts have the time to show their guests around to the extent Therese describes here. In fact, some of the people I interviewed told me stories of being given a key to their host's apartment and then not seeing their host again during the visit. These kinds of experiences reflect a somewhat instrumental use of the network, and do not necessarily exemplify what CouchSurfing encounters are 'supposed' to be about. A favourite motto that circulates among CouchSurfers is 'It's not about the furniture!' In other words, these hospitality encounters are not just about providing someone a bed for the night, though of course offering a space to rest is crucial to the endeavour. Instead, these encounters are about giving each other insight into your home, your town and yourself. Far more common are stories about hosts inviting their CouchSurfers on daytrips, taking them to festivals or blueberry picking, showing them around the city, going on hikes or taking bike rides together. These kinds of experiences, including the one Therese relates above, challenge the idea that hospitality is a static encounter or an encounter in which only the guest/traveller is mobile. Instead, hospitality is produced through both stillness and mobility, with hosts and guests quite literally on the move together.

Therese's story, along with my experiences of CouchSurfing with Noelle in Montreal or at Jack's farm, reveals a second feature of this conviviality: it is embodied. Brushing lint off Noelle's coat or eating warm cherry pie on a cool New Mexico evening exemplify the visceral qualities of this networked hospitality. CouchSurfing encounters are defined less by the exchange of emails that precede them than by the embodied activities of preparing meals, eating and drinking together ('feasting' and 'carousing'), walking around a city together, or sharing intimate living spaces like kitchens, bedrooms and bathrooms. In some cases, hosts and guests will even in engage in romantic and sexual relations. Although the CouchSurfing website downplays this potential, many of my respondents acknowledged that it was inevitable that hosts and guests should occasionally 'hook up'. In fact, some members use the site primarily to target potential sexual partners while on holiday, such as female European travellers who use CouchSurfing to meet available men in Tunisia (Carpenter-Latiri and Buchberger 2010).

A third key feature of CouchSurfing conviviality is its ephemerality. Although there are certainly exceptions, most CouchSurfers stay with their hosts for just a few nights, and guests and hosts may never see each other again. For example, Therese only stayed with her host for one night. The mobile and often temporary nature of CouchSurfing encounters has the effect of 'quickening', as Dylan put it, a feeling of intimacy and togetherness between strangers, both in the sense of bringing it into being and in the sense of speeding up that process. In her study of CouchSurfing, Bialski (2007: 12) explains that CouchSurfing interactions are often spontaneous 'short segmented periods . . . removed from the normality of . . . everyday life'. The relative brevity of CouchSurfing encounters adds to the sense that these interactions are fluid and fleeting. These encounters between strangers are thus better thought of as making the most of moments of conviviality rather than as negotiating long-term patterns of living together.

Therese's story also illustrates the way walking intersects with talking; walking around the town with Therese allows her host's narrative to unfold. This intertwining of moving and talking points to a fourth key feature of mobile conviviality: it is deeply conversational. Like 'conviviality', the term 'conversation' derives from the Latin roots *conversationem* – 'act of living with' – and *conversari* – 'to keep company with'. In the context of CouchSurfing, conviviality between strangers is not about keeping each other at arm's length, but rather about bringing the stranger physically and emotionally close through intimate verbal exchange. When I first looked at Therese's CouchSurfing profile, I noticed that the word 'conversation' was used more than forty times in the references people left for her. She had also written on her profile that what she likes best is 'conversar y viajar', a Spanish phrase that loosely translates as 'to talk and to travel'. When I asked Therese to explain what she meant by this phrase, she told me that she saw talking and travelling as combined in two ways. In one sense, conversations can be a form of travelling:

> [C]onversation take you places and it shows you things, so I guess you could stay in your home . . . and through CouchSurfing travel the world [through] conversation. . . . [A] conversation can take you to a place you haven't been, show you things.
>
> (Interview transcript)

In another sense, though, the appeal of travel is precisely to talk. She goes on to explain that in addition to experiencing places, one of the attractions of travelling is meeting new people. In this case, she explains:

> [Travel] is intrinsically tied with conversation because it's intrinsically tied with meeting people. And what do we do when we meet people? We talk. . . . [G]enerally when you meet someone, you talk and talk and talk for hours and that's how you eventually share all this information, feelings, and questions, and a sense that you got to know that person.
>
> (Interview transcript)

For Therese, conversation not only constitutes the social encounter itself, it also forges a connection between strangers by allowing for shared information, emotions and knowledge.

One of the CouchSurfers I spoke with was Beth, an educator from New Mexico, who had used the site only a few times to host or surf with other members. In our interview, she described her first meeting with Kaya, another CouchSurfer, and two other women. Beth described what meeting and talking with these strangers was like:

> So we met and it was really interesting because right away I just felt [a] connection with [Kaya]. . . . It was easy to talk with her. And the conversation was really interesting because . . . we got into a conversation about intuition and how we kind of have intuitive hits on things. . . . [T]he whole conversation just kind of evolved. . . . It felt like we found the meat of . . . something that we were all dealing with on a deeper level, and that the conversation went there was kind of interesting to me, how it evolved. Kaya . . . made a comment at one point about her experiences with CouchSurfing, that that almost always happens. That the conversation goes to this place that's just like really real and really important in terms of whatever is happening with people.
>
> (Interview transcript)

The way Beth described this exchange to me, it was clear that she saw it as out of the ordinary. She even told me that she was fascinated by how quickly the conversation between these four strangers went to such a 'real' and 'important' place. CouchSurfers often express surprise at the level of intensity and the depth of sharing that CouchSurfers experience in their conversations – sometimes within only a few hours of meeting each other.

In her ethnography of CouchSurfing, Bialski (2007) is concerned precisely with answering this question: why did the exchanges she experienced and observed between other hosts and guests become 'so deep so quickly' (Bialski 2007: 17)? Besides the fact that common ground has already been established online, what are the conditions for this kind of instantaneous conversational intimacy and, just as importantly, what are its effects? Bialski offers several explanations for the speed and intensity with which CouchSurfers connect and converse. One reason is that conversational intimacy is a kind of 'equalization process' that makes sharing one's private space with a stranger seem less strange. Through conversation, people who do not know each other can establish a level of emotional intimacy that aligns better with the physical intimacy of shared living space. One of her respondents suggests that CouchSurfers skip small talk about 'superficial things' and immediately delve into deeper conversations because they know they only have a short time to get to know each other. Bialski agrees with these notions, but thinks they do not go far enough to explain why CouchSurfing conversations become so deep and personal in such a short window of time.

In pushing for a more robust explanation, Bialski argues that CouchSurfing conversations are actually part of a broader modern project of identity construction. Drawing on theories from Giddens (1991) and Gergen (1997), Bialski suggests that for individuals today, the self is a project, and identity involves a process of self-reflexivity. 'An individual today is inclined to be in a state of reflexivity' and so 'relationships with others allow the individual to pursue that reflexivity which then leads to identity formation' (Bialski 2007: 42). She concludes that the majority of CouchSurfers see interactions with others – especially in the form of deep conversations that focus on personal qualities, thoughts and emotions – as opportunities to learn about others, about the world, and especially about the self. By engaging in meaningful conversations, CouchSurfers are not just expressing who they are, but working to develop into the selves they want to be.

It is important to note, however, that shared conversation relies on a shared language. When CouchSurfers create their profiles, they are invited to list the various languages they speak. This item on the profile suggests linguistic diversity, but in reality, the vast majority of CouchSurfers speak English as a first or second language (see Chapter 2). English, the lingua franca of the CouchSurfing community, constitutes yet another implicit filter that includes some strangers while excluding others. In her study of CouchSurfing in Taiwan, for example, Chen (2011) explains that Taiwanese members who do not speak English find it difficult to participate not only in the online community, but also in local CouchSurfing happy hours and meet-ups. English dominates both online and offline encounters in the Taiwan CouchSurfing community, and only those cosmopolitan locals who speak English can fully participate, she argues. Furthermore, Chen's respondents note that potential hosts abroad will often discriminate against non-English-speaking guests from Taiwan, finding it too 'boring' to host people with whom they cannot converse. Language can thus be a point of intense connection between strangers, but it can also be a point of missed connections and even alienation.

The mobile, conversational and brief, but emotionally intense, conviviality of CouchSurfing encounters is not surprising, especially if we consider these encounters to be part of a broader form of 'network sociality' (Wittel 2001; Urry 2003). In Chapter 1, I introduced Wittel's theory of network sociality, which he positions in contrast to the stability, coherence, proximity and endurance of place-based community. According to Wittel (2001: 51) modern social relations are characterized precisely by the kind of fleeting and transient exchanges and 'ephemeral but intense encounters' we see in CouchSurfing. In this context, he argues, 'strangers become potential friends,' (ibid.: 71) with the caveat that friendship is being redefined around 'focused, fast and over-loaded social ties' (ibid.: 66) rather than around relationships that unfold and evolve over time.

Picking up on these features of network sociality, Urry goes on to explain that brief and intermittent interactions, embodied meeting and face-to-face conversations have become defining elements of contemporary social life. He explains that travelling to be physically together with friends, colleagues, family members and acquaintances has become necessary to cement weak social ties, especially now that these ties are increasingly at a distance. At the core of these face-to-face meetings, Urry argues, are 'rich, multi-layered and dense conversations' (2003: 164). Through conversation, people are able not only to verbally share information, stories and 'troubles', but also to physically exchange touches, eye contact, and other gestures that help to establish the emotional connections and shared trust that keep the social tie going (see Boden 1994; Boden and Molotch 1994). Urry also notes that in these intermittent face-to-face conversations, 'there is an expectation of mutual attentiveness' (2003: 165). This is quite unlike what Goffman describes as civil *in*attention among strangers in public. We might expect this exchange of 'mutual attentiveness' between friends who have not seen each other for some time, but what does it mean when it occurs between strangers, as it does in CouchSurfing?

Conversation works as a kind of social glue that holds strangers together in short-lived moments of face-to-face interaction, requiring individuals to negotiate shifting patterns of spatial proximity and social distance. Simmel saw these shifting relations of proximity and distance as a fundamental feature of modern social life, which he tried to capture in his figure of 'the stranger'. In fact, Simmel's observation that the stranger often becomes a confidante and confessor seems a quite fitting description of the way CouchSurfers entrust each other with deeply personal intimations. But, whereas Simmel compared the mobile stranger to a geographically-rooted group, CouchSurfing allows us to peer into a community where everyone is (potentially) mobile and everyone is a stranger (but also a potential friend) to one another. What we find is that mobile conviviality within this group is characterized not by mutual inattention or efforts to keep one another at a distance, but rather (or also) by moments of emotional and embodied intimacy with strangers. Online social networking and hospitality exchange networks like CouchSurfing give individuals a new social repertoire for negotiating risk, for performing hospitality and for thinking about and interacting with strangers.

The features of mobile conviviality I have described in this section are not an exhaustive description of what all CouchSurfing encounters look and feel like. As I noted earlier, exceptions certainly exist across the network and even within an individual CouchSurfer's experiences. Not all encounters are as conversational, or emotional or rewarding as the ones I have described here. Furthermore, as I have repeatedly pointed out throughout this chapter, the sense of connection between some strangers relies on the systematic, if implicit, exclusion of other strangers, whose 'otherness' positions them too far outside the cosmopolitan ideals of the community. Nevertheless, CouchSurfers see their participation in the network as resisting, if imperfectly, the stigmatization of strangers and the commodification of social life. The sentiments expressed by the CouchSurfers in this study suggest that CouchSurfing offers a model for alternative forms of mobility, sociality and hospitality; for living with difference.

## Conclusion

In this chapter, I have described the way CouchSurfing translates online connections and technical systems into embodied, face-to-face and often intimate social connections between strangers. The Internet makes it possible for strangers to find each other and to establish trust with one another online to the extent that they feel comfortable inviting each other into their homes. As I have suggested, this phenomenon constitutes a new form of hospitality that challenges the distinction between hosts and guests, and is premised on the non-commercial exchange of generosity and trust. It also illustrates several features of a newly emerging form of mobile sociality.

Through a complex interplay of vulnerability and trust, CouchSurfers both reproduce and resist the logic of risk that characterizes modern society. In one sense, CouchSurfing exemplifies the disembedding of social relations into technical systems of trust and virtual interactions among distant network members. On the other hand, however, CouchSurfing re-embeds and re-embodies these social relations in the form of mobile conviviality; new ways of physically and emotionally connecting with strangers. Instead of keeping the stranger at a distance, CouchSurfers decide to trust one another and to bring strangers dangerously close. The danger at stake is not necessarily the threat of violence, but the threat of becoming obligated in mutual responsibility for others – keeping each other safe, reciprocating hospitality to other travellers, negotiating non-commercial exchanges of generosity and supporting alternative mobile lifestyles. Many of the CouchSurfers I spoke with saw their acts of hosting and surfing as forms of resistance to the distancing forces in modern social life: a mass-mediated culture of fear that vilifies strangers; the commercialization of the Internet; or the corporatization of social life.

This is not to say that all CouchSurfing encounters operate according to this ethos, or that all members of the network subscribe to the project's broader mission. As I have explained, in some cases CouchSurfing reproduces a consumerist tendency that objectifies social connections. Furthermore, many participants really are just looking for a free place to crash or a no-strings-attached sexual partner. For the most part, however, the discourses I have described throughout this chapter work in powerful ways to structure the way members participate in the network and make sense of their hosting and guesting encounters with strangers. The Internet and sophisticated networking technologies are central to these hospitality encounters. Not only does CouchSurfing re-imagine the relationship between the host and the guest as fluid, hybrid, non-commercial and networked, it also points to a broader re-configuration of patterns of embodied togetherness among mobile strangers. In the example of CouchSurfing, we can discern the way mobile sociality revolves around an interplay between closeness and distance, trust and risk, inclusion and exclusion, emotional intimacy and brief connections, and embodied and virtual connections.

Throughout this chapter, I have argued that online networking technologies help establish trust among strangers. In the next chapter, I consider the opposite possibility: that new technologies can potentially be used to deceive and misrepresent. This brings us, in a somewhat roundabout way, to another paradigm that has long shaped tourism studies: authenticity.

# 6   Authenticity

## Representation, commodification and re-enchantment

In 2003, Matt Harding, a video game designer from Connecticut, quit his job and used his modest savings to travel around the world. Along the way, he published a blog titled *Where the Hell is Matt?* to keep his family and friends updated about his journey. A few months into the trip, a friend shot a short video of Matt in Vietnam, directing him to 'Do that dance you do'. So Matt started doing his signature dance – an awkward but amusing jig – in the middle of a busy Hanoi street with motorbikes whizzing past in the background. In 2005, Matt combined that footage with a series of similar video clips of him dancing badly in front of famous and not-so-famous scenes around the world. When he posted the final product on YouTube, the video quickly went viral, attracting thousands of views per day and catching the attention of the marketing team at Stride gum. In 2006, Matt packed up his video camera and travelled around the world again, this time under Stride's sponsorship. He shot more video, edited another montage of himself dancing badly around the world, posted it on YouTube and attracted even more online viewers. A year later, Stride agreed to sponsor yet another round-the-world dancing tour, only this time Matt did not dance alone. In each of the eighty destinations featured in the video, Matt was joined by local people who danced along as he did his silly jig. The result is a heart warming montage set to an uplifting score based on the poem 'Stream of Life' by the cosmopolitan Bengali poet Rabindranathe Tagore. The video from this third trip was posted on YouTube in June 2008 and by December of that year had been viewed seventeen million times.*

While most of the comments posted in response to the YouTube video were positive – many of them thanking Harding for capturing the joy of life and reminding us of our shared humanity – a number of sceptics cast doubt on the video's veracity, suggesting that the footage had been digitally altered or perhaps shot in front of a green screen. Debates over whether the video, or at least parts of it, were fake raged in the wake of the video's release in 2008. While some viewers posted 'evidence' that the images had been manipulated, and expressed extreme disappointment over the revelation of fakery, others refused to believe that the video was fake. Still others accepted that the video might be fake, but were willing to overlook this fact in light of the authentic emotional response they felt while watching it. This scepticism was fed not only by an underlying suspicion of technologies of representation – in the postmodern digital age, images can be easily made to lie – but by misgivings about the commercialization of Harding's project. Many viewers attributed the video's fakery, if it was indeed faked, to the fact that his trip had been subsidized by a corporate entity: Stride gum. In other words, Matt had sold out in more ways than one. In December 2008, the sceptics were vindicated when Harding confessed to the audience at the Entertainment Gathering conference in Monterey, California, that the video was, indeed, a fake.

In his talk, Harding admitted that he and his production team had created the video without travelling anywhere at all. Matt confessed that he was actually an actor, not a video game designer or a world traveller, and proceeded to confirm rumours that the imagery in the video had indeed been manipulated using Photoshop editing software. He described how his production team had constructed some of the trickier shots and had used animatronic puppets to create the impression that thousands of people were dancing with Matt in various destinations around the world. News of Matt's confession spread through the blogosphere, replacing suspicions of one hoax – the video itself – with suspicions of another – Matt's confession. Which scenario was more absurd: that a young white backpacker from the United States would travel to dozens of places around the world and convince people in each place to dance with him in front of a video camera, or that a corporate marketing team would go to extreme lengths and substantial expense to simulate such a journey in a sound studio?

Indeed, one month after his admission to the Entertainment Gathering conference, Matt made a different kind of confession at the MacWorld Expo in San Francisco, California. In an interview with David Pogue, Matt revealed that the hoax was itself a hoax. Matt assured the audience that all three of his videos were, of course, real. His confession had been nothing more than a joke, staged to destabilize the rumours of fakery circulating around his dancing videos. Whether Matt's stunt quelled those rumours was perhaps beside the point. More to the point was the fact that his confessions to fakery and fake confessions drove traffic to his Stride-sponsored video on YouTube, validating his budding reputation as a viral marketing sensation. To date, the video in question has been viewed more than thirty-seven million times. What began as scepticism about the manipulability of imagery in the digital age combined with more generalized anxieties around world travel and corporate marketing into a full-blown episode of public uncertainty. Matt's story may be extraordinary and even amusing, but the issues it raises about the way digital technologies, physical and virtual mobilities and the corporatization of social life shape our modern sensibilities about what counts as 'real' are very familiar. At stake in the doubts expressed by so many of Matt's viewers, and in his subsequent admission to the elaborate hoax, is a concept that has animated and haunted tourism studies for decades: authenticity.

*The video is available at: www.youtube.com/watch?v=zlfkdbWwruY (site accessed 30 July 2011).

## Introduction

Authenticity, the topic of this chapter, is certainly not a recent concern, nor is it confined to the realm of tourism. Since Plato, it has occupied a significant place in philosophical thought and has been a central theme in disciplines from religion and psychology to art and museum studies, to name a few. Nevertheless, there is no doubt that tourism studies and the concept of authenticity share a special relationship. When the field of tourism studies began to take shape in the late 1970s, it did so in large part around the question of authenticity. Initial concerns about the impact of tourism development and touristic commodification on the authenticity of 'primitive' and fragile cultures soon developed into more metaphysical debates about tourism as a quest for authenticity, or authenticity as an existential experience.

At the heart of these debates is a familiar, if contested, narrative that casts authenticity as an antidote to the alienation and disenchantment of modern social life and then proposes travel as a way of recapturing that authenticity, at least momentarily. As we will see, authenticity, whether defined as a quest, as a social construct or as a subjective experience, is essentially a product of modernity. In much the same way that the 'original' is born out of the process of simulation, 'authenticity' only appeared once modernity made its absence felt. The loss of authenticity may be a symptom of modernity, but the concept of authenticity is a modern invention, and therefore reflective of modern values, norms and assumptions. These norms and assumptions are reproduced when we use authenticity as a way of valuing certain objects, practices and relationships. New digital devices, technological practices and mediated interactions are certainly included in this accounting. Discourses of authenticity, including critiques of inauthenticity, help produce a new technology's social meaning and prescribe its social uses. The objective of this chapter is to bring some empirical specificity to the conceptual link between authenticity, tourism and technology, in part by asking how the emergence of mobile technologies and social media onto the travel scene reshapes existing concerns about authenticity and poses new ones.

In this chapter, I ask what is at stake when some digital travel practices are judged to be authentic or to facilitate authentic connections while others are not. What kinds of assumptions are at play when a cultural product, such as Matt's video, is deemed to be a hoax? I address authenticity here not as a descriptive quality of objects, cultures or experiences, but rather as a discursive construct through which certain technological practices and mediated connections are made meaningful by tourists and by scholars alike. In the discussion that follows, I try to avoid the temptation to make determinations about what is or is not authentic in any objective or subjective sense, or to dwell on the way the mobile developers, travel bloggers and CouchSurfers in my study make such determinations (though I am sure that, to some extent, we all participate in this kind of assessment). Instead, I pay attention to the way interactive travellers' references to authenticity (and to fakery) make new digital technologies and technological practices socially meaningful. In this sense, I see authenticity – along with landscape, the tourist gaze and hospitality – as a framework for making sense of how tourists relate to people and places, to each other and to the world around them while they are on the move.

I begin this chapter by outlining the trajectory the concept of authenticity has taken in the field of tourism studies and framing the questions it raises about technologically mediated forms of social life. Next, I examine the way travellers negotiate certain anxieties and aspirations about their technological practices through the concept of authenticity. These anxieties about new technologies coalesce around some predictable concerns, such as fears about misrepresentation, deception or the commodification of social life, as well as some new ones, such as worries about the effects of (dis)connection. At the same time, however, interactive travellers project a variety of hopes onto these new technologies, among them fantasies of opening up more authentic modes of social connectivity and re-enchanting a disenchanted modernity.

## Authenticity in tourism studies

MacCannell's analysis of authenticity in the 1970s secured the concept's place at the centre of a decades-long debate within the sociology of tourism. In his groundbreaking analysis, MacCannell (1973, 1999[1976]) asserted that what really motivates tourists to travel is a 'quest for authenticity' born out of the alienating and isolating effects of modernity. Because the modern condition is bereft of a sense of tradition and coherence, MacCannell argues, 'modern man [sic] has been condemned to look elsewhere, everywhere, for his authenticity, to see if he can catch a glimpse of it reflected in the simplicity, poverty, chastity or purity of others' (1999 [1976]: 41). Here, otherness and authenticity are conflated in ways that validate tourists' desires to, as MacCannell puts it, ' "get off the beaten path" and "in with the natives" ' (ibid.: 97). Unfortunately for the dispossessed modern subject, authenticity is made impossible by the vicious cycle of the quest itself: the more tourists seek the authentic, the more local cultures put authenticity on display to satisfy tourists' thirst for it, a process that ultimately strips those local cultures of their authenticity. Drawing on Goffman's social schema of 'front stage' and 'back stage' performances, MacCannell concludes that what tourists are actually exposed to is 'staged authenticity', an experience constructed to make tourists believe they are getting a glimpse 'behind the curtain', though what is behind the curtain is, itself, a fabricated version of authenticity.

MacCannell's notion of 'staged authenticity' has generated lively debate and vigorous critique ever since, with tourism scholars applying, improving upon, modifying or debunking his reading of authenticity from a variety of perspectives. A number of scholars have countered MacCannell's claim that tourism is a quest for authenticity, arguing that authenticity is just one of many things tourists may seek (Graburn 1989). Others point out that some tourists desire *in*authenticity rather than authenticity, as with Urry's (1990) 'post-tourists' who delight in the kitsch and irony of simulated representations. In other studies, scholars have taken up the theme of authenticity not only to describe what prompts tourists to travel, but also to classify various styles of travel (Boorstin 1961; Cohen 1988), to assess the effects of commodification on local cultures and tourist experiences (Cohen 1988; Greenwoodd 1989; Halewood and Hannam 2001; Cole 2007) and to make sense of tourists' subjective experiences and embodied performances (Pearce and Moscardo 1986; Wang 1999; Shaffer 2004; Steiner and Reisinger 2006; Kim and Jamal 2007). So far, however, surprisingly little research has addressed the impact of technology on tourists' quest for authenticity.

The approaches outlined above have tended to present one of three perspectives on authenticity: objectivist, constructivist or existentialist (Wang 1999). The objectivist perspective sees authenticity as something that inheres in objects, performances or other cultural products. The uneasy relationship between authenticity and commodification is a case in point. Critics taking an objectivist approach, including many tourists themselves, see tourism's overarching tendency to commodify everything in its path as a serious risk to authenticity. They argue that when artefacts are reproduced as souvenirs for the tourist market, they cease to be authentic elements of cultural practice and become, at worst, inauthentic kitsch (Potter 2010: 97). Likewise, backpackers condemn overly commercialized tourist destinations or dealings with guides and hosts that involve the exchange of money as necessarily inauthentic (see Desforges 1998). The constructivist perspective, on the other hand, sees authenticity as a negotiable, situated and contingent quality that emerges in particular social contexts (Bruner 1994; DeLyser 1999). In other words, authenticity is in the eye of the beholder. Constructivists are far less concerned with the effects of commodification, in part because commodification cannot strip an object of something it does not contain in the first place. On the contrary, they argue, the process of commodification can breathe new life into cultural practices and infuse cultural products with new meanings that are perceived as authentic for both locals and tourists (Cohen 1988; Crang 1996; Halewood and Hannam 2001; Cole 2007).

Related to the constructivist perspective is a third perspective: existential authenticity. The existential perspective locates authenticity in the tourist's subjective experience. It refers to emotional impact, heightened bodily sensations or personal connections; what matters is not that something *is* authentic, only that it *feels* authentic. This perspective acknowledges that tourism is an inevitably commercialized industry, but recognizes that even commodified experiences can feel authentic to the tourist (Kim and Jamal 2007). Central to existential authenticity is a sense of *connection*, as Hall (2007: 1140) explains:

> Authenticity is derived from the property of connectedness of the individual to the perceived, everyday world and environment, and the processes that created it and the consequences of one's engagement with it . . . Authenticity is born from everyday experiences and connections which are often serendipitous. . . . Connectedness that leads to authenticity can be provided anywhere as authenticity is not intrinsically dependent on location although place, in the sense of everyday lived experiences and relations, does matter. . . . Authenticity lies in connections, not in separation and distance.

Hall captures here the idea, implicit in much of the tourism literature, that the quest for authenticity entails some form of physical, emotional or existential connection. From this perspective, authenticity is a useful framework for making sense of how travellers connect to (or remain disconnected from) people and places – and themselves – while on the move; it is more about performances and relationships than it is about objects and artefacts. Handler and Saxton (1988: 243) reiterate this point, suggesting that an authentic experience 'is one in which individuals feel themselves to be in touch both with a "real" world and with their "real" selves'. For example, in her analysis of backpacking, Shaffer (2004: 139–40) argues that the backpacker's journey 'is a carefully choreographed performance of a self who strives toward "authenticity"'. As we will see, in the context of interactive travel, what it means to 'be in touch' and what constitutes the 'real' are complicated by the emergence of the Internet, virtual cultures and mediated communication.

## Authenticity in interactive travel

Scholars often describe authenticity as something that 'evaporates under scrutiny' (Oakes 2006: 233), like a mirage that recedes into the distance just as you approach it. In this chapter, authenticity evaporates and recedes, leaving in its place questions, hopes and fears about technology. In this sense, the analysis I present in this chapter is less about authenticity than it is about technology, and it is less about either authenticity or technology than it is about a particular worldview related to western modernity. Just as public reactions to new technologies have always revealed more about the cultural *zeitgeist* of the era than about the technologies themselves (Marvin 1988), so, too, does 'the distinction between what is "real" and what is "fake," or what is authentic and what is inauthentic, tell [us] a lot more about the person making the judgment than it does about what is being judged' (Potter 2010: 224).

As Marvin (1988: 232) observes, new technologies enter the social milieu 'as a set of concrete opportunities or threats to be weighed and figured into the pursuit of ongoing social objectives'. Because authenticity is almost always freighted with positive connotations that cast it as a 'Good Thing' (Potter 2010: 6), it serves as a handy measure for doing this kind of weighing and figuring. In other words, technological forms that enhance authenticity or provide access to authentic connections are seen as fulfilling technology's promise of social cohesion and self-realization, while those technologies that seem to threaten the real or generate inauthentic cultural forms or illicit connections are perceived as a threat to these ideals. In this way, references to authenticity reflect very little about authenticity or technology in and of themselves, but say very much about the deep-seated anxieties and aspirations that shape modern social life more generally. What I hope will become apparent in the discussion that follows is that authenticity continues to hold explanatory purchase in the realm of interactive travel, primarily as an expression of travellers' hopes and fears about technology and mobile relationships in modern life. I am interested in how people deploy authenticity – and related terms that are (not unproblematically) suggestive of authenticity, such as 'real', 'insider', 'local' or 'off the beaten path', and inauthenticity, such as 'hoax' or 'virtual' – to express deeply held assumptions about what social life *might* be like, for better or for worse, in the digital age.

In the empirical analysis that follows, I consider two contrasting discourses that emerge in the research material. Using Matt Harding's dancing videos as a starting point, I explore how his blog and video become pivot points around which *anxieties* about representation, reality and commodification are expressed. After discussing the way authenticity is used to express certain anxieties about the modern condition, I then consider the counter argument: the way certain *aspirations* about uniting humanity or re-enchanting the 'beaten path' are attached to technology through the language of authenticity, access and 'real' selves. I alluded to some of these concerns in earlier chapters in relation to mobile technologies, online social media and social networking technologies. In this chapter, I return to all three of these cases – travel blogs, CouchSurfing and mediated urban tours – this time to interrogate them through the lens of authenticity.

### Technological anxieties

A closer look into the accusations of fakery surrounding Matt Harding's dance videos reveals some of the anxieties about technology, mobility and the status of the 'real' at play in modernity. According to sceptical viewers, Harding's video was suspicious on two counts: Did the video show what Matt claimed it showed? Were Matt's motives genuine or were they manufactured as a corporate marketing ploy? The crisis of authenticity evident in this public expression of uncertainty revolves around three related threats to authenticity: digital (mis)representation, corporate commodification and disconnection.

### (Mis)representation

The outcry around the authenticity of Harding's videos is in many ways a question of representation and misrepresentation: Are you *who* you say you are? Are you *where* you say you are? The introduction of the Internet and then mobile phones into everyday social life raised anxieties around identity, self-representation, location and reality. A cartoon published in *The New Yorker* in 1993 captured this uncertainty with an image of a dog typing at a computer keyboard underlined by the now-famous caption, 'On the Internet, nobody knows you're a dog'. And the fact that so many people asked 'Where are you?' as a standard feature of mobile phone conversations was seen as indicative of the spatial uncertainty wrought by mobility and technology (Laurier 2001). Such anxieties around representation and technology are certainly not new. Ever since telegraphy and photography made it possible for users to extend 'true' representations of themselves across space and time, these same technologies have also made 'false' representations possible. In her account of communication technologies in the nineteenth century, Marvin (1988) details various examples of people using the then new technologies to misrepresent themselves in order to gain access into closed social circles, make illicit contact with members of the opposite sex or swindle unsuspecting victims.

In earlier chapters, I described the way mobile technologies reconfigure the spatiotemporal framework of social life, making possible new forms of mobile togetherness such as 'absent presence' (Gergen 2002) and 'virtual proximity' (Bauman 2003). These technologies introduce a level of uncertainty into mediated, mobile and geographically dispersed social relations, blurring the distinction between presence and absence and proximity and distance. Mediated or virtual presence always begs the question of 'real' presence. Where are you, really? Are the journeys travellers display online representations of real, physical mobility or the effect of digital fabrication? Are travel bloggers, or CouchSurfers and their hosts for that matter, really who they say they are online? Such technologies make representations of identity or location more transparent and accessible, but also more easily manipulated, and therefore more suspect. In this sense, technologies that mediate presence also produce anxiety and uncertainty. Sometimes this opens up playful possibilities like Harding's hoax, but sometimes it creates possibilities for something more sinister.

As I noted in Chapter 4, interactive travellers will often implement location-based technologies on their blogs (for example, embedding Google maps into blog posts or using GPS devices to signal their location to friends), but then manage their blogs in ways that purposefully cast doubt on their own whereabouts. As I described, some travellers deliberately delay updating their blog entries as a security measure to keep the Internet public-at-large a bit behind their actual itinerary. But, travellers sometimes take advantage of the uncertainties around mediation and representation to dupe their own families. For example, in several instances travellers have secretly flown home to surprise parents who assumed, based on the status updates on their blogs, that the travellers were still abroad. This was the case with Lee and Sachi, a couple from the United States who documented their year-long journey on the blog *The World is Not Flat*. Unbeknownst to Lee's parents, the couple arranged to end their trip in time to attend his parents' fiftieth anniversary party. In a video posted on their blog after the fact, Lee explains how they kept his parents in the dark about their early homecoming:

> Our website says we're in Zaragoza, Spain. But we're not. We're in Dublin and catching a flight to New York City right now. And then arriving in North Carolina on Saturday to make my parents' 50th wedding anniversary. And they have no idea.
>
> (Blog entry posted on *TheWorldisNotFlat.com*)

Lee and Sachi were able to exploit the spatiotemporal uncertainty of the Internet and digital communications to produce a surprise moment of physical co-presence, the effects of which were captured in photos and on video for the blog.

Jodi, a Canadian traveller and former lawyer who has been travelling the world on her own for several years, carried out a similar ruse. On her blog, *Legal Nomads*, she recounts flying from Bangkok to New York to surprise her family at the holidays. Jodi tried to carry on the impression via email and mobile phone that she was still travelling:

> I decided to show up at the door [on New Year's Eve] – and hoped they wouldn't find out about my being in North America beforehand. This was a bit of a tricky situation since my mum and I correspond via email almost

daily, but I tried to keep my replies as hazy as possible without lying – i.e. 'I'll be in touch in the next few days. I left Thailand on a whim. My Thai cell phone doesn't work outside of Thailand,' etc.

(Blog entry posted on *LegalNomads.com*)

Without deliberately manipulating her online presence (as Lee and Sachi had done), Jodi plays on an assumption of physical distance implied by her travel blog and, in a sense, lets the technology lie for her. What makes Jodi's situation particularly tricky is the fact that she is in daily contact with her mother, even while she is travelling. The very same technologies that Jodi and her mother use to carry on a sense of virtual proximity are now employed to maintain virtual distance. It is precisely this capacity to reorder the spatiotemporal arrangements of mobile social relations – whether to mediate a sense of closeness or to manufacture the illusion of distance – that casts a sense of uncertainty on mobile technologies and social media.

Representation always entails the possibility of misrepresentation, a fact that Matt Harding's hoax exploits. Harding is not the only travel blogger to play with this ambiguity by staging a hoax. Gary, a long-term world traveller from the United States who publishes the popular travel blog *Everything-Everywhere*, plays an April Fool's joke on his audience every year. In 2008, a year into his journey, Gary posted the first of these jokes on his website. In an entry resembling Harding's hoax, Gary confessed that he was an imposter who had concocted the entire blog. He admitted that he was actually a 47-year-old, morbidly obese shut-in from Georgia named Roy DeWitt. He described how he created the blog by fictionalizing travel stories based on somebody else's travel blog and illustrating them with photos he found on Flickr.com, a photo sharing site. In this fake narrative, Gary touches on some of the same fears that Harding's videos raised: On the Internet, not only is your identity always in question, so is your mobility. Did you really take those photos? Did you really do the things you say you did? Are you really travelling?

Though most of Gary's readers immediately got the joke (which Gary clarified the next day in a post that read: 'Not real. Fake. Pretend. Fantasy. Fiction.'), one reader's comment sums up the sense of uncertainty that accompanies such misrepresentations of the 'real', 'Man. I don't know what to believe'. What this comment suggests is less a concern over the blurred distinction between the real and the fake than a fear of believing the wrong thing. In a world where digital simulations abound and the 'real' recedes into the distance, believing something to be true or not may be more a matter of choice than the fact of the matter. It is better not to believe something that turns out to be true than to believe something that turns out to be false. The fear of being duped always accompanies concerns for authenticity, especially in the case of corporate advertising. As we will see later, the difficulty in discerning what is and is not an advertisement online exacerbates this worry.

These uncertainties can easily expand into full-blown anxieties. Not knowing what to believe can be fun in the context of a prank or a well-intentioned surprise, but threatening in other circumstances. For example, anxieties around authenticity and representation emerged in many of my interviews with CouchSurfers as they reflected on questions of risk and safety associated with the practice of Couch-Surfing. For them, one of the key risks involved in the project was getting involved with someone who had wilfully misrepresented themselves in their profile, possibly with malicious intent. In some ways, the architecture of the CouchSurfing platform mitigates representational ambiguity. The complex profile questionnaire and the website's verification and references systems work to shore up the eroding boundaries between real and fake. In fact, what seems to comfort many Couch-Surfers is the amount of work someone would have to go to in order to create fake profiles and forge references in order to deceive other members. In this case, Internet technology poses the solution to its own problem, but not entirely. Most savvy CouchSurfers say that just because the verification process is able to confirm a member's name and address does not guarantee that the 'self' they present in their profile is authentic; that their personality is genuine. When it comes to representing the 'real', technology is a double-edged sword that can be used to obscure and misrepresent, to protect from deceit or to express one's true self (as if such a thing exists).

*Commodification*

A second anxiety related to technology and authenticity stems from commodification. While the initial debate over Harding's round-the-world dancing video revolved around the technical question of the video's veracity, subsequent debates focused, instead, on the authenticity of Harding's *motives*. To put it simply, he had sold out. According to Harding's detractors, a video that had started as an organic expression of joy and silliness had morphed into nothing more than a commercial. One disappointed viewer, who referred to the video as an example of 'corporate whoring', posted the following comment in an online blog forum where the video was under debate, 'I'd never seen the video before and at first watch it was magical. Finding out that it was a viral video to sell gum just made me really sad'.[1]

What bothered this viewer, and several others on the forum, was not that the images in the video were 'photoshopped' (as far as they were concerned, that was still up for debate), but that the video was a commercial. They thought they were watching a 'magical' and inspirational travel video, only to discover that they were, in fact, watching a clever piece of marketing. The seamless flow between commercial and non-commercial practices that often characterizes online social networking and social media spaces had blunted their ability to discern between the 'authentic' and the 'ad', and this seemed to offend them even more than the ambiguity between 'real' and 'fiction'. In many cases, as with viral campaigns, marketers deliberately blur the line between what is and is not an advertisement (O'Barr *et al.* 2009). They take advantage of – and help to produce – an online environment in which an ad can appear anywhere and anything can be an ad. In such an environment, various forms of self-expression can slip easily into the realm of commerce.

For other observers, whether the video was real or fake, an advertisement or not, was not the key issue. It was Harding's deal with Stride that had undermined the authenticity of his travels, as the following comments posted on the *BootsnAll.com* travel forums express:

> Matt's story is that he ... moved to Australia for work. When his time was up there he back packed for about 6 months home. He started dancing then. After he got back St[r]ide paid for trip number two. ... On his second trip he went some where, danced, and left. Didn't really see anything. ... I do love the videos. But I don't really consider flying to a place, dancing, and leaving as actual travel.[2]

According to this summary of Matt's story, what started out as a legitimate six-month backpacking journey turned into a simulation once it was co-opted by corporate marketers. Under their sponsorship, Harding showed up, shot the video and left, leaving viewers with the impression that he was just going through the motions without 'really' seeing anything or doing any 'actual' travel.

Authenticity takes on a familiar role in these comments where it is put to work shoring up the symbolic status boundaries between 'real' travellers and everyone else on the road. One of the best-known examples of this argument is found in Boorstin's *The Image*, a biting critique of mid-twentieth century mass culture. Here, in a chapter titled 'The lost art of travel', Boorstin makes an acerbic distinction between tourists and travellers. According to Boorstin, tourists move through foreign lands as if in a bubble, happily consuming artificial stand-ins for 'real' culture. In contrast is the traveller, a heroic figure who is hard at work searching for authentic experiences. He writes:

> The traveller, then, was working at something; the tourist was a pleasure-seeker. The traveller was active; he went strenuously in search of people, of adventure, of experience. The tourist is passive; he expects interesting things to happen to him. ... Thus foreign travel ceased to be an activity – an experience, an undertaking – and instead became a commodity. The rise of the tourist was possible, and then inevitable, when attractive items of travel were wrapped up and sold in packages (the 'package tour').
>
> (Boorstin 1961: 85)

Similar efforts to establish the categorical distinction between tourists and travellers have persisted ever since mass tourism was born (Fussell 1980; Culler 1981; Enzensberger 1996 [1958]). Today, the debate over what distinguishes a 'real' traveller from a tourist remains a favourite topic among backpackers in hostels and in online forums (Anderskov 2002; Uriely *et al.* 2002; Welk 2004). While some travellers claim not to care about this distinction, these debates continue to crop up in many travel blogs and online travel forums, often citing the familiar norms of authenticity articulated in Boorstin's critique: travel is an art, an arduous and usually solitary adventure into remote places; tourism is commercialized, passive, crowded and inauthentic.

However, this debate is rarely about definitional accuracy and more often about taste, lifestyle, snobbery and identity work. 'Authentic' travel is seen as a source of status and cultural capital, whereas tourism is not. As Desforges (1998: 185) notes in his study of young backpackers, 'by using travel as a form of cultural capital which serves as a sign of distinction, travellers gain access to a social class and its consequent privileges'. The problem is, as O'Reilly (2006) points out, travel styles that were once seen as status-enhancing practices, such as backpacking, are now becoming more and more mainstream. As these forms of travel become more accessible to a wider range of travellers, the less effective they are as signs of exclusivity. This leads, in some backpacker circles, to a kind of rivalry around certain 'status indicators' – tighter budgets, smaller backpacks, deadlier diseases and lonelier travel to ever more remote destinations – that set 'real' backpackers apart from tourists, certainly, but also from other backpackers (Anderskov 2002; Sørensen 2003).

The growing trend of flashpacking is also implicated in what O'Reilly (2006) identifies as this mainstreaming of backpacking. According to Matt, a traveller in his twenties from the United States and author of the travel blog *Nomadic Matt's Travel Site*, flashpacking is not just a new subset of backpacking; it is *the* predominant form of backpacking today. In a blog entry titled 'Are we all flashpackers now?' he explains that if flashpackers are defined by their more generous budgets, higher standards of comfort, and constant use of digital technologies, then few backpackers today are immune from this trend:

> I believe we have all morphed into a "flashpacker." The old way of travel – a backpack, a few bucks, a worn guidebook is well behind us. When I first started traveling in 2006, I hardly ever saw someone with a cell phone and barely a few people with a SLR camera and never with a laptop. ... Now everywhere I go, I see mobile phones, wi-fi available, netbooks, and SLR cameras. ... In short, backpackers today are much more wired today than they used to be. ...

> Back in the "real world," people are used to being digitally connected. We're used to having our cameras and our phones taking pictures. What used to be expensive and inconvenient on the road and, thus only available to "flashpackers", is now cheap and easy for all. ... Moreover, now that backpackers seem to have some extra money, there is a whole network of backpacker services looking to help them spend it. Travelers seem to be taking more tours, more hop on/hop off buses, and staying at nicer and more expensive accommodation. ...

> I don't see this freight train stopping anytime soon. I suspect as common as iPods are today, computers will be tomorrow. But the rising affluence of most

travelers means that even those who are "broke" will still carry their toys and comforts on the road with them. For me, that's OK so long as once in awhile they unplug, take out the iPod, and interact with the destination they spent so long saving to interact with.

(Blog entry posted on *NomadicMatt.com*)

This brings us to a question that has not yet been fully explored in research on backpacking: what role do digital technologies play in the negotiation of status and authenticity in the backpacker imaginary? These comments suggest that, because it is a more commercialized form of travelling, flashpacking poses a threat to the authenticity of backpacking. Relatively affluent flashpackers can afford tour buses and upscale accommodations that do not require them to rub elbows with local people on public transportation or in campgrounds and homestays, for example. But, they also suggest that the more travellers are 'plugged in' to their digital devices, the more disconnected they may be from the local people and places they have travelled to experience in the first place. This leads to a third anxiety around technology and authenticity: the threat of disconnection.

### *Disconnection*

In a cultural imaginary that associates 'authentic' travel with a connection to the local culture, the social significance of these technological practices is unsettled at best. In fact, Nomadic Matt's final comment – 'that's OK so long as once in a while they unplug . . . and interact with the destination' – alludes to an undercurrent of apprehension around the *dis*connections that flashpacking also makes possible. Reflecting on these remarks, several fellow travellers expressed their anxiety that digitally connecting to 'elsewhere' comes at the expense of connecting with local people and places (see Figure 6.1). Consider the way this debate unfolds in two of the comments posted in response to this blog entry:

To travel means to leave your normal life behind, get out of your comfort zone, live a different lifestyle and dive into uncertainty. The way these flash-packer travel today seems like the most efficient way to avoid all of this. You basically take your online life with you on the road. You are connected with your friends in the same way as from your small appartment [sic]at home. Your heads are docked to your computer screen the same way your [sic] are at home. Anything uncertain gets elimited [sic] by being able to access all the information you need about your next destination. Asking for the way used to be the easiest way to get in contact with locals. Now with GPS'ed phones people even managed to avoid that. . . . Technology has made it very easy, comfortable and risk free to do the 'backpacking thing.' [I]t's not a commit-ment anymore as it used to be. It's traveling minus the adventure. Seems very boring to me. I kind of feel sorry for them, cause they are missing out so much of what i[t] could be like.

*Figure 6.1* Backpackers using the computers in the guest house common room in Cusco, Peru.

Everyone seems to be drinking the flashpacker Kool-aid without looking at the downside. It blows my mind to be in a guesthouse where 10 people are in a common area and all of them are looking at a glowing blue screen, talking to the people back home instead of the ones right beside them. Why travel if you're going to spend every night on Facebook and Twitter just like you do at home? Same routine, different place. That's an improvement?

(Reader comments posted on *NomadicMatt.com*)

These comments focus primarily on the way digital technologies connect or disconnect travellers from local people and places, but another common concern expressed in such discussions is whether constantly connected flashpackers are able to connect to *themselves*, so to speak. In this case, flashpacking appears to pose a threat to existential authenticity as well. Critics argue that 'finding oneself' becomes impossible when young backpackers, in particular, are able to stay in constant touch with friends and parents back home (Murphy 2009), connected by what one blogger calls the 'electronic umbilical cord' (Potts 2009). In this case, flashpacking undercuts the idealized image of the 'authentic' backpacker as a solitary traveller, along with other norms of 'authentic' travel: immersion in local cultures, getting out of one's comfort zone, experiencing uncertainty, connecting with local people and committing to the hard work of travel. What Boorstin (1961) termed the 'tourist bubble' is also articulated here as a comfortable, risk free safety net of digital connectivity: flashpackers take their online lives with them, connecting on the road to the same friends, routines and computer screens that they connected to at home.

Although this online discussion on *Nomadic Matt's Travel Site* emphasizes how *new* these new technologies and travel practices are, the conversation that unfolds on this blog is less about the novelty of 'technical efficiencies in communication' than it is an 'arena for negotiating issues crucial to the conduct of social life; among them, who is inside and outside, . . . who has authority and may be believed' (Marvin 1988: 4). According to Marvin, it is precisely in these inchoate moments, when new media and communication technologies have not yet gelled into commonplace social practices, that 'the struggle of groups to define and locate themselves is most easily observed' (ibid.: 5). Indeed, what is evident in the debate on *Nomadic Matt* is the way some travellers seek to (re)establish certain forms of backpacking as authentic, distinctive and status-enhancing in the face of perceived threats posed by flashpacking. In this debate, technological practices are measured against a benchmark of authenticity in order to value some forms of travelling and connecting over others.

The remarks cited above are among the more sceptical responses Matt's blog entry received, but other respondents acknowledged that they enjoyed using digital technologies while on the road and did not see these emerging practices as disconnecting them from local experiences. One traveller wrote:

> I don't think it's a case of talking on twitter every night and ignoring those around you. I might spend an hour on a computer each day or so when i'm [sic] travelling. I will be talking to friends back home/emailing them etc. during that time but when i'm [sic] finished I come off and mix with the friends i've [sic] made at the hostel for a large part of the day. For me, I think it's important to do both. Going travelling is all about the experiences you have, but at the same time, if I want to call up my parents on skype, chat to an old flatmate, or just catch up with some people i've [sic] not heard from in a while I like to know I can.
>
> (Reader comment posted on *NomadicMatt.com*)

Just as new technologies can illuminate deeply held anxieties, so too do they prompt expressions of the desires and aspirations people attach to new media and communication technologies. Here, new technologies do not just allow this traveller to stay in touch at a distance, but to make choices about whom or what she wants to connect with and when. I will return to this example in the next chapter when I discuss the way travellers frame this desire for choice in terms of escape. For now, however, I want to continue by exploring the way new technological practices provoke not just anxieties about authenticity, but also fantasies of getting closer to or deeper inside local cultures.

### Authentic aspirations

The scepticism surrounding Matt Harding's dancing videos, along with the flash-packing debate on *Nomadic Matt's Travel Site*, convey deep uncertainties about shifting patterns of social interaction in a digital, corporatized and mobile world. Not only do Harding's travel videos destabilize boundaries between what is or is not real, and what is or is not an advertisement online, his corporate dealings are seen as undermining 'real' connections with local cultures while on the road. Furthermore, flashpackers' digital practices also raise concerns about the status of 'real' connections and 'authentic' travel. These debates, couched in the overlapping discourses of authenticity and commodification, are less about travel and technology than they are about negotiating power, authority, knowledge and representation amid shifting spatial and social boundaries. The ambiguity of absence and presence, the digital manipulation of online images and identities, and the commodification and digitization of travel experiences threaten to dupe, exclude or disconnect some travellers and travel practices. This exploits another anxiety travellers harbour in relation to technology, which is that it will disconnect and separate them from the very experience they want to feel most deeply. The flip side is that these technologies also promise to help travellers access precisely those experiences. So what is at stake, in many cases, is not a question of 'the real', but rather a question of connecting and managing the very real possibility that these technologies are machines of connection *and* disconnection.

As I have argued so far, concerns about authenticity often harbour deep-seated anxieties about the social and spatial impacts of new technologies, but negotiations of authenticity just as often express the aspirations and fantasies people attach to these technologies. In this case, using digital technologies to perpetrate hoaxes or to sell out is met with cynicism and contempt, but using them to promote 'authentic' connections is seen as a social 'good', a tool that can potentially unite humanity, help travellers immerse themselves more meaningfully into local cultures, and ultimately re-enchant modernity.

### Uniting humanity

Earlier, I focused on the anxieties that Matt Harding's videos and fake confession provoked amongst observers, but most of the viewers who posted comments found the dancing videos to be amusing, light hearted, moving and inspirational. A common theme running throughout the hundreds of thousands of comments posted on YouTube was that the video, regardless of its technical authenticity, had evoked an authentic emotional response of human connectedness. Viewers acknowledged that they were 'touched', 'choked up', 'moved to tears', and left 'smiling' and feeling 'warm and fuzzy' by the silliness of the dance and the sense of humanity expressed in the video, as in the following comments left in response to the video:

> This is an incredible and beautiful portrait of our world. Can't help but get choked up when [I] watch this. Goes to show just how everyone is the same regardless of nationality or race.

> It might just look like a silly dance being done over the entire world, but look what it does! Look at all those smiles in the video's [sic] and as you watched

this video, weren't you smiling too? Videos like this bring hope in a world full of pain and separation. Keep on dancing people!

Guys, this makes me feel so connected with everyone.

This is just SO BRILLIANT!! How wonderful to enjoy our beautiful world and see it presented with such harmony for mankind.

[I] can only say man u made me cry im [sic] touched one man in such a simple way made the world so small.

there's something about this video that i really like. i guess it's the sense of togetherness in a world where we are seperated.

LONG LIVE HUMANITY!!!!!!!!

Lets [sic] promote peace and love. For the sake of humankind. Your video is great and a source of inspiration. I like you Matt :D

An absolutely incredible video. Truly an inspiration. May the spirit of humanity live on and flourish.

[I] know that the whole thing is fake, but nevertheless watching it makes me feel happy and restores my faith in humanity.[3]

These comments speak to the sense of emotional authenticity that viewers experienced *despite* the concurrent debate in these forums about the video's technical and commercial authenticity. Potter (2010: 138) notes that 'emotive authenticity' is relatively unconcerned with 'historical accuracy' as long as the message has universal appeal and 'feels' true. As the final comment excerpted above suggests, rumours of digital manipulation or deception cannot detract from what viewers *feel* to be real about the video: its evocation of a sense of common humanity. The authenticity of this emotional connection is facilitated by the technology, not diminished by it. In other words, what viewers feel to be authentic about the video has less to do with its technical accuracy or with the purity of Harding's motives, but rather with the fantasy of human connectedness, global cohesion and 'small-world-ness' that viewers attach more broadly to digital videography, online distribution and electronically-mediated communication.

Harding's viewers are certainly not the only or the first to perceive within new media and communication technologies a promise to unite humanity. These sentiments recall the fantasies of erasing cultural differences and promoting the 'kinship of humanity' that accompanied the telegraph in the nineteenth century (Marvin 1988). According to Marvin, the moral influence of the telegraph was described at the time in terms of uniting the world as 'one family' sharing a 'common, universal, simultaneous heart throb' (ibid.: 199). At the time, this fantasy was premised, somewhat ironically, on another fantasy: connection without contamination. Thanks to the immediacy and accuracy of telegraphic communication, Marvin explains, correspondents on different sides of the world could interact with each other without undertaking the risk of physical travel and embodied encounter.

This meant that for a public comfortably ensconced in western society, reaching out to other cultures was rarely associated with 'any obligation to behave as a guest in the Other's domain, to learn or appreciate the Other's customs, to speak his language, to share his victories and disappointments, or to change as a result of any encounter with him' (ibid.: 195).

Here, authenticity points to technological fantasies about bringing humankind together, but this togetherness is experienced from afar, safely mediated and thus freed from the obligations of attention, hospitality and self-examination that embodied encounters might require. Clearly, this fantasy has been recycled in the discussions surrounding Harding's video, but another version of this fantasy – of abandoning one's comfort zone, veering off the beaten path, and getting physically and emotionally close to the other – is at work in some of the other technological practices I have described in this book, including the mobile mediated walking tours I described in Chapter 3 and hospitality exchanges I discussed in Chapter 5. In the next section, I consider how these mobile tour developers and CouchSurfers alike use terms like 'insider', 'local', and 'off the beaten path' to imagine mobile technologies and social media as facilitating more 'authentic', often embodied and emotional, encounters with places and with people. These technological practices are not seen as disconnecting people; on the contrary, they are framed as (re)connecting them in more focused and meaningful ways.

*Off the 'beaten path'*

With promotional materials and narratives promising access to hidden places, secret passageways and local knowledge, the mediated urban tours I introduced in Chapter 3 draw heavily on an idiom of authenticity. The mediated guides offered by Audissey, Untravel Media, PocketMetro and Urban Interactive all guarantee to give the technology-equipped tourist privileged access to stories and places. Of all the fantasies related to technology in interactive travel, perhaps the most profound one has to do with the tired trope of the 'beaten path', those predictable routes and itineraries carved out around the world by mass tourists and independent backpackers alike. Technology, with its fantastic capacity to annotate and reveal the invisible narratives inscribed on the urban landscape, holds the key to fulfilling tourists' presumed desire to get 'off the beaten path' and into the backstage and back story of the city.

Apart from revealing the 'true' story of the city, however, these mediated tours are designed to produce authentic embodied and emotional encounters with the city. Developers of these tours emphasize the technology's ability to produce embodied performances, to evoke emotional responses and to create a personal experience within the urban landscape. As I noted in my earlier analysis of the tours, their immersive narrative environment directs an intensely embodied and sensuous experience of place. Audissey's tours, for example, have been described as 'so much more emotional than somebody just spewing facts' (Lamb 2009). Likewise, the developers of the Urban Interactive adventures claim that their tours provide a more 'personal' experience than either wandering on one's own or taking a packaged guided tour of the city. For Untravel Media's CEO, Michael Epstein, mobile technologies offer the possibility to situate and inspire conversations between tourists and local people. Among the core objectives listed on the Untravel Media website are 'connect people', 'provoke reaction', 'raise awareness', and 'create the most meaningful experience possible'. This list is followed by the Untravel Media team's assertion that 'We love being able to share these values with the world using our technology!'[4] Comments like these attach a fantasy of existential authenticity to mobile devices and technological practices. Not only do mobile technologies promise access to authentic information about the city, but also to bodily sensations, personalized experiences and emotional responses that give the tourist a sense of authentic connection to the city.

Another fantasy at work here is the notion of a technologically perfectible physical and social reality. The early virtual worlds of cyberspace, for example, were pinned with optimistic hopes for a more accessible, democratic and equitable space of public exchange. Technological innovations are often embraced as a means of achieving experiences that are even more real than reality itself, just as the simulated environments at Disney World are frequently described as more natural than nature itself. The mobile mediated tours in this study do not simulate reality, of course, but they do imagine – and in many ways bring to fruition – the possibility of 'augmented reality'. The notion of augmented reality suggests that a technologically enhanced urban landscape exists that is potentially more interesting, more meaningful and more fun than plain old reality. According to Dick Paik of Urban Interactive, analogue reality offers limited options to encountering a city: 'You can validate your presence by eating. You can ... gawk at the plaques. And walk. Which is pleasant, but it really doesn't involve you at all.' Paik explains that tourists wandering around the city without a mobile device are unable to 'get involved' in the city and lack access to the stories and adventures that have been digitally tagged to that place. In contrast, mobile technologies give tourists the ability to move between digital and physical landscapes, opening up new opportunities for fantasy, narrative and play in these blended geographies. Otherwise opaque urban landscapes are revealed to be more engrossing and more meaningful than they appear to the unaided eye. Implicit in this discourse is the paradoxical notion that reality is not authentic enough on its own; authentic encounters with the city must be enhanced and accessed through digital technologies. Also implicit in this discourse is the compelling fantasy that technology can infuse the mundane and beaten paths of urban space with a sense of mystery and meaning.

A similar fantasy of access to authentic encounters with local people and places is at work in CouchSurfing. In descriptions of the project on the website, in member testimonials, on profiles and in interviews, CouchSurfers repeatedly frame the CouchSurfing network as a way of gaining direct access to 'local' life and to emotionally profound encounters, as well as to an expanded sense of self. As I noted in Chapter 5, the fact that these connections occur outside the commercial realm of monetary exchange further validates their authenticity. Appeals to authenticity emerge frequently when members attempt to describe what CouchSurfing is all about. Consider the way a discourse of authenticity structures this member's comments about CouchSurfing:

> CouchSurfing is amazing. It's a real way to know about the country you are visiting and to get in direct contact with its culture. Make friends, share ideas and tips, have experiences, learn different ways of living, etc.... It helps you grow personally. It changes your paradigms, breaks stereotypes, opens your mind and frees your spirit. It helps you know yourself much better. It makes you believe and have hope in people. It's a small world and we are connected.
> (member testimonial posted on *CouchSurfing.org*)

This testimonial interweaves several aspirations of authenticity. From the perspective of objectivist authenticity, CouchSurfing provides 'direct access' to local cultures and the intimate spheres of local life; from a more existential perspective, CouchSurfing also stimulates personal growth and helps members know themselves better; and in relation to the point I raised earlier about the fantasy of 'human kinship', CouchSurfing also reaffirms hope and a feeling of global connectedness.

Although the technology itself tends to recede into the background in Couch-Surfers' stories of face-to-face encounters with each other and with other places, networking technology is both the starting point and the endpoint of the journey. Underlying these stories is the notion that these meaningful interactions could not happen – or are unlikely to happen – without the choreographing and connecting power of technology. As Therese, the Canadian CouchSurfer I introduced in Chapter 5, explains, chances are 'slim to nil' that a traveller would randomly meet someone in a new place, start up a conversation and then get invited to their home for dinner. But with CouchSurfing, she says, 'It's basically 100% guaranteed that you're going to connect with the culture'. As much as these fantasies of authenticity coalesce around the embodied and emotional connections between CouchSurfers, it is clear that they are also attached to the technology itself. Here, technological practices that enable travellers to find, access and connect to people and places are valued and normalized through their association with authenticity. Hospitality sites like *CouchSurfing.org* are often seen as bringing to fruition the Internet's original utopian promise of global communication and community. Appealing to the Internet's early principles of democratic, inclusive and noncommercial communication, hospitality exchange networks seem to reassert what many theorists writing in the early 1990s saw as the 'true' intentions of the Internet: to create a virtual global community that would bridge political, cultural and geographical divides and replace the sense of belonging that was missing in modern social life. Twenty years on, this utopian ideal of the Internet is battered, but still very much alive.

This vision of the Internet, along with the imaginaries of authenticity at play in the responses to Harding's video, in the mobile mediated walking tours and in the CouchSurfers' remarks cited above, evokes authenticity and technology together as a response to a sense of loss of community, connectedness and belonging that characterizes the modern condition. Talking about authenticity is a way of bestowing meaning – on places, encounters and technological practices. These fantasies of technologically facilitated access to authenticity take us back, in some ways, to MacCannell's (1999[1976]) original assertion that tourists seek the authentic as an antidote to the alienation, fragmentation and ennui of modern life. The desires expressed in these discourses for both objectivist authenticity (in the form of access to local life and culture) and existential authenticity (in the form of intense emotional, personal and embodied experiences) suggest that travellers are seeking something more meaningful than their everyday lives provide.

But I want to resist, for a moment, the implied dichotomy here between modernity and authenticity. The lasting influence of MacCannell's argument suggests that this dichotomy has some explanatory purchase for tourism practices, but it leaves us with an unsatisfying, and in many cases problematic, paradox. As Meethan (2001: 91) points out, the premise of MacCannell's argument suggests that 'all that modernism brings with it will *by definition* be false, alienating, unreal and inauthentic'. This essentializes modern society as necessarily inauthentic and pre-modern cultures as authentic in a 'misplaced romanticism of traditional life' that often leads to questionable efforts to preserve what few remnants of pre-modern authenticity are left (ibid.: 91–2). Indeed, some of this is evident in the way notions of authenticity get bandied about in travellers' conversations about getting direct access to local knowledge or to local life. But, as Meethan and many others point out, thinking of tourism, modernity and authenticity in this way is a self-defeating proposition. The kind of authenticity imagined here as an antidote to modernity is, itself, a thoroughly modern invention. The concept of authenticity only came into existence by virtue of a modern realization that it was missing. This is the aporia of authenticity: it is a product of the very processes that guarantee its impossibility. From this perspective, authenticity is necessarily destroyed by the modernist projects of technological progress, global mobility and commodification. It can thus never be more than 'a phantom of modernity', and as such the idea that tourism is a quest for 'authenticity lost' offers little closure (Oakes 2006: 232). In fact, it may be the quest itself, which often morphs into a brutal form of status-seeking one-up-man-ship, rather than modernity per se that weakens the very sense of authentic community and social cohesion that modern subjects seek (Potter 2010).

This is why the aspirations of authenticity that travellers attach to new media and mobile technologies are so intriguing. How is it that these technologies operate in the cultural imaginary as both harbingers of the inauthenticity of modernity *and* points of access to authentic experiences? Surely the most 'authentic' travel experiences would be those that avoid modern technologies altogether. But as we have seen so far, this is not necessarily the case. Perhaps what the travellers in this study are searching for in authenticity is not an antidote to modernity, but a modernity they can live with. A re-enchanted modernity.

## Re-enchanting modernity

In the technological fantasies described earlier, mobile technologies and social media do not necessarily transport travellers to some traditional or pre-modern time or place, but they do, to a certain extent, re-enchant a disenchanted world. According to one version of the modernity narrative, the modern condition is a result of the disenchantment of the world. At one time, so the story goes, humans experienced the world as a divinely ordered cosmos with human beings at its centre. The sun, moon and stars revolved around the Earth, the natural world on Earth revolved around humans, and a tightly ordered social world placed humans into castes and classes based on 'natural' characteristics such as gender, skin colour or ancestry. As Potter (2010: 22) explains:

> Whatever else it might have been, this was a place of meaning, value, and purpose, with each part getting its identity from knowing its place in the whole and performing its proper function within an organic unity. . . . In this geocentric and homocentric cosmos, . . . each person's identity was entirely determined by their place in that structure.

In such a world, everything happened for a purpose predetermined by some cosmic or divine power that, for better or worse, cared about humanity. Scientific discoveries (such as the fact that the sun did not revolve around the Earth, for example) and the rise of rational thought and instrumental reason began to chip away at the certainty embedded into such 'comprehensive doctrines' of cosmic order (ibid.: 23). Once the order of the universe could be explained by the laws of science, and not the will of a divine power, humanity lost its place in this order and the world lost its sense of mystery, meaning and magic.

The destabilization of humanity's role at the centre of the cosmos was both liberating and devastating. Individuals were eventually unlocked from the rigid hierarchies of social roles and class structures and became free to create their own place and identity in the world. Indeed, as I will elaborate in the next chapter, this freedom is a hallmark of modern identity (Giddens 1991). But, it came at the expense of purpose and meaningfulness. Taylor (1991) explains that the discrediting of the cosmic and divine orders of the world resulted in the 'disenchantment' of the world and the loss of a sense of magic. He notes that this disenchantment has been described in several ways: as the loss of a heroic dimension to life, the loss of a higher sense of purpose, a lack of passion and a narrowing down to a focus on the self with little concern for others or for society. The effect of modern reason, he argues, is that human beings have been triply divided 'within themselves, between themselves, and from the natural world' (Taylor 1991: 94). In other words, the existential realization that there is no deeper purpose and no divinely ordered structure to life lends the modern condition its sense of ennui and its sense of alienation – from the self, from others and from nature.

The technological practices described throughout this book – mobile mediated walking tours, travel blogging and CouchSurfing – are tasked through their association with authenticity with restoring a sense of mystery, magic and meaning to this disenchanted world. Mobile digital technologies and social media are seen as re-enchanting the spatial and social experiences of travel, either by re-animating the aura of the 'pleasure periphery' or reinserting a sense of social order and purpose into interactions between strangers. As I described in Chapter 3, mobile mediated tours of the city are often billed as launching tourists off the beaten path, but, in many ways, these tours actually *re-enchant* the beaten path. By layering digital narratives and invisible but technologically accessible data over well-worn physical trajectories through the city, these tours and the tourists who follow them co-create new blended landscapes that can be discovered with the help of a mobile device. Companies like Untravel Media and Urban Interactive deliberately use mobile digital technologies to reinstate a sense of mystery into the city. As I described earlier, for example, Urban Interactive's adventures construct the city as an enigmatic space and position the tourist as a detective. Likewise, Untravel Media's most recent project, a 'walking cinema' piece based on the famous 1849 murder of George Parkman in Boston's Beacon Hill neighbourhood, envelops tourists into a mobile murder mystery that transports them around the city and back through time while revealing location-specific clues about Parkman's murder. The kind of mystery on offer in these tours is both educational and entertaining, though clearly not on the order of a cosmic regime. What is significant, though, is that these projects attach to digital technologies these aspirations of creating more engaging and meaningful encounters with urban spaces.

The same is true of the notion of common humanity that I introduced earlier in relation to Matt Harding's dancing video and CouchSurfing. In these cases, technology is seen as bringing some kind of order to the otherwise fragmented chaos of humanity. Travellers impart to digital video and networking technologies the ability to highlight what it is that all humans have in common, and to place our differences in a context of shared humanity. Furthermore, at least in the case of CouchSurfing, networking technology is put to use making new personal connections across the cultural and spatial boundaries. The electronic web of social connections made possible via the Internet pose a remedy to the fragmenting and dislocating effects of the modern condition. New media and communication technologies are thus enrolled in a fantasy of global social cohesion that has been lost in a fragmenting and alienating modern world. So to the extent that technological progress is seen as abetting the disenchantment of the world, it is also conceived of as a fix for modernity's loss of meaning and mystery. Technology does not, in and of itself, provide a sense of purpose and order to the world, but for many of the travellers I have introduced throughout this book, it is a potentially powerful tool in a variety of re-enchantment projects.

My intention here is not to suggest that these technologies do, in fact, restore a sense of purpose and order to a de-mystified modern world, but rather to show how the social significance of emerging technological practices gets negotiated through this fantasy of enchantment. Just as new technologies touch a nerve of anxiety around deception, alienation, commodification and the collapse of social and spatial boundaries, so too do they inspire dreams of wholeness and of (re)connecting in emotional and embodied ways with places, people and the self. This discussion is also intended to show how these technological practices destabilize the dichotomy between authenticity and modernity. Of course, authenticity is still called upon under the guise of tourism to lock some cultures and people under the protective cloak of nostalgic romanticism, but authenticity is also deployed to make other kinds of claims about mobility, technology, connection and togetherness that resist the binary distinctions between modernity and authenticity.

## Conclusion

Authenticity is undoubtedly one of those places where tourism and modernity are stitched together. For many critics, this relationship is an uneasy one. Some have suggested that MacCannell's notion that tourism entails a quest for authenticity results in a problematic dichotomy between modernity and authenticity (Meethan 2001), while others have argued that the concept of authenticity is too slippery to be of any analytical use at all (Reisinger and Steiner 2006). A desire for authenticity is prompted by conditions of modernity, but performative of those conditions as well (Shaffer 2004; Jacobs 2006). If authenticity retains any explanatory power for practices of travel and tourism, it is neither as an antithesis to modernity nor as the object of a 'quest' for something lost, but rather as a touchstone for the ambivalence of modern life. Oakes (2006: 237) reminds us that:

> Modernity does not simply represent a privileging of reason over experience, or a celebration of progress over the death of tradition, but more accurately conveys the ambivalence between reason and experience, and the sense of loss and nostalgia that progress entails.

Indeed, travellers appeal to authenticity in order to negotiate a series of paradoxes: the way technology both uproots and reconnects spatial and social arrangements; fantasies of using technology to get close to the other and fears that these same technologies will separate travellers from 'authentic' experiences; playing with virtual presence and mediated representations while remaining duly sceptical about manufactured realities or commercial motives online. The ability to stay connected while physically on the move requires travellers to embrace modernity and the technological innovations it brings with it. The fear that this mobility and mediated presence might enable people to fool each other is tempered by the hope that it will also root them in new forms of togetherness.

Clearly, technological progress and related processes of commodification entail both losses and gains in the realm of social life, but authenticity does not necessarily fall on the 'loss' side of this tally. Through the prism of authenticity, we see how travellers adjust to new social patterns afforded by mobile digital technologies and social media, negotiating the perceived threats to a familiar social order on the one hand, and playing with the new possibilities for communicating and communing with distant strangers and loved ones on the other. In the end, it is neither the loss of authenticity nor the search for authenticity that characterizes modern travel, but rather the way authenticity reveals travellers' hopes and fears about new social patterns, technological practices and ways of communicating on the move. In this context, authenticity is not necessarily the antithesis of modernity, but perhaps a way of coming to terms with, and even embracing, a modernity shaped around technology and mobility. If this is the case, then we must also rethink another paradigm that has been used to make sense of tourism – the idea of tourism as an escape from modernity.

# 7 Escape

## Unplugging from modernity

Eva and Jeremy are self-proclaimed 'foodies' whose round-the-world travel blog, *Forks and Jets*, revolves primarily around food and beer. Filled with stories of epic meals and photographs of food and drink from around the world, the blog documents a mobile feast. So, it is somewhat surprising to read in the introduction to their blog that what motivated their year-long world journey was not a desire to eat, but rather a desire to escape:

> We are Eva & Jeremy and we are going to escape. We are escaping the 9 to 5, the 40 hour work week, the daily commute, cable television, apartment rent, owning furniture. We are escaping our small corner of the world, known as Los Angeles, because we believe there is a bigger world out there. We want to meet it, eat it, bump into it and get a better look at it. . . . We don't want to be content with two-week vacations once a year, sitting in front of a computer monitor and buying a home, mowing the lawn. Sometimes you have to escape the box completely to think outside it.
>
> (Blog entry posted to *ForksandJets.com*)

What Jeremy and Eva express here is a sentiment that runs throughout many of the blogs in my study. The desire to 'escape the box' reiterates a powerful cultural imaginary that equates travel and tourism with a sense of escape from the constraints of modern life. This chapter explores the way this imaginary gives structure and meaning both to travellers' corporeal mobility practices and to their technological practices. As we will see, the notion of travel and tourism as a form of escape is certainly not new, but new communication technologies have reanimated its significance for tourism studies. What does it mean for travellers to escape in a world of ubiquitous connectivity?

## Introduction

In an article published in *The Guardian*, travel writer Dervla Murphy laments that 'in this age of mobile phones, cybercafés and satellite links, it's harder than ever to truly escape' (Murphy 2009). To Murphy's mind, the digital age has produced a worrying trend in travel:

> Increasingly, in hostels and guesthouses, one sees "independent" travellers eagerly settling down in front of computers instead of conversing with fellow

travellers. They seem only partially "abroad", unable to cut their links with home. Evidently the nanny state – and the concomitant trend among parents to over-protect offspring – has alarmingly diminished the younger generation's self-reliance. And who is to blame for this entrapment in cyberspace? Who but the fussy folk back at base, awaiting the daily (even twice daily) email of reassurance.

(ibid.)

In contrast, she suggests, 'true escapist travel' should be slow and solitary – two increasingly scarce qualities in our fast-paced, always-on modern world. To the would-be escapist, Murphy's article offers a list of tips on how to slow down, get off the beaten path of commercialized mass tourism, travel on one's own and, above all, disconnect from over-protective parents. 'Abandon your mobile phone, laptop, iPod and all such links to family, friends and work colleagues,' she advises.

Murphy's description of 'escapist travel' sounds very much like the 'quest for authenticity' I discussed in the previous chapter. From some angles, authenticity and escapism do look quite similar, especially when they are framed as a reaction to modernity or to high-tech and commodified forms of tourism. But, escapism is not necessarily synonymous with a search for authentic experience; many post-tourists fulfil their fantasies of escape in simulated environments like Disney World, for example. Like authenticity, however, escape is a way of talking about and making sense of new technological practices within the context of tourism. We see this in Murphy's article, where her conceptualization of escape illustrates the extent to which the western imaginary of 'escapism' is premised on certain social, spatial and technological conditions.

Murphy sees escape as a solitary endeavour, even though the ubiquity of technology has made solitude all but impossible, 'I prefer to forget that nowadays one is never quite alone. With all those satellites, the solitary traveller may be observed picking her nose in the middle of the Great Karoo'. Murphy's notion of escape also entails a spatial dimension. She encourages travellers to 'embark on solo journeys through little-known regions where they can imagine how real explorers used to feel'. She observes that places like Asmara, Addis Ababa, Russia and Romania can still provide a sense of escape, especially if travellers do as Murphy recommends and 'stay away from the tourist trails'. Finally, Murphy's emphatic rejection of technology and disapproval of the 'new' generation, with their noses in their computers, frames escape as a state of digital disconnection, reproducing a common dichotomy that pits escape in opposition to technology. In sum, Murphy invokes a conventional mythology of escape, conjuring up a romantic image of the solitary traveller roaming alone through exotic, untouched landscapes *sans* the technological accoutrements of modern life.

The empirical reality, at least as far as my research is concerned, looks quite different. Interactive travellers like Eva and Jeremy do call upon a discourse of 'escape' to make sense of their mobility practices, but the relationship between escape, technology and modernity is not as dichotomous as Murphy's account might imply. The gap between the romanticized myth of escape that Murphy paints in her article and the complicated 'escape attempts' (Cohen and Taylor 1992 [1976]) we see in practices of interactive travel constitutes a paradox that I explore further in this chapter. There is an irony in suggesting that interactive travel – so deeply implicated, as it is, in mobile and technological forms of modern social life – constitutes an escape from modernity. This irony is perhaps best exemplified by the travel blog *I Should Log Off*, which I introduced in Chapter 4. The blog's motto is 'Log off and live' and on the homepage, backpackers Danny and Jillian explain that they 'want to meet new people, explore new places and find a way to exclude the constant "on call" from our daily lives'. When I interviewed them, I asked Danny and Jillian to explain the significance of their blog's title. Jillian replied, 'We thought it fit well for the blog, given that we've sort of logged off from "the" path. The irony of a blog named "I should log off" isn't lost on us though!' To add to that irony, Jillian explained later in our interview that the blog is like a full time job. Far from 'logging off', they find themselves spending entire days on the road updating the blog's layout, composing posts and uploading photos. As Jillian observed, 'We spend a lot of time working on the website'.

*I Should Log Off* embodies a complicated tension between escape, technology and modernity. This tension – which includes the paradox of 'logging off' while remaining 'logged on' and the interweaving of digital and social connectivity – underpins the questions I ask in this chapter. Under what conditions does it make sense for a travel blog chronicling the experiences of two highly connected interactive travellers to be called *I Should Log Off*? What understandings of escape, mobility, technology and modernity enable travellers to see logging off and constant connectivity as congruent practices?

To begin to address these questions, I turn first to the tourism studies literature to show how the paradigm of escape has been used to make sense of tourism motivations and tourist practices. In previous chapters, I have asked how existing paradigms have helped us understand how tourists and travellers connect to people and places while on the move. In this case, I suggest that the concept of escape foregrounds *dis*connection rather than connection. Next, I ask how the emergence of mobile technologies and social media reshape this paradigm, drawing on examples from my fieldwork to show how interactive travel both reproduces and challenges the conventional mythology of tourism as escape. Interactive travellers situate their practices and desires within a familiar discourse of escape, but they reshape this discourse along the way to address the new possibilities of escaping 'the cubicle', 'getting lost' and 'unplugging' in a digital world.

## Tourism and the paradox of escape

To describe tourism as a form of escape begs at least two questions: Escape *to* where or what? And, escape *from* where or what? Tourism marketers answer the first question in vivid detail, associating escape with images of tranquil spa resorts, secluded beaches or unpopulated wilderness destinations. Certain places like the countryside, the beach, islands, the desert or the Orient are clearly branded within the tourist imaginary as places to escape *to* (see Jacobs 2006). Meanwhile, academic accounts of tourism as escape tend to focus on the latter question, suggesting that tourism constitutes an escape *from* the 'unpleasant aspects of modernity' (Berger 2004: 23; and see Fussell 1987; Rojek 1993). According to this understanding of tourism, the modern subject on holiday temporarily shrugs off personal routines and the associated domestic, work and social duties of daily life.

In addition to escaping the grind of one's personal daily life, tourism also promises an escape from the grid-like structure and 'pressures of ordered existence' that characterize modern life more generally (Westerhausen 2002: ix; and see Rojek 1993; Wang 2006). Long term independent travel, in particular, represents an escape from the overbearing monotony of a corporate career, epitomized by a 9-to-5 schedule worked in a non-descript office cubicle. Through tourism, the modern individual can escape the stress and structure of modern work life, the conformity of consumer society, the constraints of moral norms and even the ordered hierarchies of social class identity (Fussell 1987; Berger 2004; Smith 2009). Call it what you will – boredom, ennui, stress, anomie, alienation, or the tedium of 'paramount reality' (Cohen and Taylor 1992[1976]) – modernity clearly requires an escape.

As with the quest for authenticity, the desire for escape entails its own impossibility, which is epitomized by a series of paradoxes that unravel the simple dichotomy between modernity and tourism. To begin with, critics argue that even though touristic escape is almost always described in academic accounts as an escape *from* modernity, tourism itself is a thoroughly modern practice. Franklin puts it succinctly: 'It is a nonsense to imagine tourism as an escape from modern ways of life when it is *par excellence* the way of modern life' (Franklin 2003: 43). Second, scholars have pointed out that tourism cannot possibly constitute an escape from consumer society as it is itself a commodified practice. Third, several theorists argue that thinking of tourism as escape relies on an illusion of freedom, even though tourism practices are tightly contained within cultural conventions and encoded with social norms. As we will see, exploring the way travellers express and negotiate a desire to escape often leads to questions of *disconnection* rather than connection, but before we can appreciate the nuances of that story, we must understand the paradoxes inherent in the idea that tourism constitutes an escape from modernity in the first place.

### The paradox of tourism as escape from modernity

On the other side of the argument that tourism is an escape from modernity is the recognition that tourism, itself, is a thoroughly modern practice. Tourists and tourism are integral to modern processes of 'economic restructuring, globalization, the consumption of place and the aestheticization of everyday life' (Franklin and Crang 2001: 19). The more tourism and everyday modern life come to resemble each other, the less tourism makes sense as a form of escape from modernity. When Lash and Urry (1994: 259) pronounced the 'end of tourism', their argument was not that people would stop travelling, but rather that everyday life had become so 'exoticized' and 'aestheticized' that people were now tourists whether they left home or not. This is true partly because everyday life is now infused with media images and consumer goods from around the world, and partly because tourists always bring 'home' with them when they travel abroad. Larsen (2008b: 28) stresses that tourists 'never just travel *to* places: their mindsets, routines and social relations travel *with* them'. As do their bodies. Travel writer Alain de Botton (2002) laments the fact that mundane bodily concerns – a sore throat, a headache and the need to visit the bathroom – inadvertently join him in his attempts to escape to an island paradise. This comes as no surprise to feminist critics who have long argued that tourism is far more likely to reinforce structural inequalities tied to embodiment than it is to escape them (Jokinen and Veijola 1997; Jacobs 2006).

Tourism is also implicated in another modern development: the de-differentiation of work and leisure. The emergence of the Internet and mobile technologies have significantly reconfigured the distinction between work and leisure, leading theorists to conclude that 'the pleasures of new leisure geographies are not an *escape* from work, but are *connected* to changing work practices' (Bassett and Wilbert 1999: 183, emphasis added). Tourists hoping to escape from the demands of their jobs or the controls of corporate culture more generally are now increasingly obliged (whether by their bosses or by their own compulsions) to remain in touch with the office or to conduct work while travelling. This seems to be especially true for travel bloggers, like Danny and Jillian, whose idea of 'logging off' actually entails working extensively online to publish their blog while travelling. Of course, there is nothing inevitable about the way technology allows work to seep into the domestic or leisure realm. For example in his advocacy of slowing down the pace of life, Honoré (2004: 209) argues that 'instead of using BlackBerrys, laptops and cellphones to extend the workday, we can use them to rearrange it'. This is precisely what many interactive travellers aim to do. As I will discuss in more detail later, these shifting patterns of work and leisure require travellers to conceptualize escape as a carefully orchestrated state of disconnection as much as a state of physical displacement.

These perspectives show tourism to be deeply intertwined with the structures, routines and emotions of everyday modernity, which certainly makes tourism a dubious form of escape from modernity. Furthermore, the very possibility of travel and tourism relies on the tools, technologies, subjectivities and privileges of modern lifestyles. In her study of romance tourism in the Sinai, Jacobs (2006: 125–6) points out that the European women who 'escape' to the Sinai are only able to do so thanks to their position in the modern world:

> [I]t is the very technologies and privileges of modernity . . . that allow women in Europe to travel [to the Sinai] in the first place. And it is these privileges of travel inherited from the West's colonial legacy – the sovereign subject status of the First World traveler/tourist – that give the women the confidence to travel, often alone. Furthermore it is the dualistic nature of modernity that

helps to construct a world divided into spaces of work and leisure, of those who travel and those who are traveled upon, of the modern developed nations and the undeveloped – that encourages the modern subject to travel, to go on holiday, and to 'get away from it all'.

Jacobs pinpoints here a fundamental paradox inherent in the idea that tourism offers an escape from modernity: the ability to even imagine and enact tourism relies on a world order established by post-colonial modernity. Tourism is thus not an escape from modernity, but rather an extension of it and, indeed, 'a significant modality through which ... modern life is organized' (Franklin and Crang 2001: 6–7).

### *The paradox of tourism as escape from consumer society*

A second paradox is the idea that tourism, itself a commodified and highly marketed practice, constitutes an escape from the corporatization and commodification of everyday consumer society. Rojek (1995) explains that 'dreams of escape' initially emerged amidst the rise of nineteenth century consumer capitalism in western societies. During this time, newly modern subjects were in awe of the 'vast surplus of commodities ... generated by capitalism', but they were also coping with related developments of industrialism such as the expansion of the metropolis and the increasing regularity of work and social life (ibid.: 75). Within this context, Rojek argues, 'one can easily see that dreams of escape were especially vivid and compelling' (ibid.). Of course, mass tourism only became possible thanks to the technologies and infrastructures put in place by industrialization, not least of all the concept of 'packaging' trips. Tourism marketers channelled this desire for escape into their advertising campaigns, creating around tourism a 'symbolic universe of escape and fulfillment' (ibid.). Rojek notes the irony involved in marketing tourism as a form of escape from consumer society: 'In tourism, escape experience is packaged in intensely commodified form. For example, we are told that paying for a trip abroad will enable us to "get away from it all"' (ibid.: 58). Rojek extends this irony even further, pointing out that only those individuals rich in both time and money were able to pursue the promise of escape from the consumer world. In the end, tourism only 'pretends to be a relief from the world of commodities' because, in fact, an 'industry has been established to manufacture deliverance from the industrial world; travel beyond the world of commodities has itself become a commodity' (Enzensberger 1996[1958]: 133; 129).

Research on alternative forms of travel reveals that even travel practices that seek explicitly to avoid the consumer model of tourism end up conforming to predictable travel patterns and commodified structures (Cohen 1973; Richards and Wilson 2004b; O'Reilly 2006). Desforges (1998) found such a development among young backpackers, whose attempts to escape the commodified experiences of mass tourism delivered them, instead, into an equally commodified industry aimed at independent travellers. In some cases, this leads backpackers to escape from escape as they then try to distance themselves not only from other tourists, but also from other backpackers. This search for alternatives to alternative travel results in a 'spiral of escape [that] keeps spinning and spinning and spinning' (Welk 2004: 89).

### Escape and the illusion of freedom

Escape entails a third paradox, one that revolves around freedom and control. Escape promises freedom from the routines and constraints of modernity, even though in practice tourism is highly routinized and culturally encoded. Many theorists argue that this freedom is nothing more than an illusion, a 'mass deceit' (Enzensberger 1996[1958]: 135). While the desire to escape underpins tourism fantasies, tourists often retain familiar routines and embodied habits related to work, domesticity and social relations while they are on the road (McCabe 2002; Edensor 2006, 2007, 2009; Veijola 2006; Germann Molz 2008; White and White 2008). Furthermore, as Edensor (2009: 545) explains, tourism is culturally encoded with 'rigid conventions of its own, habits, and routines that shape the particular practices and experiences of tourists'. The notion that tourism frees the modern individual from the constraints and control of modern life overlooks the taken-for-granted social roles, the enactment of quotidian routines and the everyday habits and desires that tourists embody and therefore carry with them wherever they go. In his analysis of tourist itineraries, Wang (2006: 76) concludes that 'while tourism begins with an attempt to escape from the control by ... modernity, it ends up as a return to that control'.

This is not to say, however, that escape is a complete ruse. Tourism may not constitute freedom *per se*, but the fantasies and mythologies surrounding escape do help to constitute tourism. Edensor suggests that tourism is best understood not just as escape, but as a constant negotiation between escape and conformity. He observes that tourists are constantly 'escaping' from overbearing familiarity by seeking out the pleasures of the unfamiliar, and from the unpredictability of the unfamiliar by seeking out the pleasures of the everyday. The modern subject is, as Edensor (2006: 44) explains, an effect of both highly commodified and regulated structures *and* encounters with difference:

> Tourism, then, often consists of a movement between distinctive spaces and dispositions, namely between an embrace of familiar comforts and the sensualities of the unfamiliar. ... The interweaving of apparently paradoxical dispositions toward the sensual produces embodied subjects and fluid places that are distinctively modern.

Edensor's understanding of tourism situates tourist practices within a broader modern ambivalence between familiarity *and* contrast, conformity *and* escape and order *and* disorder. From this perspective, escape is not a disavowal of the modern condition, but a complex and compelling articulation of it. Minca and Oakes (2006: 17) explain that travel 'has long been seen as evoking a distinctly modern subjectivity of freedom ... from routine and obligation [that] ... mirrored the bracing freedom of modernity itself'. The experience of detachment enabled by tourism, they explain, was both liberating and terrifying, not unlike the experience of modernity itself. In which case, it makes sense to wonder whether tourism constitutes an escape *from* modernity, or *to* it? This question is especially salient when we consider the various technological strategies travellers juggle in order to 'log off' and yet stay connected while on the move.

## Redefining escape

The always-on, always-available connectivity enabled by mobile communication technologies contributes to the stress and pressures that travellers claim to be escaping. Yet, in many cases, the ability to stay connected on the move and at a distance contributes to travellers' feeling of liberation from the constraints of consumer society, from the stress of corporate culture, or from the sense of alienation that accompanies modern life. Mobile technologies represent both the fast-paced, always-on modern lifestyle travellers are fleeing, and a means of escape from the very modernity that technology epitomizes. So, in addition to escaping from the routinized structures, stifling tedium or rampant consumerism of modernity, travellers today are also figuring out how to – and whether to – escape from the mobile digital technologies and social media platforms that have become such a ubiquitous feature of modern life.

New technologies prompt new definitions of what it means to escape in the first place. Discourses of 'escape' are shifting within contexts of the information society and the 24-hour, always-on, always-available culture. Instead of imagining escape as a form of physical displacement from home, for example, modern subjects increasingly imagine escape as a form of electronic disconnection. As we will see in the sections that follow, escape is now as likely to refer to 'unplugging' or 'logging off' as to travelling to a foreign land. At the same time, however, we will also see that many travellers consider technology itself as a means to escape, or at least as complicit in their escape attempts. In this sense, technology plays a complicated role, simultaneously undercutting, redefining and facilitating escape.

The ambivalent role in which travellers cast technology mirrors broader public concern about the effects of new mobile communication and media technologies on social life. In many ways, these new technologies are so conflated with the hectic, always-connected character of modern life that when we talk about 'escape', it is not clear whether we mean escape from modernity or escape from technology, or both. Portable, personal technologies like smartphones and laptop computers have become such a familiar presence in everyday life that it has become almost impossible to coordinate our work and social lives without them. And, those are just the technological devices that we carry with us, to say nothing of the vast technological systems and infrastructures of communication and transportation that make modern life *possible* day in and day out. The ubiquitous presence of technology has become a favourite topic of public debate. A variety of technology-themed moral panics fill the air waves and news media as the public engages in continuous worry about drivers texting while behind the wheel, teenagers sending inappropriate pictures of themselves via their mobile phones or bullying each other on social networking sites, or people contracting brain cancer from cell phone radiation. Now that mobile phones and social networking sites double as always-on homing devices, debates also swirl around the privacy of our emails and status updates, parents using mobile devices to keep tabs on their teenagers, and our diminishing ability to get lost in this digital world (see Ratliffe 2009).

Many people report feeling besieged by the constant inundation of mundane updates from 'friends' who are barely friends. Worried that their 'real' relationships and ability to have 'downtime' were jeopardized by the amount of time and attention they spent on online networking, many users have deleted their Facebook accounts, erased their presence from Twitter and downsized their online presence (Cava 2010). These debates proliferate throughout the corporate world as well. In 2005, *USA Today* reported that thanks to mobile communication technologies, almost half of workers surveyed in the United States were planning to work while on holiday (Armour 2005), even while business magazines like *Fortune* and *Fast Company* were touting the benefits of unplugging and logging off (Miller and Miller 2005). Hillary Billings, a CEO quoted in *Fast Company*, complained that 'the price of being available 24/7 is the loss of time for reflection, creative thinking, and connections with our loved ones' and suggested a solution: stepping away from such constant connectivity every once in a while (Billings 2003: 104).

Several years and an economic crisis later, workers seem more concerned with finding and keeping jobs than 'escaping' the corporate grind, but the apparent inescapability of technology continues to strike a chord in the public consciousness. We remain obsessed over our obsession with technology. An article published in the *New York Times* titled 'Hooked on Gadgets, and Paying a Mental Price' is case in point. Reporting on several scientific studies, the article suggests that a steady influx of mediated information and constant interactivity have potentially dangerous social and biological effects:

> [J]uggling e-mail, phone calls and other incoming information can change how people think and behave. They say our ability to focus is being undermined by bursts of information. ... The stimulation provokes excitement – a dopamine squirt – that researchers say can be addictive. In its absence, people feel bored.
>
> (Richtel 2010)

The article profiles Kord Campbell, a 43-year-old software entrepreneur whose addiction to technology has cost him the ability to focus on his work and family, to complete projects, to be creative or to engage in deep thought. Worst of all, according to Campbell's wife, the gadget-addict is constantly online or on the phone even when the family is on vacation. She says, 'I would love for him to totally unplug, to be totally engaged'. This article aligns with a broader discourse in which technology, with its apparently addictive and fragmenting qualities, is blamed for cognitive, emotional and social troubles.

It is tempting to follow the logic of this discourse back to the technology itself and to the idea that the physical and social effects described in these stories flow directly from some aspect of the technology – its design, perhaps, or its portability or stimulating qualities. But, mobile phones, laptop computers, online social networking sites and travel blogs are neither intrinsically escapist technologies, nor do they necessarily require escape. The fantasy of escaping from technology more often than not stands in for other desires. The emergence of new devices constantly re-animates these discussions, but the ensuing debates are less about the technology itself than they are negotiations about power, social propriety, aspirations and anxieties. Concerns over mobile phones and constant connectivity are actually about how a society values things like privacy, intimacy, freedom, attention and childhood, or worries about things like cognition, addiction or familial relations. Debates over 'escape' thus reveal the ongoing drama around shifting social patterns, reconfigurations of work and leisure, newly articulated social obligations, new modes of presence and togetherness and, above all, fantasies of – and fears about – control at-a-distance (Marvin 1988).

It makes little sense, therefore, to think about 'escape' as a literal phenomenon of either touristic displacement or technological disconnection. Rojek and Urry (1997) concede that 'escape' fails to provide a unifying theory of tourism; and besides, White and White (2007) conclude, interactive travel is not about escape, but rather about remaining connected with one's social world. Yet there persists a certain 'mythology of escape' (Rojek and Urry 1997: 2) that not only motivates travellers to journey in the first place, but that also structures the way travellers make sense of their tourism mobilities and technological practices while they are on the road. In the analysis below, I approach escape not as a literal practice, but rather as a fantasy around which travellers negotiate their competing desires to log off and stay connected. According to Enzensberger (1996[1958]: 135), tourism is an 'inarticulate rebellion'; 'nothing but a gigantic escape ... [that] criticizes that from which it withdraws'. This rebellion is distinct from a disavowal or from indifference in that it engages with the very things it critiques: mobility, modernity, technology. From this perspective, escape must be considered alongside embrace.

### Escaping/embracing technology

In the sections that follow, I consider the way interactive travellers project certain hopes and fears onto technology via a discourse of escape. When travellers invoke the language and images of escape, they are not just describing the way they cope with the structures, pressures and disaffection of modernity; they are coming to terms with what it means to live a technological form of social life, conducted online, on the phone or in otherwise mediated formats. Escape helps them to make sense of new social patterns and to devise new strategies for connecting and disconnecting while on the move and at a distance. As Löfgren (2002: 269) puts it, 'getting away from it all might be an attempt to get it all back to together again'. The three fantasies of escape I analyse below – escaping the corporate cubicle or the constraints of consumer culture, getting lost or off the beaten path, and unplugging and logging off – rub up against other desires; staying in touch with friends and family, belonging to a mobile community of travellers, and remaining ensconced in a social network. As we will see, it is this tension between the impulse to escape and the 'impulse to sociability' (Simmel 1950) that shapes the contours of mobile sociality.

### Escaping the cubicle

> Living vicariously from my beige cubicle...
> (Reader comment posted on *GoBackpacking.com*)

The cubicle has become a powerful symbol of the insipid grid-like structure of modern corporate life. These modular workspaces have come to represent the uniformity and depersonalization of the modern workplace, offering the illusion of self-direction and privacy amidst control and surveillance. Nothing conveys modern ennui like a beige cubicle. So, when travellers refer to their corporeal and virtual mobilities as an escape from the 'cubicle', the 'cube farm' or the 'box', they are critiquing a particular configuration of corporate life and, by extension, consumer society.

To some extent, we have already seen how technology is employed to circumvent the corporatization of tourism encounters. In Chapter 3, for example, I argued that smart tourism entails civic and social imperatives that resist the commodifying logic of the market economy. And in Chapter 5, I described how CouchSurfers use networking technology to organize host–guest encounters outside of the commercialized framework of the hospitality industry. In these examples, travellers turn to technology to create alternatives to market-driven tourism. Travel blogging entails a similar critique, this time aimed more directly at the corporate logic of daily life. Travel blogging constitutes an escape from the cubicle in two ways: first, travel blogs provide a kind of virtual escape for office-bound workers; second, the increasing professionalization and monetization of travel blogging offers an alternative livelihood to the corporate career structure.

As I explained in Chapter 4, travel bloggers and their readers see travel blogs as a way to travel virtually and vicariously, and many explicitly frame this practice as an escape from their desks, cubicles and daily work routines. A comment posted on Beau and Meggan's blog, *The World Effect*, illustrates this sentiment:

> What a fascinating trek. I love this stuff. I've been following the posts. I think I'm just getting more and more envious of your travels. Keep the good stuff coming. It's my mid day escape from work.
> (Reader comment posted on *TheWorldEffect.com*)

Kirsty, a web-savvy Canadian traveller who has been travelling since 2001, makes a similar observation on her blog, *Nerdy Nomad*, that 'people stuck at a desk sometimes use blogs to escape during their work day. ... Yes, it's an escape, particularly if these are blogs about travelling and working in cool places'.

For some readers, the online blog entries, photos and videos offer a short but satisfying break from their desks. But for many, travel blogs tap into a deeper desire to quit their jobs and escape for themselves. Conversations to this effect crop up consistently on the blog *Nomadic Matt's Travel Site*, in part because Matt periodically posts practical advice for would-be travellers. He advises them on how to save money for their journeys or what to pack, but also on overcoming their fears and working up the courage to 'break free from the cubicle'. Consider, for example, the following blog entry and subsequent reader responses posted on the site. Matt writes:

> I get a lot of emails asking me for my secret ... to escaping the cubicle and being a nomad ... I am finally going to spill the beans. ... The big secret to travelling long term is ... nothing. There is no secret. There I said it. ...
>
> Vagabonds, nomads, and long term travellers are nothing special. We have no super powers or secret Swiss bank accounts. I used to think they were special – unique for what they were doing. They had found the secret to breaking free from the cubicle I was so chained too [sic]. I was jealous. I was envious. But once I got on the road I saw that their secret was there was no secret. Lots of people did this. It wasn't special. It wasn't unique.
>
> (Blog entry posted on *NomadicMatt.com*)

Judging from the number of comments and heated discussions that erupt whenever Matt frames travel as an escape from cubicle life, as he does in this posting and elsewhere on his blog, it is clear that this topic touches a nerve with many people. Readers respond with descriptions of their own cubicle-defying adventures, philosophical remarks on the risks and rewards of taking a different path in life, or, as in the following comment posted in response to Matt's 'travel secret' entry, frustration:

> Matt – that's what separates you from us (me) with a 9–5 job. you have the GUTS to do it . . . that's not nothing. . . that's something!! case in point. everyday that i drag myself to the dungeon, i go through a dilemma: i like my cubicle job because it pays the bills, have great healthcare benefits, it keeps me sharp, it feeds our family and pays for trips. but at the same time, i hate my cubicle job because i know i can be somewhere else, doing what i love instead of THIS HELL ... so everyday, i try to devise a plan of escape. i start with my blog. . . then i dream of travelling and/or starting some career in travel. . . as to when i will actually have the GUTS to do it? ... I don't know. . . so, kudos to you.
>
> (Reader comment posted on *NomadicMatt.com*)

According to this reader, the 9-to-5 cubicle job is both a prison – a dungeon to which he drags himself everyday – and a safety net that offers stability and financial security for his family. These competing desires for the thrill of adventure and the familiarity of home repeat a common refrain of escape/embrace in response to modernity. It is also worth noting that in this account, technology is not a tether, but rather an escape route into a dream world of virtual travel and, perhaps eventually, physical travel. The discourse of escape expressed in this exchange thus reflects the deep ambivalence – and sometime intense emotions – with which travel bloggers and their readers confront modernity, and the complex role technology plays in this drama.

*Nomadic Matt's Travel Site* also exemplifies the second way in which technology serves as a means of escape from the 'cubicle'. Like many other travel bloggers in my research sample, Matt does not need to work at a 9-to-5 office job because he has 'monetized' his blog. This means that he is able to generate income by striking lucrative deals with affiliates or selling advertising space on his blog. Kirsty, the author of *Nerdy Nomad*, has also capitalized on her site and she publishes a monthly report indicating how much money she makes from each revenue stream. Like many other travel bloggers, she earns enough money from her blog to stay on the road indefinitely. Dave, author of *Go Backpacking*, played with several income-earning ideas on his blog when he started travelling. Originally, he launched a 'dare-me' feature in which he would complete dares posed by readers in exchange for cash donations. He later wrote about the dares in an e-book that is available on his revamped site. His blog has since been transformed into a profitable travel advice site and although the e-book is free to subscribers, he does sell a 12-week course that teaches other travel bloggers how to make money from their sites. Matt has also written an e-book, titled 'Monetize Your Travel Blog', that helps others do the same. These monetized travel blogs seem to epitomize the commodification of the form. Not only have Dave and Matt figured out how to make money from their blogs, they have also commodified their knowledge about commodifying their blogs. In other words, they have escaped the corporate cubicle precisely by embracing the commercial potential of the Internet.

Monetizing one's travel blog to support a travelling lifestyle is part of a broader trend toward 'digital nomadism' and 'lifestyle design', both of which encourage people to fulfil their desires for leisure and adventure by harnessing the liberating potential of mobile technologies (Makimoto and Manners 1997; Ferriss 2007). Mobile technologies have largely enabled the corporate world to re-imagine the geography of work. Work now extends into leisure space and time, just as leisure practices have infiltrated spaces of work. Travellers who 'blog to travel' or who are able to do freelance work via the Internet from anywhere in the world benefit enormously from this development. They are able to escape physically from the 9-to-5 grind epitomized by the cubicle while still earning enough money and flexibility to travel the world.

These trends also institutionalize the modern ideal of the self as a project. Modern identities are no longer given by virtue of birth and tradition, but rather fashioned through a constant process of self-narration, self-adjustment and self-reflexivity. This is the gift and the curse of the disenchanted world I discussed in the previous chapter. In the modern world, individuals are not relegated to identities, but rather have the freedom to change, explore and develop themselves as they wish. Indeed, they are required to do so, and resignation to given identities is seen as a failure of self-knowledge and self-expression. In this sense, the 'cubicle' also represents succumbing to an identity pre-formed by consumer society. Eva and Jeremy, the travellers cited at the beginning of this chapter, capture the contours of this pre-established identity in their description of the modern lifestyle:

> 9 to 5, the 40 hour work week, the daily commute, cable television, apartment rent, owning furniture ... two-week vacations once a year, sitting in front of a computer monitor and buying a home, mowing the lawn.
>
> (Blog entry posted on *ForksandJets.com*)

Travel, in contrast, is associated with personal growth and self-development, key ingredients in the construction of self. Two competing but interrelated versions of modern identity are at work in these discourses of escape: the cubicle dweller who fulfils the modern aspiration toward order, control, efficiency and rationality, and the digital nomad who fulfils the equally modern fantasy of mobility, self-determination and freedom. In their efforts to escape the cubicle, travellers clearly reject the former and embrace the latter, even though as Minca and Oakes (2006: 17) observe, this freedom is both liberating and terrifying.

The freedom to find and follow one's unique passion in life can become, in itself, a tyranny. This helps to explain the sense of ambivalence travellers express toward work and technology. The cubicle may represent fear and imprisonment, but it also represents safety, stability and order. And, as much significance as they invest in getting 'off the grid' and leaving the technological accoutrements of modernity behind, travellers acknowledge that these devices have become necessary to their new mobile lifestyles. In these accounts, then, escape is not necessarily a rejection of modernity or technology or even work, but rather an effort to configure all of these elements in a meaningful and liveable way.

### Getting lost

In the realm of travel, escape is often associated with the fantasy of 'getting lost', even though interactive travellers seem obsessed with *not* getting lost. For example, the mobile walking tours I introduced in Chapter 3 are designed precisely to enable tourists to explore the city without getting lost. And in Chapter 4, I described the various technologies travellers use to ensure that their friends and family never lose track of them. Indeed, travellers encourage their online audience to follow and monitor them as they move around the world. New mobile technologies and online social media offer travellers a sense of security premised on control and mastery of space and location, but they have also provoked a nostalgic desire for the emotional and phenomenological pleasures of getting lost. In a world of ubiquitous computing, we must now engineer opportunities for getting lost. As locative media critic, Andre Lemos (2009), urges:

> Create situations to lose yourself in. Fear of losing oneself is a correlate of the fear of meeting someone. But in losing oneself, one may find something. Disorientation is a method for appropriating space! To locate, map and index everything is symbolic death: fear of the imponderable, of meeting with chance; avoiding a vital dimension of existence.

Only by getting lost, Lemos suggests, can one hope to find something. Getting lost may entail an unpleasant sense of disorientation, but it also involves the thrill of the unknown, the frisson of danger and the appeal of disappearing. Here, again, escape evokes a dual impulse toward order *and* disorder.

In a world made utterly navigable and transparent by portable GPS devices and location-aware mobile applications, what *does* it mean to get lost anymore? To address this question, I turn to one of the travel blogs in my research sample, aptly titled *The Lost Girls*, to consider the complex desires and anxieties involved in getting lost in the context of travel, technology and modernity.

*The Lost Girls* documents the journey of Amanda, Jennifer and Holly, three friends in their mid-twenties who left their media jobs in New York to travel around the world for a year. In the introduction to their travel blog, the three authors explain the origin of the blog's title, and why they left to travel:

> It was in New York City, dead-of-winter 2005, when we – Amanda, Jen and Holly – found ourselves in the midst of a collective quarter life crisis . . . long workweeks at stress-driven offices had taken their toll. Despite having creative gigs that fueled our passions, we were frustrated that we'd let our careers become our identities. We were starving for real connections with family, friends and significant others . . .

> It turns out, we weren't alone. Like millions of young women in our generation, we were plagued with doubts about the paths we were choosing. Though intense workdays left us little time for contemplation, we often found ourselves asking: What exactly were we doing with our lives? . . . On our own, with no parents, advisers or a syllabus to guide us, you could say that we were a little, well, Lost. Okay, very Lost. So before making the ultimate choice of which way to go as (gulp) adults, we decided to take a major detour, one we hoped might provide a little insight into these questions and just maybe, a road-map to our futures.

> Kissing our jobs, boyfriends, apartments, families and our beloved Manhattan goodbye, we officially became "The Lost Girls," and started making plans for a yearlong, 60,000-mile journey around the globe. Loosely building an itinerary that begins in South America and crawled eastward through Africa, the Middle East, India, Southeast Asia and Australia, we plan to explore the

cultures, mindsets and lifestyles of our international counterparts, getting to know thousands of strangers so we may better know ourselves.

We have no idea what the next year will hold – or where the future will lead us – but we can't wait to start the journey. ... We hope that you'll stick with us every step of the way.

(Blog entry posted on *LostGirlsWorld.com*)

In this description, 'getting lost' is laden with multiple, somewhat contradictory, connotations. First, being lost epitomizes a modern sense of alienation wrought by the stress of corporate work and the daunting project of life. Only in their mid-twenties, these three women already feel burned out by their intense jobs, alienated from 'real connections' with the people in their lives, and excited but overwhelmed by the prospect of constructing a meaningful life for themselves, a task akin to the modern self-as-project I discussed earlier. They resolve to 'get lost' as a response to feeling lost in these modern circumstances. Second, getting lost is associated with leaving home and travelling the world. It entails a physical displacement thousands of miles from home and across several continents. According to this second connotation, getting lost represents personal growth and self-reflexivity attained through mobility and encounters with otherness. By meeting 'thousands of strangers' in places like Africa, India and Southeast Asia, they expect to better know themselves. Getting lost is a way of 'finding yourself'.

In this case, 'lost' describes both the problem with modern life and its solution. Technology plays a complicated role here. For one thing, these three travellers spent their year abroad working online in social media, even after escaping from stressful media jobs in the city. For another, they encouraged their readers to stick with them 'every step of the way'. How 'lost' could they get while maintaining an online presence with an eager audience checking up on them as they travelled? Yet, elsewhere on the blog, Jennifer writes that her 'favorite way to "get lost" ' is by 'disconnecting from all email and internet'. And, as we will see in the story below, one of Amanda's desires was to 'disconnect' during her 'lost' year. Clearly, getting lost involves a negotiation between connecting and disconnecting, as well as a complex arrangement of disconnection and displacement.

All of these elements come into play in the following story about Amanda and Holly's travels in Burma. The two women had left Jennifer in Bangkok and flown to Burma to take a river cruise with Amanda's family, who had flown to Southeast Asia from the United States to travel with her. The story begins when, before embarking on the cruise, Holly and Amanda decide to finalize some online tasks:

Hol and I decided ... to check our email and perhaps, post a blog entry. She went ahead to reserve us a computer while I ran up to the room to grab my daypack. When I returned, she was already walking out of the business center with a strange look on her face. "There's no internet," she said flatly. "No email."

"No email in the hotel?" I asked, about to suggest that we leave the hotel to find an internet cafe to do our work. "No. There's no email in the whole country." . . . Incredulity gave way to utter disbelief. Myanmar had to have internet. Every country in the world did. To me, saying that a place didn't have internet was like saying that it didn't have air to breathe or water to drink. How could locals survive without Gmail? Yahoo? Skype?!?

We quickly learned that the militaristic government, well known for repressing the rights of its citizens, had all but banned web-based email in an effort to control the flow of information in and out of the country. The internet itself wasn't illegal (there were plenty of cafes which offered online services), but email was strictly monitored by the government.

While I wasn't sure if this was the whole truth (who could I ask without stirring up trouble?), I did know that this was my opportunity to accomplish the very thing I'd set out to do eight months ago. . . Unplug. Disconnect. Log OFF.

For the first time on our entire trip, Holly and I would have no cell phones and no computers and no communications devices. We'd be forced to just hang out, absorb some culture and not check in with anyone for an entire week and a half. 10 days. 240 hours. 14,400 minutes.

(Blog entry posted on *LostGirlsWorld.com*)

Amanda's story illustrates the dialectic between connecting and disconnecting that characterizes mobile sociality more generally. As with many interactive travellers and travel bloggers, her desires to stay in touch with distant friends or update her blog jar with a fantasy of unplugging. It is not until she travels to a place where connecting to the Internet is out of the question that certain assumptions underpinning this fantasy of disconnection and escape become apparent.

For one thing, the sudden absence of an Internet connection reveals the extent to which checking email and updating the blog had become habitual practices in the context of the journey. As Amanda notes, she had not been without a communication device throughout the entire trip. Until this point, being 'lost' had not meant actually logging off. At the same time, Amanda clearly associates unplugging with connecting locally, seeing her enforced disconnection as an opportunity to hang out and absorb the local culture. This story also imagines 'being lost' as a condition of displacement *and* disconnection. Escape is not just about travelling away from home, but also about unplugging from the constant connectivity of the digital world. Burma offers the opportunity to do both. Perceived as both physically and digitally remote, Burma occupies a particularly significant place in the imagined geography of escape. In a world that, from Amanda's perspective, is so universally connected that access to the Internet is as taken-for-granted as access to air and water (a fairly hefty assumption in itself), Burma represents the possibility of escape not only from modernity, but from technology as well.

Travel bloggers are well aware of Burma's reputation as an 'unplugged' place, a place-myth they perpetuate in their own discourses. For example, before leaving for Burma, Jodi, author of the blog *Legal Nomads*, used Twitter to warn her friends and followers not to expect any online updates from her while she was there and Kirsty, author of *Nerdy Nomad*, commented at length on her blog about the challenges of working online from Burma. Kirsty writes in a blog posting on *Nerdy Nomad*, 'You probably won't get any work done online but, hey, we all need a vacation from it now and then and Myanmar is a great place to come to escape the net'. In response, one of her readers comments, 'Sounds like a good place to visit if you want to unplug'.

Kirsty notes elsewhere on her blog that 'Myanmar [Burma] isn't really on the map as far as wifi access goes'. Burma is on the map, of course, but in these accounts it is located on the geographical and political periphery of the modern world, and on the wrong side of the global digital divide. This is good news for western travellers seeking to fulfil a particular fantasy of physical and technological escape, but bad news for the country's citizens, whose government, as Amanda points out, exerts oppressive control over the flow of information and people. Whereas the lack of Internet access poses little more than an inconvenience for western travellers, one that they gamely revise into an opportunity for escape, for the citizens of Burma disconnecting – being lost, excluded from the global flows of information and capitalism – is not a choice, but the result of authoritarian control. To some extent, this lack of choice further situates Burma in the imagined geography of escape as a place on the margins of the civilized West and a modern life overwrought by too much choice.

The matter of choice is itself a complicated notion here. Is the choice to disconnect, like the choice to connect, a luxury afforded only to some? Is connection necessarily a choice at all? In this story, Amanda draws on a common trope in popular discourses of technology and constant connectivity: addiction. Later in the story, she compares herself to a smoker going 'cold turkey', her search for an Internet connection to a quest for illicit drugs and her eventual Internet access to getting a 'fix':

> Looking for web-based email in a country that has banned it can only be compared to looking for drugs. ... We finally got our fix at an upstanding internet and long-distance calling shop outside the center of town. By asking the right guy the right questions, we were able to sneak into our respective email accounts without alerting the suspicions of the internet police.
>
> (Blog entry posted on *LostWorldGirls.com*)

This trope frames constant connectivity as irresistible; the addict has *no choice* but to plug in and log on. Travellers feel that they lack control over their Internet use or technological habits. This metaphor of addiction exemplifies the belief that our social lives have become so mobile and geographically dispersed that we have no choice but to conduct them via mobile phones and other communication technologies. The term 'addiction' derives from the Latin word *a-ducere*, meaning 'to lead away', which also taps into an anxious suspicion among travellers that connecting online means separating from interactions with co-present people or from the local environment. As in the *New York Times* article I cited earlier, this discourse of addiction pathologizes technology use and frames technology itself as something that must be escaped. One way to reassert control over technology is by unplugging.

### *Unplugging*

As I noted at the beginning of this chapter, there is widespread public concern about addiction to technology, and no shortage of popular and professional advice on how to 'unplug' from this wired way of life (see Gordon 2001; Dutwin 2009; Cava 2010; Powers 2010; Maushart 2011). This advice extends into the realm of travel as well, as we saw in Murphy's (2009) admonition that true escapist travel is technology-free: no cars, no airplanes, no mobile phones, no computers. A similar philosophy underpins the Slow Movement, and the related trend of Slow Travel, which advocates travelling slowly in order to better savour the local culture (Honoré 2004; Gardner 2009; Germann Molz 2009). Slow travellers tend to choose environmentally friendly modes of transportation, like walking or cycling, over high-speed carbon-emitting transportation technologies, especially airplanes. This is not to say that supporters of the Slow Movement and Slow Travel are technophobes, far from it. However, they do promote a more mindful and controlled use of technology that often involves switching it off. In his book describing the Slow Movement, for example, Honoré (2004: 40) recounts one proponent's dream of opening the world's first 'Slow Hotel': guests will arrive by steam train, horse-drawn carriage or on foot; they will enjoy slow, technology-free pursuits like hiking, gardening and yoga; and 'all hurry-inducing technology – televisions, cellphones, laptops, Palm Pilots, cars – will be banned'. Today, several luxury hotels and resorts offer 'technology break' packages and 'tranquility suites' that require guests to surrender their gadgets at check-in (Tergesen 2011).

This discourse equates unplugging and disconnecting with escaping the grip of technology; turning off the mobile phone creates a little oasis of calm amidst the frenzy of modern life. This line of reasoning that disconnecting from technology enables us to connect, on a more human level, with the people and places around us certainly inflects the way interactive travellers make sense of their own technology practices. A desire to 'unplug', or at least a recognition that they should *want* to unplug, weaves through travel blog entries and online discussions. And yet, as with the thought of escaping the cubicle or getting lost, travellers express ambivalence about unplugging while on the road. In a blog posting on *Nomadic Matt's Travel Site* titled 'Staying in Touch on the Road', Matt writes:

> When I first traveled overseas . . . I only needed to occasionally call my parents, but still wanted to remain unconnected from the world at large. Having a cellphone just didn't seem like I was getting off the grid. It was bad enough I was at an Internet cafe all the time! Wasn't the point of travel to get away from the trappings of modern life?
>
> (Blog entry posted on *NomadicMatt.com*)

Matt's comments reveal the extent to which interactive travellers constantly negotiate the desire to stay in touch with friends, family and other travellers against the
desire to escape the 'trappings of modern life' and get 'off the grid'.

These competing desires are the topic of much debate on Matt's site and
throughout the online travel community. In the previous chapter, I cited one of
Matt's blog entries titled 'Are We All Flashpackers Now?' in which he observes
that almost everyone he encounters on the backpacker trail seems to be toting laptops and smartphones or logging on to Facebook instead of chatting with the other
people in their hostel. I included a few of the comments that readers had posted
in response to his remarks in order to illustrate the way technological connections
engendered anxieties about authenticity. Here, I introduce a few more reader comments from this blog entry in order to consider the way travellers also negotiate a
deep ambivalence about the desires and effects of 'unplugging'.

In their responses to Matt's post on flashpacking, two readers defend the decision to stay in touch while travelling, arguing that digital connectivity is 'normal'
and that staying in touch offers a sense of security:

> Coming from an IT career its [sic] been very normal for me to think to take my
> macbook, iphone etc with me. . . . As time goes by we become more and more
> digitized and with technology getting cheaper its [sic] perhaps opened the
> door for more people to travel as they can still be connected to friends/family
> at home. Having the safety of that connection is a comfort perhaps?

> This is a trend of people being able to retain some of their "normal life" rou-
> tines while they travel. Perhaps it will mean a greater volume of travelers, as
> there are plenty of people who want to see new places without being com-
> pletely out of their element. iPhones, laptops, facebook – all of these tools
> make it more difficult to unplug from your routines and get "lost" somewhere
> new. Maybe that isn't such a good thing, but I'll be sure to blog about it on
> my MacBook while I'm away.
>
> (Reader comments posted on *NomadicMatt.com*)

Because mobile technologies make it possible for travellers to maintain their 'normal' routines, they are also seen as undermining the point of travel, which is 'to
unplug from your routines and get "lost" somewhere new'. Although this reader
disapproves of this aspect of interactive travel, he does so with irony, noting that
he will blog about his critique while he travels. The extent to which this debate
assumes that connecting and disconnecting are a matter of choice is striking. There
are few stories of *unintentional* disconnection – forgetting to recharge batteries,
misplacing power cords, failing to make a wireless connection work – and when
they do appear, they are either framed as temporary hiccups or rewritten, as in
Amanda and Holly's case, as a blessing in disguise. Technological connection is
the norm against which disconnection becomes a meaningful choice.

For two other readers commenting on Matt's blog post about flashpacking, it is the ability to work while on the road that normalizes their mobile

technology practices and supersedes other concerns about staying connected while travelling.

> [I]f you're not making money working, freelancing or keeping your ad-supported blog updated, taking Facebook, Twitter, etc on the road just tethers you to the world you're traveling so far to escape.

> I've noticed quite a few people like myself that have work we can do while travelling thanks to internet access being available in more places. The flash-packing trend has made my new life on the road is possible, so I'm more grateful than I can say. That said though I'm looking forward to going to out of the way places and being able to disconnect and truly take vacations from modern life. I guess I'm hoping to have the best of both worlds.
>
> (Reader comments posted on *NomadicMatt.com*)

Technology is both a bane and a blessing to these interactive travellers. For those who are able to make money via the Internet, staying connected becomes an indispensable element of a mobile lifestyle. At the same time, however, these readers' comments express a suspicion that as much as technology liberates them, it also acts as a tether 'to the world you're traveling so far to escape'. Even in defence of technology, these readers associate escape and a 'true' vacation with unplugging and disconnecting. This assumption is especially evident in the following two comments:

> Great post, Matt and SO true! I noticed the same trends in myself and others. Though I confess I absolutely love those far flung places where neither cell phones nor laptops are available. It's there I truly relax and experience.

> This article is very true. When I first started travelling I'd see maybe one or two people with laptops and most hostels didn't have wireless. On my most recent trip, it was absurd – everyone had laptops, iphones, cell phones, ipods, the works. I have succumbed to this style of travel in the past because it is convenient, but I ditched all the technology on my last trip (just had a cell phone which I left switched off – for emergencies only). It was such a liberating experience! I had the most fantastic time, I spent more time meeting and talking to fellow travellers and locals rather than being so focused on Facebook and what was going on back home. I spent more time out and about and less time chained to the computer. I didn't feel the need to update my status every day with where and what I was doing. Apart from the occasional email to home to let them know I was alive, and checking the odd bus timetable, I simply didn't have time to be using a computer! . . . Best way to travel!
>
> (Reader comments posted on *NomadicMatt.com*)

Both of these comments celebrate 'unplugging' as liberating, relaxing and the 'best way to travel', in part because they associate unplugging with a deeper connection to co-present people and local experiences. Yet neither reader rejects technology out of hand. Both admit to falling in with the flashpacking trend, even though they both suspect that travelling without technology may result in a more meaningful experience.

These debates around 'unplugging' are not about the technology itself, but rather constitute a collective discussion about how to use the technology, not in the technical sense, of course, but in a social and cultural sense. As 'normalized' as mobile information and communication technologies have become, technological practices remain open to interpretation and innovation. What communication should be like in person and at a distance, what travel should be like, and how mobile technologies, social media and travel should intersect are all up for negotiation. In this conversation, certain practices are deemed worthy and valuable (working online to fund a mobile lifestyle) while other practices are condemned (letting technology get in the way of 'true' experiences) as travellers try to reconcile a desire to stay connected with other culturally informed fantasies about what constitutes 'true' travel. In other words, a range of possible social performances are afforded and contained, not just by material or technical capacities, but also by the hopes and fears travellers bring to bear on them.

What seems to be at stake in this particular exchange of views is not so much a rejection of technology (implied by the term 'unplugging'), but rather an appeal to mindful or intentional engagement with technology. Consider how this tension plays out in the following two comments, one of which I also discussed in the previous chapter, in response to Matt's blog posting:

> Everyone seems to be drinking the flashpacker Kool-aid without looking at the downside. It blows my mind to be in a guesthouse where 10 people are in a common area and all of them are looking at a glowing blue screen, talking to the people back home instead of the ones right beside them. Why travel if you're going to spend every night on Facebook and Twitter just like you do at home? Same routine, different place. That's an improvement?

> I don't think it's a case of talking on twitter every night and ignoring those around you. I might spend an hour on a computer each day or so when i'm travelling. I will be talking to friends back home/emailing them etc during that time but when i'm finished I come off and mix with the friends i've made at the hostel for a large part of the day. For me, I think it's important to do both. Going travelling is all about the experiences you have, but at the same time, if I want to call up my parents on skype, chat to an old flatmate, or just catch up with some people i've not heard from in a while I like to know I can.
> (Reader comments posted on *NomadicMatt.com*)

In the first comment, travellers who use technology unreflexively are seen as dupes who have imbibed the 'flashpacker Kool-aid' and unwittingly tethered themselves to the routines and concerns of home. According to this logic, if travellers stay connected to home while on the road, they have missed the point of travel entirely. However, the response to this comment suggests that technology use is not as mindless as it may appear. This reader notes that she chooses when to go online and when to disconnect. Thanks to these communication technologies, she is also able to choose whom she wants to socialize with – parents and friends who are at a distance or new friends she has met while travelling. Like the reader cited earlier who hopes to 'have the best of both worlds', this reader also thinks 'it's important to do both'.

For these travellers, unplugging is not in polar opposition to staying connected. It is not the case that 'escape from modernity' entails a rejection of technology. On the contrary, the practices of 'escaping the cubicle', 'getting lost' and 'unplugging' that I have described in these sections involve a complex negotiation of choice and control over technology. Because the meanings and uses of mobile technologies and online social media are contextual and constantly negotiated, travellers implement these technologies in various ways. Travellers may want to escape from some aspects of modernity, but they do not necessarily want to escape from their social networks or from a sense of connection to the wider world. In other words, their desire to escape is more a desire to have a choice in the matter – to decide whether to log on or log off, when and where to connect, and with whom – than a desire to completely disengage or 'get away from it all'. This is why travellers like Danny and Jillian, authors of the blog *I Should Log Off*, are able to consider blogging, connecting online *and* 'logging off' as congruent practices.

This desire for choice returns us back to the paradoxes I outlined at the beginning of the chapter. Travel and tourism may be constructed in the cultural imaginary as an escape from modernity, but, as Jacobs (2006) argues, such fantasies and their correlating practices are premised inextricably on the material and symbolic conditions of the very modernity tourists seek to escape. The ability and desire to travel rely on modern infrastructures and technologies and access to economic and cultural capital made available to those living in the 'modern' First World such as passports and currency that are welcome the world over, or the confidence to travel abroad (Jacobs 2006: 126, 133). Today's travellers are 'using the trappings and technologies of modernity – the privileges of life in the West – in order to escape it' (ibid.: 149). Above all, this notion of escaping modernity depends upon and reproduces the thoroughly modern privilege of choice. The travellers described throughout this book belong to what Bialski (2007: 71) refers to as a 'society of choice'. If modern life is characterized on the one hand by stifling constraints, it is at the same time characterized by choice, freedom and self-determination. Travel is thus not an escape from modernity, but an articulation of the modern self fashioned out of choice.

## Conclusion: escape strategies and mobile sociality

For interactive travellers, mobile technologies and online social media represent strategies of escape *from* modernity, but also *to* modernity, bringing the possibility of the exotic and the unknown to an overly structured daily existence and, at the same time, a sense of order and control to a fragmented and disorderly world. Travellers draw on a discourse of escape to frame their travel practices simultaneously as breaking free from the constraints and alienating effects of modernity and as articulating their choice, freedom and self-determination as modern sovereign subjects. Interactive travel is about escaping *and* embracing technology; escaping *and* embracing modernity. The decision to live a mobile lifestyle, which includes using information and communication technologies to stay in touch while on the move and at a distance, is a function of the modern understanding of identity-as-choice.

As I have described, technology does not always mesh easily with fantasies of escape. The debates posted on Nomadic Matt's blog suggest that technology has made the choice of a mobile lifestyle available to more and more travellers. Yet, as the public concerns noted earlier suggest, the modern subject is in constant danger of being controlled by technology rather than the other way around. Travellers must work diligently to ensure that they remain in control of their mobile technologies and social media use; that they harness these technologies to *increase* their options of mobility and communication. This is why such intense anxieties are aroused when technology begins to feel more like an obligation or addiction, and less like a choice.

In this sense, interactive travel is best understood as involving 'escape strategies'. In a world of ubiquitous computing and constant connectivity, the fantasy of escape is redefined. The various forms of presence that mobile technologies and online social media make possible – virtual proximity, virtual distance or absent presence – mean that escape is now as much about strategic connections and disconnections as it is about physical displacement. Travellers can use new technologies and social media to virtually or physically escape from 'the cubicle'. Getting lost is now a matter of choice rather than circumstance, contrived as much by travelling abroad as by intentionally connecting or disconnecting from mobile technologies and the Internet. Conditions of in person or mediated availability and absence can also be engineered by strategically logging on or unplugging. Interactive travellers can connect with friends and family back home when they a need dose of familiarity or comfort; or they can strategically manage their online availability to maintain a needed sense of distance, as I described in Chapter 4. Escape is thus about determining where, when, how and with whom to travel and communicate. From this perspective, escape is not about becoming liberated from the structures of modernity or the social obligations of everyday life, but rather about being able to stay in touch – on the traveller's terms – with established networks and relationships while on the road.

This version of escape is a far cry from the image of the gadget-free solitary adventurer painted in Murphy's (2009) account of escapism. Instead, escape is imagined and practiced here not in solitude but as a sociable endeavour, which makes sense if we consider the fact that 'many tourists do not experience the world through a solitary "romantic gaze" . . . , but in the company of friends, family members and partners' (Larsen 2008b: 28). Indeed, tourism is less about travelling to exotic places in search of difference than it is about being together and reconnecting with loved ones, as Larsen argues:

> Most tourism performances are performed collectively, and this sociality is in part what makes them pleasurable. ... [T]ourism is not only a way of

practising or consuming (new) places but also an emotional geography of sociability, of being together with close friends and family members from home. While travelling together, couples, families and friends are actually together, not separated by work, institutions, homework, leisure activities and geographical distances.

(ibid.)

Larsen points out that much of what makes travelling pleasurable is participating in sociable exchanges with significant members of our social networks. He focuses in this comment primarily on the opportunities tourism presents for physical co-presence, but his argument extends as well to the various forms of socializing at a distance and mediated and virtual presence that travellers enact with distant loved ones. Escape is better understood as a desire for sociability rather than a desire for solitude. A reconfigured concept of escape thus has much to tell us about mobile sociality, especially regarding the way mobile sociality dissembles dualisms between escape and embrace, solitariness and sociability, home and away, order and disorder, work and leisure or connection and disconnection. Mobile sociality – practices of being together on the move and at a distance – is about negotiating the complex intersection between these categorical pairs rather than keeping them in diametric opposition.

# 8  Conclusion

## Performing mobile sociality

> The metaphor of vacationing as a cultural laboratory makes sense, but what kind of experiment is it to be? It can be a new awareness of the body, the luxury of regressing into playful childhood, the feeling of freedom of choice or the luxury of not having to choose. It may be the challenge of handling new social relations or redefining old ones ... stretching old rules or even transgressing them. ... Perhaps the most important tourist experiments concern daydreaming and mindtraveling, skills of transcendence, which vacationers explore and practice. Here, you learn to move simultaneously through landscapes and mindscapes, in time travel and flights of the mind, as fantasy turns into social practice in constant interaction with the very concrete materiality of technologies and flows of media.
>
> (Löfgren 2002: 270)

### Introduction

I began this book with a story about Mark, a tech-savvy backpacker who used his laptop computer to connect from the courtyard of an Indonesian guest house to his friends back in the United States. Like Mark, the travellers featured in this book are people at play, experimenting with new technologies, trying on different social roles, testing alternative versions of co-presence, probing the elastic boundaries between the material and the digital and working out new rules of engagement. If there is one thing that tourists and travellers do well, it is play. Travellers have always been among the first to try out new communication technologies – from postcards and telegrams to phone calls and faxes and now emails, texts and blogs – while on the road and far from home. To some extent, the Internet and mobile digital devices can be seen as the latest mode of fulfilling a familiar desire to stay in touch while on the road. However, the immediacy, interactivity and ubiquity of new mobile and media technologies have afforded travellers unique ways of engaging with, as well as detaching from, distant social networks while on the move. Interactive travel offers a glimpse into these new technological and social practices in the making. It also offers a glimpse of who we are, as a society and as individuals, and who we want to be.

The uses, meanings and effects of these technologies may be in play, but this does not necessarily mean that the possibilities are endless. As I have argued, new technologies emerge into (and most certainly out of) existing social conditions. Travelling, as Löfgren (2002: 269) notes, 'carries an emancipatory potential, to try something different, or to keep the world as it is (was)'. Interactive travellers' experiments with new technologies are thus bounded on one side by a desire to bring a new world into being, and on the other by a desire to keep things the way they are. These experiments thus reveal our aspirations for social transformation, but also our anxieties over what kinds of losses or obligations this transformation might incur. Travel connections, and the hopes and fears they provoke, thus reflect what is at stake as we shift toward a mobile, mediated and networked mode of social life.

## Tourism and togetherness in the twenty-first century

Clearly, tourism is good to think with, but how should we think about tourism? I have addressed this question in various ways throughout the book. To begin with, I argued, we must understand tourism as a fundamentally sociotechnical practice. Travelling with technology has become the norm, especially among middle-class travellers from wealthy societies, but even travellers who are not necessarily 'flash-packers' find their experiences on the road shaped by tourism's entanglement with technology. This means that the theoretical frameworks we use to analyse tourism must account for the fact that tourism is a 'technological form of life' (Lash 2001), one in which social and spatial connections have become interwoven with digital connections to the extent that one is practically unthinkable without the other. One of the book's objectives, therefore, has been to revise some of the key paradigms in tourism studies in light of new technological developments.

In the preceding chapters, I detailed the various ways in which new mobile and media technologies challenge our notions of tourist landscapes, the tourist gaze, hospitality, authenticity and escape. I argued in Chapter 3 that tourist places are now blended geographies where the material and the virtual converge. Mobile devices offer tourists new opportunities to connect with and create an augmented urban landscape, one that may be as much a site of civic engagement as it is a site for consumption. The tourist gaze is similarly transformed. The tourist gaze has always been a technological accomplishment, but as I argued in Chapter 4, online social media platforms like blogging have mobilized and mediated the tourist gaze in new ways. In this context, technologies of representation, such as the digital camera or the travel blog, do more than just represent; they become interactive points around which distant and dispersed friends collaborate and 'do togetherness'. Advances in online networking technologies have also afforded new possibilities for togetherness, not just between friends but between strangers as well. This is especially evident in the context of online hospitality exchange networks like *CouchSurfing.org*, where travellers revise the accepted norms around encountering strangers. As new methods for managing risk and establishing trust online emerge, so too do new possibilities for 'living with' strangers materialize.

Innovations in communication and networking technologies have also provided new screens onto which travellers project anxieties and aspirations about our technological futures. Quests for authenticity or escape, familiar tropes in tourism discourse, take on renewed significance in interactive travel, revealing in their wake travellers' thoroughly modern anxieties over the ambiguous nature of reality, the commodification of everyday life, and the possibilities of controlling and being controlled at-a-distance or having too much but not enough choice. At the same time, however, these concepts reveal travellers' abiding desires for meaning, mooring and a sense of togetherness in a mobile world.

I noted in the introductory chapter that these foundational paradigms in tourism studies were developed before mobile information and communication technologies had emerged on the travel scene, and therefore needed to be reconsidered in light of current technological affordances. It is also worth noting that these paradigms were developed at a time when tourism was defined around a fairly clear-cut set of dualisms: production/consumption, everyday/extraordinary, home/away, real/fake and work/leisure. These distinctions made sense in the solid modernity of the twentieth century, but they fall apart in the liquid modernity of today, eroded in large part by the ubiquity of mobile information and communication technologies that challenge the distinctions between here and there, home and away, real and virtual. What might these twentieth century frameworks have to tell us about twenty-first century tourism? As it turns out, quite a bit. In part, the continuing relevance of concepts like landscape, the tourist gaze, hospitality, authenticity and escape can be explained by how rooted these notions are in the tourist vernacular. Anyone who has been a tourist will know that places remain undeniably central to tourist experiences, as do practices like gazing, photographing, sightseeing, hosting and being hosted. Similarly, tourists and tourism marketers continue to frame travel in the public imaginary as a search for authenticity and a means of escape. These theoretical frameworks have been adept at capturing significant empirical realities, even as tourism practices and paradigms alike have shifted over time. However, I also attribute the enduring analytical power of these frameworks to the critical questions they ask about togetherness in the midst of mobility. At the heart of each of these frameworks is an impulse to better understand how travellers connect to themselves, to others, to places and to the world while on the move. In addressing this key question about the nature of sociality in the context of mobility, these paradigms have become more, not less, relevant in the twenty-first century.

In order to see what these frameworks can tell us about what social life is like in a mobile, mediated and networked world, I have suggested that we need to rethink and revise some of their underlying assumptions. To do this, I have turned again and again to the emerging literature on performance in tourism studies to think about the everyday, embodied and lived experiences of interactive travel and mobile sociality. The 'performance turn' offers a compelling challenge to the traditional frameworks in tourism studies and I engage with it here not to replace concepts like landscape, the tourist gaze, hospitality, authenticity or escape, but rather to demonstrate how a performance perspective can reanimate these concepts for a contemporary critical tourism studies. In this concluding chapter, I engage the theoretical lens and conceptual language provided by the performance turn to synthesize the key themes presented in this book and to gesture toward an emerging theory of mobile sociality.

## Interactive travel and the performance turn

The 'performance turn' in tourism studies is evident in a growing body of scholarship that has been more concerned with tourists' multi-sensuous mobilities, embodied enactments and productions of place, than with the representational world of place myths, semiotic readings and signifying practices (Edensor 1998, 2000b, 2001; Franklin and Crang 2001; Coleman and Crang 2002; Bærenholdt *et al.* 2004; Sheller and Urry 2004; Minca and Oakes 2006; Haldrup and Larsen 2010). In fact, the performance turn constitutes an explicit departure from the dominant visual and representational approaches in tourism studies that have traditionally privileged the eye over other embodied senses and authoritative cultural readings over everyday lived practices (Urry 1990; Shields 1991; MacCannell 1999[1976]). In their place, theorists have proposed a dramaturgical model of tourism that envisions tourists as expressive and creative performers, tourist places as emergent stages, and tourism practices as improvised and hybrid choreographies of bodies, technologies and material objects. The performance turn:

> shift[s] the focus to ontologies of acting and doing [to reveal] the corporeality of tourist bodies and their creative potentials, as well as the significance of technologies and the material affordances of places ... [T]he performance turn dislocates attention from symbolic meanings and discourses to embodied, collaborative and technologized *doings* and *enactments*.
>
> (Haldrup and Larsen 2010: 3, emphasis in original)

Instead of framing tourism primarily as a form of visual consumption or representation, then, the performance turn encourages us to see it as a fundamentally material, embodied and social endeavour. It is precisely by thinking about interactive travel in terms of 'embodied, collaborative and technologized doings and enactments' that we can understand it as a form of 'doing' togetherness on the move; in other words, as a performance of mobile sociality.

According to Haldrup and Larsen (2010), thinking of interactive travel in terms of performance entails recognizing it as an embodied engagement with material places as well as symbolic environments; as both choreographed and creative; and as embedded in everyday practices. It also means thinking about the way the complex networks of bodies, mobilities, materialities and technologies that make up interactive travel afford some performances while precluding others. Following this perspective, we can identify the key features of interactive travel and begin to see how they shape the distinctive qualities – and paradoxes – of mobile sociality that have emerged throughout this analysis.

### *Embodied encounters*

As we have seen in earlier chapters, interactive travel entails bodily encounters with other embodied travellers, with digital devices and with hybrid tourist landscapes. To suggest that interactive travel is embodied may seem counterintuitive, given its emphasis on mediated connections and its potential to virtually transport the traveller 'elsewhere'. As I noted in Chapter 3, however, mobile devices can be used as much to facilitate travellers' embodied immersion in place as to virtually remove them from the physical locale. Likewise, just because bodies encounter one another at a distance does not mean those encounters are disembodied; mediated togetherness may be embodied in new ways. In Chapter 4, I argued that travel blogging frames the traveller's body as an object of care and concern, even from afar, and described the way travellers' stories and images of corporeal mobility can viscerally move their online readers. Central to interactive travel and the forms of mobile sociality it affords, then, are these embodied performances of mobile devices, online social media and social networking technologies. This is particularly evident in CouchSurfing, where online connections translate into embodied forms of conviviality that involve eating, drinking, talking and walking together in bodily proximity. These face-to-face encounters may be brief and intermittent, but they may also be quite close and intimate, and in both cases they require travellers to choreograph their embodied performances around mobile communication and networking technologies.

## *Performing places*

One of the central concerns of the performance turn is the relationship between these embodied performances and the tourist places where they occur. The dramaturgical model that informs the performance turn suggests that we can think of tourist destinations as stages where tourists' embodied performances are 'staged' by the material backdrop and props of the environment (Bærenholdt et al. 2004). This is not to suggest, however, that the stage is a static location merely waiting for the show to begin. Tourist places shape, but are also constituted by, tourists' performances in and of them. Edensor explains that 'the nature of the stage is dependent on the kinds of performance enacted upon it. … [S]tages can continually change, can expand and contract. For most stages are ambiguous, sites for different performances' (2001: 64). For the most part, these studies of tourist places refer to physical tourist locations like beaches or museums or heritage sites, but their emphasis on the fluidity, ambiguity and hybridity of tourist places helps us understand the complex spatial dimension of interactive travel as well. Where does interactive travel take place, and what kinds of places does interactive travel make? Franklin and Crang (2001: 16) suggest that hybridity 'muddies up … the location of the visitor experience'. As I described in Chapter 3, interactive travellers meet in and move through hybrid geographies of material places and digital landscapes that alter what it means to be 'present'. They also bring these places into being with their performances by materializing their own geographies of the city or creating travel blogs where they can 'get together' with distant friends and family members. Haldrup and Larsen point out, then, that tourists are not just consuming places, but also producing them. In fact, this complex interplay between production and consumption is another central element of the performance turn.

### Consuming and producing

In tourism performances, acts of consumption meld into acts of production. According to Haldrup and Larsen (2010: 4–5):

> Portraying tourists solely as consumers disregards the fact that they *produce* photos and place myths; in the act of consuming, tourists turn themselves into producers. The act of 'consumption' is simultaneously one of production, or reinterpreting, re-forming, redoing, or decoding the encoded. ... The performance turn acknowledges that in the act of consuming tourists turn themselves into producers; they create, tell, exhibit and circulate tales and photographs.

Throughout this book, I have suggested that interactive travel is as much about producing places and experiences as it is about visually consuming them, and indeed this is one of the key challenges interactive travel poses to foundational paradigms such as landscape or the tourist gaze. While I have gestured toward some of the ways in which interactive travel is commodified, I have resisted the suggestion that flashpackers, travel bloggers and CouchSurfers are merely passive consumers. Instead, I have characterized interactive travellers as creative, collaborative and productive agents, arguing that they share, as all tourists do, 'the urge to narrate, to depict, to memorize, and communicate' (Löfgren 2002: 73).

Until recently, the tourist gaze has been associated primarily with consumption, and a kind of disembodied visual consumption at that. From a performance perspective, however, we can see how new technologies mobilize and mediate the tourist gaze in ways that enable tourists to make and share stories and images in the moment. In fact, new technologies have substantially enhanced the productive possibilities for tourists:

> [S]tudies of tourist performances highlight how tourists not only consume experiences but also co-produce, co-design and co-exhibit them, once they enact them and retell or publish them afterwards. Publication has escalated with the significant rise of user-generated Web 2.0 sites such as social networking sites (e.g. Facebook, MySpace), photo communities (e.g. Flickr, Photobucket) and travel communities (e.g. VirtualTourist, TripAdvisor), where users produce web content as well as consuming it.
>
> (Haldrup and Larsen 2010: 5)

This is certainly true of the mobile mediated walking tours I described in Chapter 3, which encourage travellers to engage creatively with the urban landscape rather than merely consuming it visually from behind a bus window. With the concept of 'smart tourism', I aimed to capture the innovative and intelligent aspects of these tours. Likewise, the travel bloggers I profiled in Chapter 4 display a creative impulse to design, illustrate, compose and collaborate online (see Bruns 2008). Not only do travel bloggers' stories and images become part of the web content, but so too do the comments and postings from readers who interact with the travel bloggers and with each other online. The pleasure of interactive travel derives not only from consuming sights and experiences, but also from producing and publishing them as sites of interaction with friends, family members and other travellers. In doing so, interactive travellers often find themselves folding innovative practices into existing social codes, using new technologies in fabulously new ways to fulfil old desires and obligations involved in staying in touch with the familiar/familial. This overlap between the extraordinary and the everyday is another aspect of tourism that a performance approach reveals.

### Extraordinary and everyday

Tourism scholars have tended to focus on tourists' desires for the extraordinary and the exotic, even though tourism is also made up of many banal, unremarkable, everyday practices. Because the performance turn encourages us to focus on embodied and material practices, it makes visible the small and habitual ways in which tourism is intertwined with everyday life. In fact, one of the key claims of the performance turn is that we must understand tourism not in contrast to everyday life at home, but as an extension of it.

For one thing, tourists inevitably carry 'home' with them in the familiar objects that they pack in their luggage (including their phones and laptops) as well as in the unreflexive embodied habits that shape their daily routines (Edensor 2007; Germann Molz 2008; Haldrup and Larsen 2010). As Larsen (2008b: 25) explains:

> '[T]ourist escapes' are full of everyday practices such as eating, drinking, sleeping, brushing teeth, changing nappies, reading bedtime stories and having sex with one's partner, as well as co-travelling mundane objects such as mobile phones, cameras, food, clothes and medicine.

In other words, tourists travel with an embodied habitus, reproducing familiar routines and quite ordinary activities in new surroundings. Some of these routines include online habits, such as logging on to the Internet to send emails, updating status on social networking sites, or checking up on friends (Germann Molz 2004). Here, we can detect routines of sociability, namely keeping up and staying in touch with loved ones. Tourism is a thoroughly sociable endeavour, which the performance turn acknowledges by '*explicitly* conceptualiz[ing] tourism as intricately tied up with ... significant others, such as family members and friends, but co-residing and at-a-distance' (Larsen 2008b: 26, emphasis in original). The relationships that constitute our everyday lives – friends and family, in particular – are not left behind. Families travel together; friends visit friends elsewhere. And if friends cannot join the traveller physically, they do so virtually thanks to new communication technologies.

The extent to which tourism performances revolve around everyday objects, embodied habitus and mundane routines returns us to a point I made in the previous chapter: we must rethink our notions of escape. To think of tourism, and especially interactive travel, as an escape from the everyday – our everyday routines, social obligations or even the technology we use on a daily basis – overlooks the extent to which the *pleasure* of travel emerges precisely around the ability to do things like stay in touch, care and share at a distance, or collaborate and create with a mobile community of travellers. In this sense, interactive travel is as much about embracing technological forms of social life as it is about escaping the everyday. In fact, by emphasizing the ways in which tourism is embedded in the everyday, the performance turn underscores the broader implications of a study like this one. Interactive travel is not an escape from modern social life, but rather indicative of a profound shift in contemporary society. When interactive travellers use their mobile phones to connect to a new place, log on to upload their blogs, or network online (and face-to-face) with friends and strangers in another country, they are participating in the increasingly dominant mode of 'doing togetherness' in a mobile, mediated and networked world. Interactive travel is emblematic of the kind of sociality that characterizes modern life more generally, one that now takes place online, on the phone and on the road. The form this sociality takes has been one of the main concerns of this book. What kind of 'mobile sociality' emerges out of the complex networks of bodies, mobilities, materialities and technologies that make up interactive travel?

Throughout this book, I have explored the embodied and sociable performances that new mobile communication and networking technologies afford, focusing especially on the way these technologies enable togetherness on the move and at a distance. I have argued that while communication technologies afford some sociable performances, they preclude others; they enable connections, but also disconnections. And they afford contradictory performances with unpredictable outcomes. The complex interface between humans, technology and the material environment reproduces existing social codes, but also leaves room for innovation, creativity and debate. It is in these debates, which often coalesce around the fragmenting versus cohering effects of new technologies, that we get a sense of who we are and who we want to be, what kinds of technological futures are probable and possible and which of these futures we want to bring into existence.

## Toward a theory of mobile sociality

In his analysis of the social implications of the mobile phone, Arnold (2003) suggests that we should see mobile technologies as 'Janus-faced', a metaphor meant to emphasize the paradoxical performances these technologies afford. Like the Roman deity Janus, who was cursed and blessed with two faces, one looking backwards and the other forwards at the same time, mobile phones cannot be reduced to a single perspective or linear trajectory. Instead, the performances they afford are multiple, unpredictable and, frequently, contradictory. With its capacity to mobilize and make the user 'available' anyplace, anytime, Arnold argues, the mobile phone affords a whole range of roles and performances, some of which align and others which do not: mobile and fixed, vulnerable and secure, independent and co-dependent, private and public, consumer and producer, busy and available, important and not so important.

In order to make sense of these multiple possibilities, Arnold draws on Haraway's notion of irony: 'Irony is about contradictions that do not resolve into larger wholes, even dialectically, about the tension of holding incompatible things together because both or all are necessary and true' (Haraway 1985: 65, cited in Arnold 2003: 233). From this perspective, sociotechnical performances of mobile sociality need not be either/or; in fact, it is more likely that they will be both/and. Arnold (2003: 232) goes on to explain:

> [T]echnologies are not simply a mechanism for achieving a given outcome, where desires, means and ends can be understood in reasonably unambiguous, linear and stable terms. Rather, their performance reconstitutes desires and ends, as well as mechanisms, and to account for this reconstituted sociotechnical landscape, we need an approach that allows theoretically and empirically for contrariness, paradox and irony to arise within the analytic frame.

A theory of mobile sociality is intended to move us in this direction. It is an attempt to describe and account for the contrary and ironic effects of being together while literally apart. It is from this perspective that we can hold together the seemingly irreconcilable elements that constitute sociability on the move and at a distance, things like absence and presence, escape and embrace, friend and stranger.

Indeed, the defining quality of mobile sociality is not necessarily togetherness, but rather the constant toggling between contradictory possibilities and ambivalent desires – to be together *and* apart, unbound *and* stable, connected *and* disconnected. The drama of mobile sociality pivots around these tensions, requiring us to work out and rework the meanings, uses and rules of new communication technologies. To be modern is to constantly navigate the ambiguous spaces between social cohesion and fragmentation; between the 'impulse to sociability' (Simmel 1950: 157) and the risk of 'embraces that are too tight' (Bauman 2003: 58). It is clear that as much as mobile communication and online social media technologies enable new ways of being together, they also raise new possibilities for disconnection and overconnection, for placelessness and confinement, and for fragmentation and solidarity. Mobile sociality is neither a utopian articulation of community nor the symbol of social dysfunction, but rather a complex and hybrid negotiation of these competing possibilities: balancing desires for cohesion, empathy and solidarity on the one hand with strategies for coping with risk, obligation and losses on the other. Throughout this book, I have pointed toward some of the paradoxical tensions that hold interactive travellers together and apart, suspended between connection and disconnection. Here, in conclusion, I summarize three of the tensions that I see as central to mobile sociality. The following sections are not meant to provide an exhaustive overview of mobile sociality, but rather to provoke additional, and I hope ongoing, debate around the qualities, textures and possibilities of contemporary togetherness.

*'Market economy' and 'moral economy'*

The first tension I traced throughout the book is one that Zygmunt Bauman (2003) presents in *Liquid Love* when he distinguishes between the 'market economy' and the 'moral economy'. As I noted in earlier chapters, many of the questions I pose in this book about the links between technology and sociality are inspired by Bauman's description of 'liquid love', a frail and fleeting form of social life held together by the loose ties of mediated communication. For Bauman, the frailty of human relations is intricately tied to the technologies through which we make and maintain our connections with others. Our social connections come to resemble our digital connections: short, sweet and easy to delete. We flit into and out of relationships, network rather than relate, and connect rather than commit. According to Bauman, this kind of sociality is deeply inflected by a consumerist logic that sees connections as currency, relationships as commodities and human beings as objects of consumption. This is what we can expect from a 'market economy' that seeks to commodify and capitalize on all aspects of social life including, especially, our tendency to stretch our relationships across considerable distances and conduct them across various digital mediums. In contrast, the 'moral economy' relies on physical proximity – not 'virtual proximity' – and involves a very different kind of exchange. In a moral economy, friends, family and neighbours trade on cooperation and generosity, shared goods and services, and mutual help and support. For Bauman, this is the bedrock on which enduring human bonds, deep commitments and a sense of solidarity can be built.

The features Bauman identifies in the shift from a moral economy to a market economy will certainly resonate with those living in post-industrial, highly technologized and thoroughly corporatized modern societies. But to what extent is the frail texture of modern social life attributable to technologies like mobile phones or social networking sites? Do mobile communication and online networking technologies necessarily result in a brittle sociality, one lacking in deep commitments and a sense of solidarity? Is the delete button really the emblem par excellence of contemporary sociality? These were the questions circulating in my mind as I considered the way interactive travellers used digital devices and online platforms to connect to people and places while on the move. These questions initially emerged in the interviews I conducted with the mobile developers who produced mediated walking tours and interactive adventures for urban tourists in Cambridge and Boston. As I described in Chapter 3, these developers envisioned mobile technologies from both a commercial perspective – as an instrument for driving tourist foot traffic to local businesses or to deliver advertisements to tourists – and from a civic perspective – as a means of promoting tourists' participation in the social and political life of the city. They sought to frame urban tourists not just as gazing consumers, but as embodied and interactive participants in the city. These developers imagined using digital technologies to promote consumption, but also to fortify social relations between people and to create meaningful and responsible connections to place. As they experimented with the locative, interactive and mobile capacities of new communication technologies, these developers were also navigating between the commercial and civic affordances of these devices.

This tension was also evident in CouchSurfers' and travel bloggers' use of online networking and social media platforms. For many of the CouchSurfers I interviewed, the networking framework of CouchSurfing produced the opposite of the frail sociality Bauman describes. On the contrary, CouchSurfers made sense of their participation in CouchSurfing and their encounters with the strangers they met there through a specific discourse of like-mindedness, shared generosity, global community and human solidarity. These aspects of CouchSurfing – evident both in the website's official documentation and in interviews with individual CouchSurfers – seem more aligned with a moral economy than a market economy. Of course, this is not the kind of moral economy Bauman has in mind. For Bauman, the moral economy emerges out of a stable and coherent community built on enduring relationships, shared history and face-to-face proximity. CouchSurfing's moral economy revolves instead around a globally dispersed network of travellers who meet online and offline, and even then only intermittently and briefly. The brevity of these encounters does not, however, guarantee that they are brittle, as Bialski (2007: 72) points out in her study of CouchSurfers:

> Somehow within the explanations of relationships within modernity, theorists began to link lightness with impermanence, depth with long-term commitment. This is where current theory misses the mark. Why is the intimacy achieved through the hospitality exchange not 'real intimacy'? Since when did time become a necessary factor in true intimacy?

CouchSurfers often experience their hospitality encounters as both fleeting and intimate, both brief and emotionally intense.

At the same time, CouchSurfing has a complicated relationship with the market economy, as Bauman describes it. In one sense, some members see CouchSurfing as resisting the corporatization of social life by offering modes of exchange outside of the commercial grid. For others, however, CouchSurfing's networking, profile and reputation systems are inherently consumerist, framing hosts and guests as commodities to be picked and chosen, and relationships between members as consumable experiences (Bialski 2007). The mobile sociality of CouchSurfing thus unfolds in various directions: resisting and reiterating commercial imperatives, undermining and underpinning solidarity and embracing strangers while keeping them at arm's length.

Travel blogs are another example of the complex ways in which technology use is simultaneously implicated in both the market economy and the moral economy. As we saw in previous chapters, notions of succumbing to a corporate career, as symbolized by the cubicle, or suspicions about commodification and corporate sponsorship provoke intense anxieties for travellers negotiating their own desires for authenticity or escape. Technology plays a central role in this drama. For some travellers, mobile and online technologies provide access to authentic experiences or to a more authentic way of life beyond the cubicle. In order to escape the cubicle, both literally and figuratively, many travel bloggers turn to commercial options to fund their mobile lifestyle. As I noted in the previous chapter, they sometimes end up commodifying their own blogs and blogging knowledge by selling advertising space on their blogs, affiliating with online retailers or marketing their own e-books on how to monetize a travel blog. At the same time, however, travellers express ambivalence around such commodification and complicity with corporate entities. Matt Harding's blog, *Where the Hell is Matt?*, and subsequent YouTube videos are a case in point. Thanks in large part to the corporate sponsorship he accepted, and which underwrote the majority of his round-the-world travels, Harding's website and online videos became a hub of debate around authenticity. At the heart of these debates was a question about the social consequences of online social media: did Matt's videos exploit unwitting consumers or generate a sense of global community? In posing this question, however, these debates were less about the authenticity of Matt's travels or web content and more about public hopes and fears around technology, commodification and community. The technologies in question afford certain performances – such as arranging free accommodation with a local host or making money online while travelling – but neither their complicity in a market economy nor their promotion of a moral economy is guaranteed by the technology itself. Mobile sociality moves between these two impulses, simultaneously escaping and embracing the commercial, civic and social potentialities of new technologies.

### *Mobile and moored*

The second tension that shapes mobile sociality revolves around mobilities and moorings. In laying out an agenda for mobilities studies, theorists have emphasized the fact that mobility is never purely mobile; it is always located, materialized and fixed in certain ways (Hannam, Sheller and Urry 2006; Sheller and Urry 2006; Bissell and Fuller 2010). Mobility – whether physical or virtual – relies upon and reproduces material infrastructures that are fixed in place, such as concrete motorways, physical ports and airports, and buried networks of copper wires and fibre optic cables. In other words, mobilities, including tourism mobilities, cannot be understood without taking into consideration their material underpinnings and the various ways in which they are physically stabilized. This interplay between mobility and mooring is central to an understanding of the lived qualities of mobile sociality.

In addressing this interplay between mobility and stillness, previous research has tended to focus either on the spatial, infrastructural and institutional moorings that support contemporary mobilities or on the social structures and power inequalities that work to slow down or de-mobilize some people while enhancing the mobility of others (Verstraete 2004; Adey 2006; Cresswell 2006; Hannam, Sheller and Urry 2006). These material and power structures certainly shape interactive travel as well, however throughout this book I have focused on a somewhat different set of moorings, what we might call the social, emotional and virtual moorings of mobile sociality. The metaphor of mooring implies particular sensibilities of stillness-in-movement that are reflected in the term's maritime connotations of safe harbour. The material infrastructure of ropes, cables, docks and anchors secure the ship amidst the fluidity of the sea:

> A moored boat is anchored at dock or in a bay, safe from the heave winds and waves of the open sea. Yet, the mooring itself must also be flexible, giving the boat some leeway to shift and move with the water.
>
> (Germann Molz and Gibson 2007: 15)

The leeway of the mooring acknowledges the traveller's need to stop, rest and breathe, but without being locked figuratively or literally into place. Moorings thus provide the traveller with physical rest and ontological security in the context of fluidity and mobility; with the intermittent moments of physical stillness, emotional connection and social embeddedness that enable travellers to connect while on the move.

A theory of mobile sociality thus requires us to discern the complex interplay between mobility and stillness. As Sheller and Urry (2006: 211) suggest, we must:

> delineate the context in which both sedentary and nomadic accounts of the social world operate, and ... question how that context is itself mobilised, or performed, through ongoing sociotechnical practices, of intermittently mobile material worlds.

As we have seen, interactive travel involves both sedentary and nomadic accounts in which travellers are intermittently mobile and still. This is not surprising, especially considering that most lived experiences of tourism are rarely ones of rarefied mobility. Tourism involves hurrying and waiting, moving and sitting, travelling and sleeping (Vannini 2009; Bissell and Fuller 2010; Valtonen and Veijola 2011). Interactive travel also involves intermittent moments of virtual mobility and immobility – surfing the web; sitting behind a computer screen; waiting for a connection, for photos to upload, for an email to send. As we have seen, mobile sociality emerges out of these interwoven moments of mobility and stillness.

CouchSurfing, for example, involves intersecting virtual and embodied mobilities as travellers communicate online and move around the world to meet up with one another. But it would hardly make sense, as a project or as a practice, if it did not involve offering a traveller a physical couch or bed for the night, a place where they can unload their backpack, rest and sleep. In this sense, mobile sociality is as much about dwelling as it is about travelling. In the case of Couch-Surfing, tourists dwell in the private spaces of people's homes and in moments of face-to-face and body-to-body encounters in which travellers are immobilized, at least temporarily. They perform these places as much by the way they dwell in them as they do by moving to and through them. Mobile sociality, and CouchSurfing in particular, is thus emblematic of the kinds of 'travelling-in-dwelling' and 'dwelling-in-travelling' that characterize contemporary sociality more generally (Clifford 1997; Urry 2000).

CouchSurfing moors the traveller with physical accommodation, but as many of the CouchSurfers I spoke with explained, it also offers a kind of emotional mooring, which they described in terms of intimate personal connections or a renewed faith in humanity. A similar sense of emotional mooring is evident among the travel bloggers I studied as well. In Chapter 4, I described the way travel bloggers and their dispersed social networks managed to share and care for one another at a distance, with the blog serving as a touchstone for this togetherness. For interactive travellers, these blogs are one of the 'virtual moorings' that ground them within their social networks even as they lead a mobile lifestyle. Paris (2010a: 40) explains that such virtual moorings 'allow backpackers to be fully integrated in their multiple networks and maintain a sustained state of co-presence ... with friends, family, work, school and fellow travellers'. A travel blog, a Facebook profile or an email address remain stationary relative to the traveller's constant geographic mobility. The blog constitutes a permanent address in the absence of a physical address, a 'homepage away from home' (Germann Molz 2008: 330). It is the relative *im*mobility of the traveller's online presence that makes mobile sociality possible. Online social media and social network sites are the places where the traveller can always be found and where they can interact and communicate with distant friends and family.

These virtual and emotional moorings illustrate the ways in which mobile social relations are simultaneously mobilized and fixed. In the process, they trouble the spatial dualisms around which tourism has traditionally been organized. Distinctions between here and there, home and away, absence and presence or proximity and distance make little sense in a mobile, mediated and networked world. Instead, we must think about the way social relations are disembedded, and also re-embedded, through the use of new technologies. Along with being both mobile *and* moored, interactive travellers and their social networks are both here *and* there, home *and* away, near *and* far. As I noted in Chapter 1, communications theorists have proposed concepts like 'connected presence' (Licoppe 2004) and 'ambient virtual co-presence' (Ito and Okabe 2005) precisely to capture this sense of embeddedness and ongoingness, even among dispersed and mobile social networks. As I have described, mobile technologies open up new ways for people to share with one another, to care for each other, and to integrate themselves into the fabric of each other's everyday lives – in other words, to provide a sense of social and emotional mooring – even when they are apart.

In between mobilities and moorings, the desire to be free to travel the world intersects with a paradoxical desire to remain connected. I argued in the previous chapter that travellers do not necessarily want to escape from their social networks and all of the routines and obligations, support, love and belonging those entail. They desire a kind of moored mobility, a connected escape. But finding this balance can be risky; a mooring can be a safe harbour, but it can also be a tether.

As Bauman (2003: 58–9) warns, the mobilizing network can easily become an incarcerating net:

> Don't let yourself be caught. Avoid embraces that are too tight. Remember, the deeper and denser your attachments, commitments, engagement, the greater your risk. Do not confuse the network – a swirl of roads to glide over – with a net: that treacherous implement that feels from the inside like a cage.

Of course, not everyone is vulnerable to the dangers of being too mobile or too moored in quite the same way. Hannam, Sheller and Urry (2006: 8) suggest that the interplay between mobility and moorings raises important questions of 'how to move and how to settle, what is up for grabs and what is locked in, who is able to move and who is trapped'. This is an important reminder that the middle-class interactive travellers featured in this book are able to move and to be still under relatively privileged conditions. As Skeggs (2004: 49) notes, 'mobility is a resource to which not everyone has an equal relationship'. The same might be argued of mooring; not everyone has the privilege of stopping and resting under safe, protected conditions or access to the material and emotional resources of a globally dispersed social network. For the most part, interactive travellers from wealthy societies control their own movement and stillness. They are free to connect with loved ones from afar and to develop strategies to avoid becoming trapped by 'embraces that are too tight'. As I suggested in Chapter 1, their lived experience of mobilities and moorings might be contrasted to that of other mobile subjects, such as refugees, migrants or trafficked people, for whom movement may be involuntary or who feel stuck rather than moored. In either case, the interplay between mobility and mooring implicates mobile sociality in relations of power, especially at the macro level of global mobilities like tourism, migration or trafficking. But mobility, power and control can also be discerned in the interpersonal relationships I have described throughout this book, which brings us to a third tension that shapes mobile sociality: choice and control.

### *Choice and control*

Interactive travellers belong to a 'society of choice', a prospect that is simultaneously liberating and terrifying (Oakes 2006; Bialski 2007). Modern subjects are free to choose a life and lifestyle; indeed, they are compelled to do so in a world where identities are no longer guaranteed by a cosmic order, rigid social roles or class structures. Unlike in pre-modern times, when social life could be carried out primarily through face-to-face and spatially-proximate interactions, modern sociality emerges 'more often as a by-product of social differentiation and specialization, the increased physical distance between us, and the capacity to choose aspects of our lives that had once been strictly proscribed' (Chayko 2002: 8). For some of the travellers in this study, this capacity to choose is both exciting and overwhelming, a paradox made all the more complicated by new communication technologies. These technologies open up an array of choices: new possibilities for performing identity and togetherness online and in person, access to new people and communities to interact with, and new avenues for earning a living while travelling, to name a few. These same technologies also curtail choice. Indeed, some interactive travellers are ambivalent about the extent to which their engagement with technology is a choice at all, especially in a world where social life is such a thoroughly 'technological form of life' (Lash 2001) that travellers describe themselves as 'addicted' to technology.

Travellers' concerns about being addicted to technology reflect larger anxieties about the status of choice and control in a mobile, mediated and networked world. To what extent do travellers choose to connect, and to what extent are they compelled to do so? Access to digital devices and online connections are so taken for granted that many travellers see *dis*connecting, rather than connecting, as the choice. In the previous chapter, I described how travellers appeal to a discourse of escape to make sense of this tension around choice, control and technology. Oakes' argument that escape 'is *empowering* in that it evokes a sense of *control* over an otherwise uncontrollable world' (Oakes 2006: 248, emphasis in original) is instructive here. Personal mobility and technological practices put the world at the traveller's fingertips and make it seem more manageable. But new communication technologies also put the traveller at the world's fingertips, enabling the travellers' social network to keep tabs on them, to watch and monitor them from afar, and to keep them tied into their existing social obligations.

This tension between choice and control is evident in the notion of 'following', which I discussed in Chapter 4 as an emerging form of relating among dispersed and mobile social networks. Following entails paradoxical effects. With its undertones of surveillance, following fulfils fantasies of control at-a-distance that have long accompanied new communication technologies, but it also provokes anxieties about being on the receiving end of such 'remote control'. On the one hand, following enables social networks to share emotional support and a sense of connectedness in the context of mobility. On the other hand, it can ratchet up expectations for constant availability and co-presence in ways that feel stifling to the traveller. Bauman (2003) argues that we will eventually come to expect of our social relations the same kind of lightness and looseness that we enjoy with 'virtual proximity'. The opposite may also be true: instead of decreasing our social obligations, mediated sociality may increase and extend them. As much as distant friends and family members can use new technologies to offer love, support and a sense of belonging from afar, so too can they use those technologies to redefine obligations and apply pressure in new ways. For example, the frequency with which travellers are expected to update their status and check in with friends and family has been recalibrated in a world of ubiquitous connectivity. Whereas an occasional postcard or phone call from a traveller may have been sufficient to alleviate parental concern a couple of decades ago, today's travellers feel compelled to be in touch weekly, or even daily, so that their friends and family will not worry about them.

In response to shifting social rules around availability, travellers devise strategies to capitalize on and manage these expectations of constant contact – not necessarily to avoid 'embraces that are too tight', as Bauman put it, but to balance that embrace with escape. All social relations entail interpersonal dynamics of power and control as well as forms of inclusion and exclusion, and mobile sociality is no exception. New mobile technologies, online social media and networking sites play a paradoxical role in this dynamic, providing new ways to extend community and a sense of human solidarity across physical and virtual spaces but also reiterating social boundaries and exclusions. The result of mediated interactions is not necessarily a frail and brittle sociality, but neither is it necessarily one of inclusive solidarity.

In her analysis of mediated connections in the Internet age, Chayko (2002, 2008) argues that online and mediated social interactions can result in a sense of profound bonding between individuals and among groups who do not meet face-to-face. The Internet is thus more likely to ameliorate the potentially fragmenting aspects of modern life than it is to exacerbate them. She notes that one of the consequences of technologies of communication and transportation is not further social fragmentation, but rather 'the discovery and development of interpersonal commonalities across space and time' (Chayko 2002: 8). In light of the modern freedom to choose our social ties and identities, for example, she notes that face-to-face meetings are no guarantee that two people will feel a connection with one another whereas online communities can be a genuine source of connection. These mediated communities, often constructed around a shared interest or common attribute, attract like-minded members and can result in a sense of affinity and connection among members, as we saw with the mobile community of travel bloggers I described in Chapter 4 and the global community of CouchSurfers that I discussed in Chapter 5.

In his study of mobile phones, Ling (2008) makes a similar argument. Like Chayko, Ling is unconvinced by studies that associate the Internet and mobile phones with the decline of intimate ties in contemporary society, arguing that, on the contrary, these devices augment the possibilities for social cohesion and help maintain and 'expand the flow of interaction beyond face-to-face meetings' (Ling 2008: 18). Within existing social groups, such as families and groups of friends, mobile phones can open up a channel of communication and shared mood that links people together, even when they are apart. To a large extent, this is true of the travel bloggers whose mediated interactions with an online audience were often marked by shared emotions, a sense of caring at a distance and the ritual sharing of banal intimacies.

Chayko (2002: 160) believes that a close reading of mediated interaction reveals that 'the social fabric is ... more densely "stitched" together; not quite so threadbare'. However, the inclusive potential that Chayko identifies with the Internet and that Ling identifies with mobile phones is certainly not without social 'fallout', as Chayko puts it. One of the risks is that social groups will become too densely stitched together. This is a point Ling raises alongside his argument that mobile communication helps to solidify a sense of group identity and cohesion. He suggests that mobile communication may be so effective at intensifying a group's sense of togetherness that it creates a kind of 'bounded solidarity' to the exclusion of outside perspectives (Ling 2008: 159). The rituals around mobile communication tend to intensify existing social ties rather than create new ones. Not only does mobile communication not lead to an attenuated sociality, he argues, it may actually result in the opposite: densely reciprocal and over-configured social ties within tightly bound groups. One anxiety is replaced with another.

This paradox of a profound and ongoing, yet exclusive and bounded, sense of togetherness was also at the heart of the debate that took place on *Nomadic Matt's Travel Site* over Matt's contention that we are all flashpackers now. Some of the respondents who participated in that debate worried that by remaining connected to friends and family back at home, flashpackers were missing out on making new connections with the other travellers in their hostel or with the local people and places they had travelled so far to encounter. They were anxious that travellers were using these technologies to fortify distant social ties at the expense of local ones. Mobile communication technologies, online social media and networking sites often revolve around this kind of exclusive inclusivity. For example, in Chapter 5 I described the paradox of global community in the case of Couch-Surfing, arguing that the website and its online security systems work to include the 'right' kind of difference and the 'right' kind of strangers while filtering out strangers who might pose a risk to the cosmopolitan aspirations of the project. The website's rhetoric of inclusion, tolerance for difference and global community conceals implicit criteria for participation, such as access to the Internet, the ability to travel, having a home in which to host other travellers, and 'like-mindedness'. In CouchSurfing, as in the other cases of interactive travel I have described throughout this book, we can see how new mobile communication technologies and social networking sites can promote solidarity as well as insularity, both enabling and containing togetherness between friends and strangers. Choice and control are thus negotiated around inclusion and exclusion, foregrounding yet again the way new technologies afford unpredictable and even contradictory potentialities.

## Conclusion

> To commute or communicate – both terms being etymological cousins of *communis* – is to realize community by some form of exchange.
>
> (Holmes 2001: 5)

In this chapter, I have turned to the concept of performance to summarize the material and embodied qualities of mobile sociality and to begin to make sense of the series of paradoxes around which it is organized. The various performances that constitute interactive travel reflect the material and social affordances of new technologies, but these performances also navigate between the competing forces of anxiety and aspiration. They emerge out of interlocking desires to escape and embrace, to log off but remain connected, to be mobile and liberated and still belong, to move and rest, to keep things light and loose and intense and solid, and to be together even when far apart. This is the 'stuff' of society; the promise and the problem of human togetherness.

Technology, mobility and sociality are intimately entwined, and my objective in this book has been to describe the work – and play – of figuring out how to live together in a mobile world. Contemporary forms of togetherness, especially as they are reflected in the case of interactive travel, now take place at the intersection between travelling and communicating. If mobile sociality has an essence, it is this hybrid sociotechnical condition and the various ambiguities and complexities it entails. Travel connections do not just hold distant friends together, they also hold together (and are held together by) competing spatial and social positions. When we pivot between ties that are too light and loose to provide sustenance, and ties that bind too tightly, or between virtual proximity and virtual distance, as Bauman describes it, we are not deciding whether to be together or apart, but working out how to be both at once. In the process, we revise the nature of things like togetherness, distance, proximity, mobility and belonging. We redefine what constitutes an opportunity or an obligation, and we rethink what it means to connect and to be social.

The mobile social world unfolding around us is not confined to travel and tourism; it is the shape of our everyday lives. As we use mobile technologies to make and maintain our social relations on the move and at a distance, we bring this world into being. The question is, of course, what form will it take? At the beginning of this chapter, I cited Löfgren's observation that in the cultural laboratory of tourism, 'fantasy turns into social practice in constant interaction with the very concrete materiality of technologies and flows of media'. As I have argued, mobile sociality is profoundly shaped by new technologies, yet the paths we take, the performances we enact, and the fantasies we turn into social practice do not flow directly from these technologies. They remain open. If we are willing to embrace the risks and bounty of human togetherness, mobile sociality can nourish a sense of solidarity and belonging and develop opportunities for deeper, smarter and more meaningful connections with people and places even in the midst of mobility. These possibilities are not confined to the realm of interactive travel. They are reflective of a broader shift in which mobile, mediated and networked relations now constitute the dominant mode of social life. Far from being an escape from the everyday, therefore, interactive travel is deeply emblematic of the 'travel connections' that make up contemporary society.

# Notes

## 1 Introduction

1 www.bootsnall.com/articles/11-06/should-you-start-a-travel-blog-for-your-round-the-world-trip.html
2 A portable multimedia MP3 player and Internet-enabled 'smart' phone, respectively, designed and marketed by Apple, Inc.
3 www.couchsurfing.org/statistics.html (site accessed 27 July 2011).

## 2 Fieldwork on the move

1 www.travelblog.org/about.html
2 www.travelpod.com
3 www.bootsnall.com
4 http://techcrunch.com/2006/06/29/couchsurfing-deletes-itself-shuts-down/
5 www.hospitalityclub.org

## 3 Landscape

1 These citations refer to the project's original website, http://www.pocketmetro.com, which is now defunct.
2 www.audisseyguides.com
3 www.untravelmedia.com/company/1/our_values/
4 urban-interactive.com/how

## 6 Authenticity

1 http://www.metafilter.com/77911/Matt-Harding-comes-clean
2 http://boards.bootsnall.com/post331495.html
3 www.youtube.com/watch?v=zlfkdbWwruY
4 www.untravelmedia.com/company/1/our_values/

# Bibliography

Acland, C. R. (1998) 'IMAX technology and the tourist gaze', *Cultural Studies*, 12(3): 429–45.

Adey, P. (2006) 'If mobility is everything then it is nothing: towards a relational politics of (im)mobilities', *Mobilities*, 1: 75–94.

Adler, J. (1989) 'Travel as performed art', *American Journal of Sociology*, 94(6): 1366–91.

Ahmed, S. (2000) *Strange Encounters: Embodied Others in Post-Coloniality*, London: Routledge.

Allen, J. (2000) 'On Georg Simmel: proximity, distance and movement', in M. Crang and N. Thrift (eds) *Thinking Space*, London: Routledge (54–70).

Allen, P. (2008) 'Framing, locality and the body in augmented public space', in A. Aurigi and F. De Cindio (eds) *Augmented Urban Spaces*, Aldershot: Ashgate (27–40).

Anderskov, C. (2002) *Backpacker Culture: Meaning and Identity Making Process in the Backpacker Culture among Backpackers in Central America*, Research report. Denmark: Department of Ethnography and Social Anthropology, Aarhus University.

Anderson, B. (1991) *Imagined Communities*, London: Verso.

Anderson, J. (2004) 'Talking whilst walking: a geographical archaeology of knowledge', *Area*, 36(3): 254–61.

Aoki, P., Grinter, R. E., Hurst, A., Szymanski, M., Thornton, J. D. and Woodruff, A. (2002) '*Sotto voce*: exploring the interplay of conversation and mobile audio spaces', in *ACM Conference on Human Factors in Computing Systems* conference proceedings, 20–25 April 2002, Minneapolis, MN.

Appadurai, A. (1990) 'Disjuncture and difference in the global cultural economy', in M. Featherstone (ed.) *Global Culture: Nationalism, Globalization and Modernity*, London: Sage (295–310).

Aramberri, J. (2001), 'The host should get lost: paradigms in the tourism theory', *Annals of Tourism Research*, 28(3): 738–61.

Arellano, A. (2004) 'Bodies, spirits, and Incas: performing Machu Picchu', in M. Sheller and J. Urry (eds) *Tourism Mobilities: Places to Play, Places in Play*, London: Routledge (67–77).

Armour, S. (2005) 'Fewer workers truly "off" on holidays', *USA Today*, 21 December 2005.

Arnold, M. (2003) 'On the phenomenology of technology: the "Janus-faces" of mobile phones', *Information and Organization*, 13(4): 231–56.

Augé, M. (1995) *Non-Places: Introduction to an Anthropology of Supermodernity*, London: Verso.

Aurigi, A. and De Cindio, F. (eds) (2008) *Augmented Urban Spaces: Articulating the Physical and Electronic City*. Aldershot: Ashgate.

Axup, J. and Viller, S. (2005) 'Augmenting travel gossip: design for mobile communities', in *The Proceedings of OzCHI 2005*, 21–25 November 2005, Canberra, Australia.

Bærenholdt, J., Haldrup, M., Larsen, J. and Urry, J. (2004) *Performing Tourist Places*, Aldershot: Ashgate.

Balabanović, M., Chu, L. and Wolff, G. J. (2000) 'Storytelling with digital photography', in *Proceedings of CHI 2000*, New York: ACM Press (564–71).

Bassett, C. and Wilbert, C. (1999) 'Where do you want to go today? (like it or not): leisure practices in cyberspace', in D. Crouch (ed.) *Leisure/Tourism Geographies: Practices and Geographical Knowledge*, London: Routledge (181–94).

Bauman, Z. (1995) *Life in Fragments*, Cambridge: Blackwell.

—— (2000) *Liquid Modernity*, Cambridge: Polity Press.

—— (2003) *Liquid Love: On the Frailty of Human Bonds*, Cambridge: Polity Press.

Beck, U. (1992) *Risk Society*, London: Sage.

Beeton, S. (2005) *Film-induced Tourism*, Clevedon: Channel View.

Bell, C. and Lyall, J. (2002) *The Accelerated Sublime: Landscape, Tourism and Identity*, Westport, CT: Praeger Publishers.

—— (2005) ' "I was here": pixilated evidence', in D. Crouch, R. Jackson and F. Thompson (eds) *The Media & The Tourist Imagination: Converging Cultures*, London: Routledge (135–42).

Bell, D. (2007) 'Moments of hospitality', in J. Germann Molz and S. Gibson (eds) *Mobilizing Hospitality: The Ethics of Social Relations in a Mobile World*, Aldershot: Ashgate (29–46).

—— (2009) 'Tourism and hospitality', in T. Jamal and M. Robinson (eds) *The Sage Handbook of Tourism Studies*, London: Sage (19–34).

—— (2011) 'Hospitality is society', *Hospitality & Society*, 1(2): 137–152.

Benveniste, E. (1973) *Indo-European Language and Society*, London: Faber and Faber Limited.

Berger, A. A. (2004) *Deconstructing Travel*, Walnut Creek, CA: AltaMira Press.

Bialski, P. (2006) 'Emotional tourism: an interpretive study of online hospitality exchange systems as a new form of tourism', *Hosp.Ex Net* (June 2006). Available online: http://www.hospitalityguide.net/hg/wiki/index.php?title=Emotional_Tourism&PHPSESSID=ca84b9f2d61106e3e9ccccdac48edb12.

—— (2007) *Intimate Tourism Friendships in a State of Mobility: The Case of the Online Hospitality Network*, MA Thesis, University of Warsaw. Available online: http://intimatetourism.files.wordpress.com/2007/07/paulabialski-thesisma-intimatetourism.pdf (accessed 29 July 2011).

—— (2009) *Intimate Tourism*, Paris: Solilang.

Billings, H. (2003) 'IdeaFest', *Fast Company* January 2003: 104.

Bissell, D. (2010) 'Passenger mobilities: affective atmospheres and the sociality of public transport', *Environment and Planning D*, 28(2): 270–89.

Bissell, D. and Fuller G. (eds) (2010) *Stillness in a Mobile World*, London: Routledge.

Blood, R. (2004) 'How blogging software reshapes the online community', *Communications of the ACM*, 47(12): 53–5.

Boden, D. (1994) *The Business of Talk*, Cambridge: Polity.

Boden, D. and Molotch, H. (1994) 'The compulsion of proximity', in R. Friedland and D. Boden (eds) *NowHere: Space, Time and Modernity*, Berkeley: University of California Press (257–86).

Boorstin, D. J. (1961) *The Image: A Guide to Pseudo-Events in America*, New York: Atheneum.

Brown, B., MacColl, I., Chalmers, M., Galani, A. Randell, C. and Steed, A. (2003) 'Lessons from the lighthouse: collaboration in a shared mixed reality system', in *Human Factors in Computing Systems* conference proceedings, January 2003, Fort Lauderdale, USA. Available online: http://www.dcs.gla.ac.uk/~barry/papers/CHIlighthousepaper.pdf (accessed 12 June 2009).

Bruner, E. M. (1994) 'Abraham Lincoln as authentic reproduction: a critique of postmodernism', *American Anthropologist*, 96(2):397–415.

Bruns, A. (2008) *Blogs, Wikipedia, Second Life, and Beyond: From Production to Pro-dusage*, Peter Lang: New York.

Buchberger, S. (2011) 'Hospitality, secrecy and gossip in Morocco: hosting CouchSurfers against great odds', *Hospitality & Society*, 1(3): 299–315.

Bull, M. (2000) *Sounding Out the City: Personal Stereos and the Management of Everyday Life*. Oxford: Berg.

—— (2004) ' "To each their own bubble": mobile spaces of sound in the city', in N. Couldry and A. McCarthy (eds) *MediaSpace: Place, Scale and Culture in a Media Age*, London: Routledge (275–93).

Burgess, J. (2006) 'Hearing ordinary voices: cultural studies, vernacular creativity and digital storytelling', *Continuum: Journal of Media & Cultural Studies*, 20(2): 201–14.

Burns, P. M. and O'Regan, M. (2008) 'Everyday techno-social device in everyday travel life: digital audio devices in solo travelling lifestyles', in P. M. Burns and M. Novelli (eds) *Tourism and Mobilities: Local-Global Connections*, Cambridge, MA: CABI International (146–86).

Büscher, M., Urry, J. and Witchger, K. (eds) (2010) *Mobile Methods*, London: Routledge.

Butz, D. and Besio, K. (2009) 'Autoethnography', *Geography Compass*, 3(5): 1660–4.

Buzard, J. (1993) *The Beaten Track: European Tourism, Literature, and the Ways to Culture, 1800–1918*. Oxford: Clarendon.

Cairncross, F. (1997) *The Death of Distance*. Cambridge: Harvard Business School Press.

Carpenter-Latiri, D. and Buchberger, S. (2010) 'Couchsurfing in Tunisia: hospitality, the female tourist and the "bezness" ', in D. Picard and C. Amaral (eds) *TOCOCU 1st Biannual Conference* proceedings, 9–12 September 2010, Lisbon, Portugal.

Castells, M. (1996) *The Rise of the Network Society*, Cambridge, MA: Blackwell.

Cava, M. (2010) ' "Friends" no more? For some, social networking has become too much of a good thing', *USA Today*, 10 February 2010: A1.

Chalfen, R. (1987) *Snapshot Versions of Life*, Bowling Green State University: Popular Press.

Chayko, M. (2002) *Connecting: How We Form Social Bonds and Communities in the Internet Age*, Albany, NY: State University of New York Press.

—— (2008) *Portable Communities: The Social Dynamics of Online and Mobile Connectedness*, Albany, NY: State University of New York Press.

Chen, D.-J. (2011) 'Global concept, local practice: Taiwanese experiences of CouchSurfing', *Hospitality & Society*, 1(3): 279–297.

Choi, J.-G., Woods, Robert H. and Murrmann, S. K. (2000) 'International labor markets and the migration of labor forces as an alternative solution for labor shortages in the hospitality industry', *International Journal of Contemporary Hospitality Management*, 12(1): 61–7.

Clarke, N. (2004) 'Mobility, fixity, agency: Australia's working holiday programme', *Population, Space and Place*, 10(5): 411–20.

Clifford, J. (1997) *Routes: Travel and Translation in the Late Twentieth Century*, Cambridge: Harvard University Press.

Cohen, A. (2010) 'The connected traveler', *Budget Travel* (December 2009/January 2010).

Cohen, E. (1973) 'Nomads from affluence: notes on the phenomenon of drifter tourism', *International Journal of Comparative Sociology*, 14(1–2): 89–103.

—— (1988) 'Authenticity and commoditization in tourism', *Annals of Tourism Research*, 15(3):371–86.

Cohen, R. K. (2005) 'What does the photoblog want?' *Media, Culture and Society*, 27(6): 883–901.

Cohen, S. and Taylor, L. (1992 [1976]) *Escape Attempts: The Theory and Practice of Resistance in Everyday Life*, London: Routledge.

Cole, S. (2007) 'Beyond authenticity and commodification', *Annals of Tourism Research*, 34 (4): 943–60.

Coleman, S. and Crang, M. (eds) (2002) *Tourism: Between Place and Performance*, Oxford: Berghahn Books.

—— (2002) 'Grounded tourists, travelling theory', in S. Coleman and M. Crang (eds) *Tourism: Between Place and Performance*, Oxford: Berghahn Books (1–20).

*Conde Nast Traveler* (2009) 'Get Smart? Testing the iPhone and the Blackberry Bold', June 2009. Available online: http://www.cntraveler.com/technology/2009/06/Get-Smart-Testing-the-iPhone-and-the-Blackberry-Bold.

Cosgrove, D. (1998) *Social Formation and Symbolic Landscape*, Madison, WI: University of Wisconsin Press.

Couldry, N. (2005) 'On the actual street', in D. Crouch, R. Jackson and F. Thompson (eds) *The Media and The Tourist Imagination: Converging Cultures*, London: Routledge (60–75).

—— (2008) 'Mediatization or mediation? Alternative understandings of the emergent space of digital storytelling', *New Media & Society*, 10(3): 373–91.

Counts, S. and Fellheimer, E. (2004) 'Supporting social presence through lightweight photo sharing on and off the desktop', in *Proceedings of CHI '04*, 24–29 April 2004, New York: ACM Press (599–606).

Crang, M. (1996) 'Magic Kingdom or a quixotic quest for authenticity?', *Annals of Tourism Research*, 23(2): 415–31.

—— (1999) 'Knowing, tourism and practices of vision', in D. Crouch (ed.) *Leisure/Tourism Geographies: Practices and Geographical Knowledge*, London: Routledge (238–56).

Crawford, K. (2009) 'Following you: disciplines of listening in social media', *Continuum*, 23(4): 525–35.

Cresswell, T. (2006) *On the Move: Mobility in the Modern Western World*, London: Routledge.

—— (2010) 'The politics of turbulence', paper presented at the Cultures of Movement: Mobile Subjects, Communities, and Technologies in the Americas conference, Victoria, BC, 10 April 2010.

Crouch, D. and Desforges, L. (2003) 'Introduction: the power of the body in tourist studies', *Tourist Studies*, 3(1): 5–22.

Crouch, D., Jackson, R. and Thompson, F. (eds) (2005) *The Media and the Tourist Imagination: Converging Cultures*, London: Routledge.

Culler, J. (1981) 'Semiotics of tourism', *American Journal of Semiotics*, 1(1-2):127–40.

Cuthill, V. (2007) 'Sensing and performing hospitalities and socialities of tourist places: eating and drinking out in Harrogate and Whitehaven', in J. Germann Molz and S. Gibson (eds) *Mobilizing Hospitality: The Ethics of Social Relations in a Mobile World*, Aldershot: Ashgate (83–102).

Dann, G. M. S. (ed.) (2002) *Tourism as a Metaphor of the Social World*, New York: CABI International.

Dann, G. M. S. and Jacobsen, J. K. S. (2003) 'Leading the tourist by the nose', in G. M. S. Dann (ed.) *The Tourist as a Metaphor of the Social World*, New York: CABI International (209–35).

Dann, G. M. S. and Parrinello, G. L. (2007) 'From travelogue to travelblog: (re)-negotiating tourist identity', *Acta Turistica*, 19(1): 7–29.

Davies, J. (2006) 'Affinities and beyond! Developing ways of seeing in online spaces', *E–Learning*, 3(2): 217–34.

de Botton, A. (2002) *The Art of Travel*, London: Hamish Hamilton.

de Certeau, M. (1984) *The Practice of Everyday Life*, Berkeley: University of California Press.

de Souza e Silva, A. (2006) 'From cyber to hybrid: mobile technologies as interfaces of hybrid spaces', *Space & Culture*, 9 (3): 261–78.

de Waal, M. (2007) 'The Mobile City: A Conference on Locative Media, Urban Culture and Identity', *The Mobile City* blog. Posting available online: http://www.

themobilecity.nl/background-information/lang_enconference-textlang_enlang_nlconfe-rentie-tekstlang_nl/ (accessed 12 December 2009).

DeLyser, D. (1999) 'Authenticity on the ground: engaging the past in a California ghost town', *Annals of the Association of American Geographers*, 89(4): 602–32.

Desforges, L. (1998) ' "Checking out the planet": global representations/local identities and youth travel', in T. Skelton and G. Valentine (eds) *Cool Places*, London: Routledge (175–92).

Destination Analysts, Inc. (2009) 'The state of the American traveler', 7 January 2009. Available online: http://www.destinationanalysts.com/SATSJanuary2009.pdf (site accessed 15 July 2011).

—— (2010) 'The state of the American traveler', 9 January 2010. Available online: http://www.destinationanalysts.com/State_of_the_American_Traveler_January2010.pdf (site accessed 15 July 2011).

—— (2011) 'The state of the American traveler', 11 January 2011. Available online: http://www.destinationanalysts.com/State_of_the_American_Traveler_January2011.pdf (site accessed 15 July 2011).

Dow, S., Lee, J., Oezbek, C., MacIntyre, B., Bolter, J. D. and Gandy, M. (2005) 'Exploring spatial narratives and mixed reality experiences in oakland cemetery', in *ACM SIGCHI International Conference on Advances in Computer Entertainment Technology* conference proceedings, 15–17 June 2005, Valencia, Spain.

Dutwin, D. (2009) Unplug Your Kids: A Parent's Guide to Raising Happy, Active and Well-Adjusted Children in the Digital Age, Avon, MA: Adams Media.

Duval, D. T. (2003) 'When hosts become guests: return visits and diasporic identities in a commonwealth eastern Caribbean community', *Current Issues in Tourism*, 6(4): 267–308.

—— (2004) 'Mobile migrants: travel to second homes', in C. M. Hall and D. K. Müller (eds) *Tourism, Mobility and Second Homes*, Clevedon: Channel View Publications (87–96).

Edensor, T. (1998) *Tourists at the Taj*, London: Routledge.

—— (2000a) 'Walking in the British countryside: reflexivity, embodied practices and ways to escape', *Body & Society*, 6(3): 81–106.

—— (2000b) 'Staging tourism: tourists as performers', *Annals of Tourism Research*, 27(2): 322–44.

—— (2001) 'Performing tourism, staging tourism: (re)producing tourist space and practice', *Tourist Studies*, 1(1): 59–81.

—— (2006) 'Sensing tourist spaces', in C. Minca and T. Oakes (eds) *Travels in Paradox*, Lanham, MD: Rowman and Littlefield (23–45).

—— (2007) 'Mundane mobilities, performances and spaces of tourism', *Social & Cultural Geography*, 8(2): 199–215.

—— (2009) 'Tourism and performance', in M. Robinson and T. Jamal (eds) *Sage Handbook of Tourism Studies*, London: Sage (543–57).

Elliott, A. and Urry, J. (2010) *Mobile Lives*, London: Routledge.

Enzensberger, H. M. (1996 [1958]) 'A theory of tourism' *New German Critique*, 68 (Spring–Summer): 117–35.

Epstein, M. (2009a) 'Moving Story', paper presented at *Media in Transition 6: Stone and Papyrus*, Cambridge, USA, 24–26 April 2009.

—— (2009b) 'A Brief History of Headphones in Public', *Untravel Media* blog. Available online: http://www.untravelmedia.com/blog/ (accessed 5 August 2009).

Epstein, M. and Vergani, S. (2006) 'Mobile Technologies and Creative Tourism', in *Twelfth Americas Conference on Information Systems* conference proceedings, 4–6 August 2006, Acapulco, Mexico.

Epstein, M., Garcia, C. and dal Fiore, F. (2003) *History Unwired: Venice Frontiers: Mobile Technology for Intelligent Tourism and Citizenship*. Report available online:

http://web.mit.edu/crisgh/www/History%20Unwired%20Final.pdf (accessed 15 June 2009).

Everett, S. (2008) 'Beyond the visual gaze? the pursuit of an embodied experience through food tourism', *Tourist Studies*, 8(3): 337–58.

Ferriss, T. (2007) *The 4-Hour Workweek: Escape 9-5, Live Anywhere and Join the New Rich*, New York: Crown Publishing Group.

Fortunati, L. (2002) 'The mobile phone: towards new categories and social relations', *Information, Communication, and Society*, 5(4): 514–528.

—— (2005) 'Mobile telephone and the presentation of self', in R. Ling and P. E. Pedersen (eds) *Mobile Communications: Re-negotiation of the Social Sphere*, London: Springer (203–18).

Foucault, M. (1970) *The Order of Things*. London: Tavistock.

—— (1976) *The Birth of the Clinic*. London: Tavistock.

Franklin, A. (2003) *Tourism: An Introduction*, London: Sage.

Franklin, A. and Crang, M. (2001) 'The trouble with tourism and travel theory?' *Tourist Studies*, 1(1): 5–22.

Fussell, P. (1980) *Abroad*, Oxford: Oxford University Press.

—— (ed.) (1987) *The Norton Book of Travel*, New York: Norton.

Gajjala, R. (2002) 'An interrupted postcolonial/feminist cyberethnography: complicity and resistance in the "cyberfield" ', *Feminist Media Studies*, 2(2): 177–93.

Game, A. (1991) *Undoing the Social: Towards a Deconstructive Sociology*, Toronto: University of Toronto Press.

Gardner, N. (2009) 'A manifesto for slow travel', *Hidden Europe* (March/April). Available online: http://www.hiddeneurope.co.uk/a-manifesto-for-slow-travel (accessed 10 October 2009).

Gaved, M. and Mulholland, P. (2005) 'Grassroots initiated network communities: a study of hybrid physical/virtual communities', in *Proceedings of the 38th Hawaii International Conference on System Sciences*, 3–6 January 2005, Big Island, Hawaii.

Gergen, K. (1997) *The Saturated Self: Dilemmas of Identity in Contemporary Life*, New York: Basic Books.

—— (2002) 'The challenge of absent presence', in J. Katz and M. Aakhus (eds) *Perpetual Contact*, Cambridge: Cambridge University Press (227–41).

Germann Molz, J. (2004) 'Round-the-world websites as global places to play', in M. Sheller and J. Urry (eds) *Tourism Mobilities: Places to Play, Places in Play*, London: Routledge (169–80).

—— (2006) ' "Watch us wander": mobile surveillance and the surveillance of mobility', *Environment and Planning A*, 38(2): 377–93.

—— (2007a) 'Eating difference: the cosmopolitan mobilities of culinary tourism', *Space and Culture*, 10(1): 77–93.

—— (2007b) 'Cosmopolitans on the couch: mobile hospitality and the Internet', in J. Germann Molz and S. Gibson (eds) *Mobilizing Hospitality: The Ethics of Social Relations in a Mobile World*, Aldershot: Ashgate (65–80).

—— (2008) 'Global abode: home and mobility in narratives of round-the-world travel', *Space and Culture*, 11 (4): 325–42.

—— (2009) 'Representing pace in tourism mobilities: staycations, Slow Travel and *The Amazing Race*', *Journal of Tourism and Cultural Change*, 7(4): 270–86.

—— (2010) 'Connectivity, collaboration, search', in M. Büscher, J. Urry and K. Witchger (eds) *Mobile Methods*, London: Routledge (88–103).

Germann Molz, J. and Gibson, S. (2007) 'Introduction: mobilizing and mooring hospitality', in J. Germann Molz and S. Gibson (eds) *Mobilizing Hospitality: The Ethics of Social Relations in a Mobile World*, Aldershot: Ashgate (1–25).

Gibson, J. J. (1979) *The Ecological Approach to Visual Perception*, Boston: Houghton Mifflin.

Gibson, S. (2006) 'A seat with a view: tourism, (im)mobility and the cinematic-travel glance', *Tourist Studies*, 6(2): 157–78.

Giddens, A. (1991) *Modernity and Self-Identity: Self and Society in the Late Modern Age*, Stanford, CA: Stanford University Press.

Gillespie, A. (2006) 'Tourist photography and the reverse gaze', *Ethos*, 34(3): 343–66.

Glavinskas, V. N. (2008) 'Who needs friends when you have an iPod?', *NBC Chicago* blog. Available online: http://www.nbcchicago.com/around-town/archive/Who-Needs-Friends-When-You-Have-an-Ipod.html (accessed 18 January 2010).

Goffman, E. (1959) *The Presentation of Self in Everyday Life*, New York: Anchor Books.

—— (1963) *Behavior in Public Places: Notes on the Social Organization of Gatherings*, New York: Free Press.

Gordon, E. and de Souza e Silva, A. (2011) *Net Locality: Why Location Matters in a Networked World*, Boston: Blackwell-Wiley.

Gordon, G. (2001) *Turn It Off: How to Unplug from the Anytime-Anywhere Office Without Disconnecting Your Career*, New York: Three Rivers Press.

Graburn, N. H. H. (1989) 'Tourism: the sacred journey', in V. Smith (ed.) *Hosts and Guests, second edition*, Philadelphia: University of Pennsylvania Press (21–52).

Green, N. (2002) 'Who's watching whom? Monitoring and accountability in mobile relations', in B. Brown, N. Green and R. Harper (eds) *Wireless World*, London: Springer Verlag (32–45).

Greenwoodd, D. J. (1989) 'Culture by the pound: an anthropological perspective on tourism as cultural commoditization', in V. Smith (ed.) *Hosts and Guests, second edition*, Philadelphia: University of Pennsylvania Press (171–86).

Hadley, B. and Caines, R. (2009) 'Negotiating selves: exploring cultures of disclosure', *M/C: Journal of Media and Communication*, 12(5). Available online: http://journal.media-culture.org.au/index.php/mcjournal/article/viewArticle/207.

Haldrup, M. and Larsen, J. (2003) 'The family gaze', *Tourist Studies*, 3(1): 23–45.

—— (2010) *Tourism, Performance and the Everyday: Consuming the Orient*, London: Routledge.

Halewood, C. and Hannam, K. (2001) 'Viking heritage tourism: authenticity and commodification', *Annals of Tourism Research*, 28(3): 565–80.

Hall, C. M. (2007) 'Response to Yeoman *et al.*: the fakery of "The authentic tourist"', *Tourism Management*, 28(4): 1139–40.

Hall, C. M. and Lew, A. A. (2009) *Understanding and Managing Tourism Impacts: An Integrated Approach*. New York: Routledge.

Hall, C. M. and Müller, D. K. (eds) (2004) *Tourism Mobility and Second Homes*, Clevedon: Channel View Publications.

Handler, R. and Saxton, W. (1988) 'Dissimulation: reflexivity, narrative, and the quest for authenticity in "living history"', *Cultural Anthropology*, 3: 242–60.

Hannam, K. and Diekman, A. (2010) 'From backpacking to flashpacking: developments in backpacker tourism research', in K. Hannam and A. Diekman (eds) *Beyond Backpacker Tourism: Mobilities and Experiences*, Clevedon: Channel View (1–7).

Hannam, K., Sheller, M. and Urry, J. (2006) 'Mobilities, immobilities and moorings', *Mobilities*, 1(1): 1–22.

Haraway, D. (1985) 'A manifesto for cyborgs: science, technology, and socialist feminism in the 1980s', *Socialist Review*, 80 (March/April): 65–107.

Hartley, J. and McWilliam, K. (eds) (2009) *Story Circle: Digital Storytelling Around the World*, Malden, MA: Blackwell.

Heath, C., Luff, P., vom Lehn, D., Hindmarsh, J. and Cleverly, J. (2002) 'Crafting participation: designing ecologies, configuring experience', *Visual Communication*, 1(1): 9–33.

Heath, C. and vom Lehn, D. (2010) 'Interactivity and collaboration: new forms of participation in museums, galleries and science centres', in R. Parry (ed.) *Museums in a Digital Age*, Abingdon: Routledge (266–80).

Hein, J. R., Evans, J. and Jones, P. (2008) 'Mobile methodologies: theory, technology and practice', *Geography Compass*, 2: 1–20.

Herring, S., Kouper, I., Paolillo, J., Scheidt, L., Tyworth, M., Welsch, P., Wright, E. and Yu, N. (2005) 'Conversations in the blogosphere: an analysis "from the bottom up"', paper presented at *38th Hawaii International Conference on System Sciences (HICSS-38)*, Big Island, HI, 3–6 January 2005.

Heuman, D. (2005) 'Hospitality and reciprocity: working tourists in Domenica', *Annals of Tourism Research*, 32(2): 407–18.

Hine, C. (2000) *Virtual Ethnography*, London: Sage.

Hofstaetter, C. and Egger, F. (2009) 'The importance and use of weblogs for backpackers', in W. Höpken, U. Gretzel and R. Law (eds) *Information and Communication Technologies in Tourism*, New York: Springer-Verlag (99–110).

Holmes, D. (2001) 'Virtual globalization – an introduction', in D. Holmes (ed.) *Virtual Globalization: Virtual Spaces/Tourist Spaces*, London: Routledge (1–53).

Holt, S. (2007) 'How to make an audio tour: ten tips from Audissey Guide pioneer Rob Pyles', *Matador Network* blog. Available online: http://matadornetwork.com/notebook/featured/how-to-make-an-audio-tour-ten-tips-from-audissey-guide-pioneer-rob-pyles/ (accessed 4 November 2009).

Honoré, C. (2004) *In Praise of Slowness: Challenging the Cult of Speed*, San Francisco: Harper.

Hooks, bell (1992) *Black Looks: Race and Representation*, London: Turnaround.

Hookway, N. (2008) ' "Entering the blogosphere": some strategies for using blogs in social research', *Qualitative Research*, 8(1): 91–113.

Howard, P. N. (2002) 'Network ethnography and the hypermedia organization: new media, new organizations, new methods', *New Media & Society*, 4(4): 550–74.

Howe, J. (2006) 'The rise of crowdsourcing', *Wired Magazine* (14 June 2006). Available online: http://www.wired.com/wired/archive/14.06/crowds.html (accessed 4 September 2009).

Ingold, T. (2000) *The Perception of the Environment: Essays on Livelihood, Dwelling and Skill*. New York and London: Routledge.

—— (2004) 'Culture on the ground: the world perceived through the feet', *Journal of Material Culture*, 9 (3): 315–40.

Ingold, T. and Vergunst, J. (eds) (2008) *Ways of Walking: Ethnography and Practice on Foot*, Aldershot: Ashgate.

Ito, M. and Okabe, D. (2005) 'Technosocial situations: emergent structuring of mobile email use', in M. Ito, D. Okabe and M. Matsuda (eds) *Personal, Portable, Pedestrian: Mobile Phones in Japanese Life*, Cambridge, MA: MIT Press (257–73).

Ito, M., Okabe, D. and Matsuda, M. (eds) (2005) *Personal, Portable, Pedestrian: Mobile Phones in Japanese Life*, Cambridge, MA: MIT Press.

Jacobs, J. (2006) 'Tourist places and negotiating modernity: European women and romance tourism in the Sinai', in C. Minca and T. Oakes (eds) *Travels in Paradox*, Lanham, MD: Rowman and Littlefield (125–54).

Jokinen, E. and Veijola, S. (1997) 'The disoriented tourist: the figuration of the tourist in contemporary cultural critique', in C. Rojek and J. Urry (eds) *Touring Cultures*, London: Routledge (23–51).

Jones, P., Bunce, G., Evans, J., Gibbs, H. and Ricketts Hein, J. (2008) 'Exploring space and place with walking interviews', *Journal of Research Practice*, 4(2) Article D2. Available online: http://jrp.icaap.org/index.php/jrp/article/view/150/161 (accessed 2 December 2009).

Jordan, F. and Aitchison, C. (2008) 'The sexualisation of the tourist gaze: solo female tourists' experiences of gendered power and surveillance in heterogeneous tourism spaces', *Leisure Studies*, 27(3): 329–49.

Jungnickel, K. (2004) *Urban Tapestries: Sensing the City and Other Stories*, Proboscis Cultural Snapshots Number Eight. Available online: http://proboscis.org.uk/publications/SNAPSHOTS_sensingthecity.pdf (accessed 15 June 2009).

Kaplan, C. (1996) *Questions of Travel*, Durham: Duke University Press.

Katz, J. E. and Aakhus, M. A. (eds) (2002) *Perpetual Contact*, Cambridge: Cambridge University Press.

Kendall, L. (2002) *Hanging out in the Virtual Pub: Masculinities and Relationships Online*, Berkeley: University of California Press.

Kern, S. (1983) *The Culture of Time and Space: 1880–1918*, Cambridge, MA: Harvard University Press.

Kim, H. and Jamal, T. (2007) 'Touristic quest for existential authenticity', *Annals of Tourism Research*, 34(1): 181–201.

Kirschenblatt-Gimblett, B. (1998) *Destination Culture*, Berkeley: University of California Press.

Kjeldskov, J. and Paay, J. (2007) 'Augmenting the city with fiction: fictional requirements for mobile guides', in *Mobile Interaction with the Real World* conference proceedings, 9 September 2007, Singapore. Available online: http://www.medien.ifi.lmu.de/mirw2007/MIRW_MGUIDES_2007_Proceedings.pdf (accessed 15 June 2009).

Kohiyama, K. (2005) 'Mobile communication and place', *Vodafone Receiver*, 13. Available online: http://www.receiver.vodafone.com/13/articles/index06.html (accessed 12 May 2006).

Kottamasu, R. (2007) 'Placelogging: mobile spatial annotation and its potential use to urban planners and designers', Masters Thesis, Department of Urban Studies and Planning, Massachusetts Institute of Technology.

Lamb, C. (2009) 'Tours off the beaten path provide business travelers, tourists a different way to see the city', *Boston Business Journal*, 25 September 2009.

Lane, G. (2003) 'Urban tapestries: wireless networking, public authoring and social knowledge', *Personal and Ubiquitous Computing*, 7(3–4): 69–175.

Langford, M. (2006) 'Speaking the album: an application of the oral photographic framework', in A. Kuhn and K. E. McAllister (eds) *Locating Memory*, Oxford: Berghan (223–46).

Larsen, J. (2001) 'Tourism mobilities and the travel glance: experiences of being on the move', *Scandinavian Journal of Hospitality and Tourism*, 1(2): 80–98.

—— (2005) 'Families seen sightseeing: performativity and tourist photography', *Space and Culture*, 8(4): 416–34.

—— (2006) 'Geographies of tourist photography: choreographies and performances', in J. Falkheimer and A. Jansson (eds) *Geographies of Communication: The Spatial Turn in Media Studies*, Gøteborg: Nordicom (243–60).

—— (2008a) 'Practices and flows of digital photography: an ethnographic framework', *Mobilities*, 3(1): 141–60.

—— (2008b) 'De-exoticizing tourist travel: everyday life and sociality on the move', *Leisure Studies*, 27(1): 21–34.

—— (2009) 'Goffman and the tourist gaze: a performative perspective on tourism mobilities', in M. H. Jacobsen (ed.) *The Contemporary Goffman*, London: Routledge (313–33).

Larsen, J., Urry, J. and Axhausen, K. (2006) *Mobilities, Networks, Geographies*, Aldershot: Ashgate.

Lash, S. (2001) 'Technological forms of life', *Theory, Culture & Society*, 18(1): 105–20.

Lash, S. and Urry, J. (1994) *Economies of Signs and Space*, London: Sage.

Laurier, E. (2001) 'Why people say where they are during mobile phone calls', *Environment and Planning D*, 19(4): 485–504.

Laurier, E. and Philo, C. (2006) 'Cold shoulders and napkins handed: gestures of responsibility', *Transactions of the Institute of British Geographers*, 31(2) 193–208.

Lauterbach, D., Truong, H., Shah, T. and Adamic, L. (2009) 'Surfing a web of trust: reputation and reciprocity on CouchSurfing.com', in *2009 International Conference on Computational Science and Engineering (CSE) Conference Proceedings*, 29–31 August 2009, Vancouver, Canada (346–53).

Lee, J. and Ingold, T. (2006) 'Fieldwork on foot: perceiving, routing, socializing', in S. Coleman and P. Collins (eds) *Locating the Field: Space, Place and Context in Anthropology*, Oxford: Berg (67–86).

Lemos, A. (2009) 'Locative media manifesto', *Carnet de Notes* blog. Available online: http://www.andrelemos.info/2009/05/locative-media-manifesto.html (accessed 4 January 2010).

Licoppe, C. (2004) ' "Connected" presence: the emergence of a new repertoire for managing social relationships in a changing communication technoscape', *Environment and Planning D*, 22: 135–56.

Ling, R. (2008) *New Tech, New Ties: How Mobile Communication is Reshaping Social Cohesion*, Cambridge, MA: MIT Press.

Löfgren, O. (2002) *On Holiday: A History of Vacationing*, Berkeley: University of California Press.

Loker-Murphy, L. and Pearce, P. L. (1995) 'Young budget travelers: backpackers in Australia', *Annals of Tourism Research*, 22(4): 819–43.

Lorimer, H. (2003) 'Telling small stories: spaces of knowledge and the practice of geography', *Transactions of the Institute of British Geographers* 28 (2): 197–217.

Lugosi, P. (2007) 'Consumer participation in commercial hospitality', *International Journal of Culture, Tourism and Hospitality Research*, 1(3): 227–36

Lundby, K. (ed.) (2008) *Digital Storytelling, Mediatized Stories: Self-Representations in New Media*, New York: Peter Lang.

Lynch, P., Germann Molz, J., McIntosh, A., Lugosi, P. and Lashley, C. (2011) 'Theorizing hospitality', *Hospitality & Society*, 1(1): 3–24.

MacCannell, D. (1973) 'Staged authenticity: arrangements of social space in tourist settings', *American Journal of Sociology*, 79(3): 589–603.

—— (1999[1976]) *The Tourist: A New Theory of the Leisure Class*. Berkeley: University of California Press.

Makimoto, T. and Manners, D. (1997) *Digital Nomad*, Chichester: Wiley.

Manovich, L. (2006) 'The poetics of augmented space', *Visual Communication*, 5(2): 219–40.

Månsson, N. (2008) 'Bauman on strangers – unwanted peculiarities', in M. H. Jacobsen and P. Poder (eds) *The Sociology of Zygmunt Bauman: Challenges and Critiques*, Aldershot: Ashgate (155–72).

Maoz, D. (2006) 'The mutual gaze', *Annals of Tourism Research*, 33(1): 221–39.

Marcus, G. E. (1998) *Ethnography through Thick and Thin*, Princeton: Princeton University Press.

Markwell, K. (2001) ' "An intimate rendezvous with nature"? Mediating the tourist-nature experience at three tourist sites in Borneo', *Tourist Studies*, 1: 39–57.

Marvin, C. (1988) *When Old Technologies Were New: Thinking About Electric Communication in the Late Nineteenth Century*, Oxford: Oxford University Press.

Mascheroni, G. (2007) 'Global nomads' mobile and network sociality: exploring new media uses on the move', *Information, Communication and Society*, 10(4): 527–46.

Massey, D. (1993) 'Power-geometry and a progressive sense of place', in J. Bird, B. Curtis, T. Putnam, G. Robertson and L. Tickner (eds) *Mapping the Futures*, London: Routledge (59–69).

Maushart, S. (2011) *The Winter of our Disconnect: How Three Totally Wired Teenagers (and a Mother Who Slept with Her iPhone) Pulled the Plug on Their Technology and Lived to Tell the Tale*, London: Profile Books.

McCabe, S. (2002) 'The tourist experience and everyday life', in G. M. S. Dann (ed.) *The Tourist as a Metaphor for the Social World*, New York: CABI International (61–75).

McLaren, D. (2003) *Rethinking Tourism & Ecotravel, second edition*, Bloomfield, CT: Kumarian.

McNaughton, D. (2006) 'The "host" as uninvited "guest": hospitality, violence and tourism', *Annals of Tourism Research*, 33(3): 645–65.

Meethan, K. (2001) *Tourism in Global Society*, New York: Palgrave.

Miller, D. and Slater, D. (2000) *The Internet: An Ethnographic Approach*, Oxford: Berg.

Miller, J. and Miller, M. (2005) 'Get a life!' *Fortune*, 28 November 2005: 38–48.

Minca, C. (2007) 'The tourist landscape paradox', *Social & Cultural Geography*, 8(3): 433–53.

Minca, C. and Oakes, T. (2006) 'Introduction: traveling paradoxes', in C. Minca and T. Oakes (eds) *Travels in Paradox*, Lanham, MD: Rowman and Littlefield (1–21).

Moles, K. (2008) 'A walk in thirdspace: place, methods and walking', *Sociological Research Online*, 13(4)2. Available online: http://www.socresonline.org.uk/13/4/2.html (accessed 14 May 2011).

Murphy, D. (2009) 'First, buy your pack animal', *The Guardian*, 3 January 2009.

Murphy, L. (2001) 'Exploring social interactions of backpackers', *Annals of Tourism Research*, 28(1): 50–67.

Nardi, B. A., Schiano, D. J. and Gumbrecht, M. (2004) 'Blogging as social activity, or, would you let 900 million people read your diary?', in *Computer Supported Cooperative Work, Proceedings of the 2004 ACM Conference on Computer Supported Cooperative Work*, 6–10 November 2004, Chicago, Illinois, USA (222–31).

Navarette, C. Huerta, E. and Horan, T. A. (2008) 'Social place identity in hybrid communities', in A. Aurigi and F. De Cindio (eds) *Augmented Urban Spaces*, Ashgate: Aldershot (125–38).

O'Barr, W. M., Tobaccowala, R., Partilla, J. and Gotlieb, I. (2009) 'Media and advertising', *Advertising & Society Review*, 10(2). Available online: http://muse.jhu.edu/journals/advertising_and_society_review/v010/10.2.o-barr.html.

O'Reilly, C. C. (2006) 'From drifter to gap year tourist: mainstreaming backpacker travel', *Annals of Tourism Research*, 33(4): 998–1017.

O'Reilly, K. (2003) 'When is a tourist? The articulation of tourism and migration in Spain's Costa del Sol', *Tourist Studies*, 3(3): 301–17.

O'Reilly, T. (2005) 'What Is Web 2.0: design patterns and business models for the next generation of software', *O'Reilly: Spreading the Knowledge of Innovators* blog. Available online: http://oreilly.com/web2/archive/what-is-web-20.html (accessed 14 March 2010).

Oakes, T. (2006) 'Get real! On being yourself and being a tourist', in C. Minca and T. Oakes (eds) *Travels in Paradox*, Lanham, MD: Rowman and Littlefield (229–50).

Okabe, D. and Ito, M. (2003) 'Camera phones changing the definition of pictureworthy', *Japan Media Review*. Available online: http://www.ojr.org/japan/wireless/1062208524.php (accessed 16 March 2010).

Okabe, D. and Ito, M. (2006) 'Everyday contexts of camera phone use: steps toward technosocial ethnographic frameworks', in J. R. Hoflich and M. Hartmann (eds) *Mobile Communication in Everyday Life*, Berlin: Frank & Timme (79–102).

Olson, T. J. (2008) 'Introducing *Wanderlust*: proposing and defending the utility of a social networking space for contemporary backpackers', MA Thesis (unpublished), New York University, Tisch School of the Arts. Available online: http://www.wanderlustlive.com/documentation/Wanderlust.pdf.

Ousby, I. (1990) *The Englishman's England*, Cambridge: Cambridge University Press.

Paris, C. M. (2009) 'The virtualization of backpacker culture', in W. Höpken, U. Gretzel and R. Law (eds) *Information and Communication Technologies in Tourism*, New York: Springer-Verlag (25–35).

—— (2010a) 'The virtualization of backpacker culture: virtual mooring, sustained interaction and enhanced mobilities', in K. Hannam and A. Diekmann (eds) *Beyond Backpacker Tourism: Mobilities and Experiences*, Clevedon: Channel View (40–63).

—— (2010b). 'Backpackers and social media: the statusphere and the blogosphere', paper presented at the Association of American Geographers conference, Washington, DC, 17 April 2011.

Pearce, P. L. and Moscardo, G. M. (1986) 'The concept of authenticity in tourist experiences', *The Australian and New Zealand Journal of Sociology*, 22(1): 121–32.

Perkins, H. and Thorns, D. (2001) 'Gazing or performing?' *International Sociology*, 16(2): 185–205.

Pink, S. (2008) 'Mobilising visual ethnography: making routes, making place and making images', *Qualitative Research*, 9(3) Art. 36. Available online: http://www.qualitative-research.net/index.php/fqs/article/viewArticle/1166/2575 (accessed 14 May 2011).

Pope, N. and Guthrie, K. (1996) 'A hypertext journal', Available online: http://www.somewhere.org.uk/hypertext/journal/index.html (accessed 29 October 2010).

Potter, A. (2010) *The Authenticity Hoax*, New York: HarperCollins.

Potts, R. (2009) 'I'm traveling to Europe this summer. Should I Twitter from the road?', *World Hum* blog. Available online: http://www.worldhum.com/features/ask-rolf-potts/im-traveling-to-europe-this-summer.-should-i-twitter-from-the-road-20090401/ (accessed 29 May 2010).

Powers, W. (2010) *Hamlet's BlackBerry: A Practical Philosophy for Building a Good Life in the Digital Age*, New York: HarperCollins.

Pultar, E. and Raubal, M. (2009) 'A case for space: physical and virtual location requirements in the CouchSurfing social network', in *ACM Conference Proceedings*, 3 November 2009.

Qian, H. and Scott, C. R. (2007) 'Anonymity and self-disclosure on weblogs', *Journal of Computer-Mediated Communication*, 12(4), article 14. Available online: http://jcmc.indiana.edu/vol12/issue4/qian.html.

Qiu. J. L. (2007) 'The wireless leash: mobile messaging service as a means of control', *International Journal of Communication*, 1(2007): 74–91

Ratliff, E. (2009) 'Vanish', *Wired Magazine*, December 2009: 144–88.

Reisinger, Y. and Steiner, C. J. (2006) 'Reconceptualizing object authenticity', *Annals of Tourism Research*, 33(1):65–86.

Relph, E. C. (1976) *Place and Placelessness*, London: Pion.

Resnick, P., Kuwabara, K., Zeckhauser, R. and Friedman, E. (2000) 'Reputation systems', *Communications of the ACM*, 43(12): 45–8.

Rheingold, H. (1994) *The Virtual Community: Finding Connection in a Computerized World*, London: Secker and Warburg.

—— (2002) *Smart Mobs: The Next Social Revolution*, New York: Basic Books.

Richards, G. and Wilson, J. (2004a) 'Drifting towards the global nomad', in G. Richards and J. Wilson (eds) *The Global Nomad: Backpacker Travel in Theory and Practice*, Clevedon: Channel View (1–13).

—— (2004b) 'Widening perspectives in backpacker research', in G. Richards and J. Wilson (eds) *The Global Nomad: Backpacker Travel in Theory and Practice*, Clevedon: Channel View (253–79).

Richtel, M. (2010) 'Hooked on gadgets and paying a mental price', *New York Times*, 7 June 2010: Technology A1.

Riessman, C. K. (1993) *Narrative Analysis*, London: Sage.

Rifkin, J. (2010) *The Empathic Civilization: The Race to Global Consciousness in a World in Crisis*, Cambridge: Polity Press.

Riley, P. (1988) 'Road culture of international long-term budget travelers', *Annals of Tourism Research*, 15(3): 313–28.

Riley, R. Baker, D. and Van Doren, C. (1998) 'Movie induced tourism', *Annals of Tourism Research*, 25(4): 919–35.

Rojek, C. (1993) *Ways of Escape*, London: Routledge.
—— (1995) *Decentring Leisure: Rethinking Leisure Theory*, London: Sage.
Rojek, C. and Urry, J. (1997) 'Transformations of travel and theory', in C. Rojek and J. Urry (eds) *Touring Cultures*, London: Routledge (1–22).
Rosa, H. and Scheuerman, W. E. (eds) (2008) *High-Speed Society: Social Acceleration, Power, and Modernity*, University Park, PA: Penn State Press.
Rosen, D., Lafontaine, P. R. and Hendrickson, B. (2011) 'CouchSurfing: belonging and trust in a globally cooperative online social network', *New Media & Society*, published online 8 March 2011.
Sanders, T. (2005) 'Researching the online sex work community', in C. Hine (ed.) *Virtual Methods: Issues in Social Research on the Internet*, Oxford: Berg (67–80).
Schivelbusch (1986) *The Railway Journey: The Industrialization of Time and Space in the 19th Century*. Berkeley: University of California Press.
Scifo, B. (2005) 'The domestication of camera-phone and MMS communication: the early experiences of young Italians', in K. Nyiri (ed.) *A Sense of Place: The Global and the Local in Mobile Communication*, Vienna: Passagen Verlag (363–74).
Selwyn, T. (ed.) (1996) *The Tourist Image: Myths and Myth Making in Tourism*, New York: John Wiley & Sons.
Sevick Bortree, D. (2005) 'Presentation of self on the web: an ethnographic study of teenage girls' weblogs', *Education, Communication & Information*, 5(1): 25–39.
Shaffer, T. S. (2004) 'Performing backpacking: constructing "authenticity" every step of the way', *Text and Performance Quarterly*, http://www.informaworld.com/smpp/title~db=all~content=t713709382~tab=issueslist~branches=24-v24 24(2): 139–60.
Sheller, M. (2004) 'Demobilizing and remobilizing Caribbean paradise', in M. Sheller and J. Urry (eds) *Tourism Mobilities: Places to Play, Places in Play*, London: Routledge, (13–22).
Sheller, M. and Urry, J. (eds) (2004) *Tourism Mobilities: Places to Play, Places in Play*, London: Routledge.
—— (2006) 'The new mobilities paradigm', *Environment and Planning A*, 38: 207–26.
Shepard, M. (ed.) (2011) *Sentient City: Ubiquitous Computing, Architecture, and the Future of Urban Space*, Cambridge, MA: MIT Press.
Sherlock, K. (2001), 'Revisiting the concept of hosts and guests', *Tourist Studies*, 1(3): 271–95.
Shields, R. (1991) *Places on the Margin: Alternative Geographies of Modernity*, London: Routledge.
Simmel, G. (1950) *The Sociology of Georg Simmel*, K. Wolff (trans.) New York: Free Press.
Skeggs, B. (2004) *Class, Self, Culture*, London: Routledge.
Smith, M. (2009) 'Ethical perspectives: exploring the ethical landscape of tourism', in M. Robinson and T. Jamal (eds) *Sage Handbook of Tourism Studies*, London: Sage (613–30).
Smith, V. (ed.) (1989) *Hosts and Guests: The Anthropology of Tourism, second edition*, Philadelphia: University of Pennsylvania Press.
Solnit, R. (2001) *Wanderlust: A History of Walking*, New York: Viking.
Sørensen, A. (2003) 'Backpacker ethnography', *Annals of Tourism Research*, 30(4): 847–67.
Southern, J. (2011) 'Co-mobility: an experiment in mobilities research and locative art practice', paper presented at the Mobilities in Motion: New Approaches to Emergent and Future Mobilities conference, Philadelphia, PA, 21 March 2011.
Steiner, C. J. and Reisinger, Y. (2006) 'Understanding existential authenticity', *Annals of Tourism Research*, 33(2): 299–318.
Stone, A. R. (1996) *The War of Desire and Technology at the Close of the Mechanical Age*, Cambridge, MA: MIT Press.
Sutko, D. M. and de Souza e Silva, A. (2011) 'Location-aware mobile media and urban sociability', *New Media & Society*, 13(5): 807–23.

Swain, M. B. (1995) 'Gender in tourism', *Annals of Tourism Research* 22 (2):247–66.

Tan, J.-E. (2010) 'The Leap of faith from online to offline: an exploratory study of Couch-surfing.org', in *3rd International Conference, TRUST 2010 Conference Proceedings*, Berlin, Germany, 21–23 June 2010, Berlin: Springer (367–80).

Taylor, C. (1991) *The Ethics of Authenticity*, London: Harvard University Press.

Tergesen, A. (2011) 'When guests check in, their iPhones check out', *The Wall Street Journal*, 5 July 2011.

Terkenli, T. S. (2004) 'Tourism and landscape', in A. A. Lew, C. M. Hall and A.M. Williams (eds) *A Companion to Tourism*, London: Blackwell (339–48).

Thompson, C. (2008) 'Brave new world of digital intimacy', *New York Times*, 7 September 2008.

Turner, L. and Ash, J. (1975) *The Golden Hordes: International Tourism and the Pleasure Periphery*, London: Constable.

Tzanelli, R. (2007) *The Cinematic Tourist*, London: Routledge.

Uriely, N., Yonay, Y. and Simchai, D. (2002) 'Backpacking experiences: a type and form analysis', *Annals of Tourism Research*, 29(2): 520–38.

Urry, J. (1990) *The Tourist Gaze*, London: Sage.

—— (1995) *Consuming Places*, London: Routledge.

—— (1999) 'Sensing leisure spaces', in D. Crouch (ed.) *Leisure/Tourism Geographies: Practices and Geographical Knowledge*, London: Routledge (34–45).

—— (2000) *Sociology beyond Societies*, London: Routledge.

—— (2002) *The Tourist Gaze, second edition*, London: Sage.

—— (2003) 'Social networks, travel and talk', *British Journal of Sociology*, 54(2): 155–75.

—— (2007) *Mobilities*, Cambridge: Polity Press.

Urry, J. and Larsen, J. (2011) *The Tourist Gaze 3.0.*, London: Sage.

Valtonen, A. and Veijola, S. (2011) 'Sleep in tourism', *Annals of Tourism Research*, 38(1): 175–92.

Van Den Bos, M. and Nell, L. (2006) 'Territorial bounds to virtual space: transnational online and offline networks of Iranian and Turkish–Kurdish immigrants in the Netherlands', *Global Networks* 6(2): 201–20.

Vander Wal, T. (2007) 'Sharing and following/listening in the social web', *vanderwal.net* blog. Available online: http://www.vanderwal.net/random/entrysel.php?blog=1937 (accessed 14 November 2009).

Van Dijck, J. (2007) *Mediated Memories in the Digital Age*, Stanford: Stanford University Press.

Van House, N. (2004) 'Weblogs: credibility and collaboration in an online world', submitted for CSCW Workshop on Trust, October 2004 [workshop subsequently cancelled]. Available online: http://www2.sims.berkeley.edu/~vanhouse/Van%20House%20 trust%20workshop.pdf.

Vannini, P. (2009) '28'23": (On) time performance and waiting as drama', *M/C Journal of Media and Culture*, 12(1). Available online: journal.media-culture. org.au/index.php/mcjournal/article/viewArticle/128 (accessed 25 July 2011).

Veijola, S. (2006) 'Heimat tourism in the countryside: paradoxical sojourns to self and place', in C. Minca and T. Oakes (eds) *Travels in Paradox: Remapping Tourism*, Lanham, MD: Rowman & Littlefield (77–96).

Veijola, S. and Jokinen, E. (1994) 'The body in tourism', *Theory, Culture & Society*, 11(3): 125–51.

Veijola, S. and Valtonen, A. (2007) 'The body in tourism industry', in A. Pritchard, N. Morgan, I. Atelejevic and C. Harris (eds) *Tourism & Gender: Embodiment, Sensuality and Experience*, Cambridge, MA: CABI International (13–31).

Verstraete, G. (2004) 'Technological frontiers and the politics of mobility in the European Union', in S. Ahmed, C. Castañeda, A.-M. Fortier and M. Sheller (eds) *Uprootings/Regroundings: Questions of Home and Migration*, New York: Berg (225–50).

Vertovec, S. (2004) 'Cheap calls: the social glue of migrant transnationalism', *Global Networks*, 4(2): 219–24.

Viégas, F. B. (2005) 'Bloggers' expectations of privacy and accountability: an initial survey', *Journal of Computer-Mediated Communication*, 10(3). Available online: http://jcmc.indiana.edu/vol10/issue3/viegas.html.

Waitt, G. and Duffy, M. (2010) 'Listening and tourism studies', *Annals of Tourism Research*, 37(2): 457–77.

Wang, N. (1999) 'Rethinking authenticity in tourism experience', *Annals of Tourism Research*, 26(2): 349–70.

—— (2006) 'Itineraries and the tourist experience', in C. Minca and T. Oakes (eds) *Travels in Paradox*, Lanham, MD: Rowman and Littlefield (65–76).

Welk, P. (2004) 'Anti-tourism as an element of backpacker identity', in G. Richards and J. Wilson (eds) *The Global Nomad: Backpacker Travel in Theory and Practice*, Clevedon: Channel View (77–91).

Wellman, B., Quan-Haase, A., Boase, J., Chen, W., Hampton, K., Díaz, I. and Miyata, K. (2003) 'The social affordances of the Internet for networked individualism', *Journal of Computer-Mediated Communication*, 8(3).

Westerhausen, K. (2002) *Beyond the Beach: An Ethnography of Modern Travelers in Asia*, Bangkok: White Lotus.

White, N. R. and White, P. B. (2007) 'Home and away: tourists in a connected world', *Annals of Tourism Research*, 34(1): 88–104.

—— (2008) 'Maintaining co-presence: tourists and mobile communication in New Zealand', in J. E. Katz and M. Castells (eds) *Handbook of Mobile Communication Studies*, Cambridge, MA: MIT Press (195–207).

Williams, M., Fleuriot, C., Facer, K., Reid, J., Hull, R. and Jones, O. (2002) 'Mobile Bristol: a new sense of place' in P. Ljungsrand and L. E. Holmquist (eds) *Ubicomp 2002 Adjunct Proceedings*, 29 September–1 October 2002, Gotëborg, Sweden (27–9).

Wittel, A. (2000) 'Ethnography on the move: from field to net to internet', *FQS: Forum: Qualitative Social Research/Sozialforschung*, 1(1), Art. 21. Available online: http://qualitative-research.net/fqs.

—— (2001) 'Towards a network sociality', *Theory, Culture and Society*, 18(1): 31–50.

Woodruff, A., Aoki, P., Hurst, A. and Szymanski, M. (2001) 'Electronic Guidebooks and visitor attention', in *ICHIM2001: Archives and Informatics Conference Proceedings*, 3 September 2001, Milan, Italy.

Wylie, J. (2005) 'A single day's walking: narrating self and landscape on the South West Coast Path', *Transactions of the Institute of British Geographers*, 30: 234–47.

xtine. (2008) 'CouchSurfing, Delocator, and Fallen Fruit: websites respond to a crisis of democracy', *M/C: Journal of Media and Communication*, 6(1). Available online: http://journal.media-culture.org.au/index.php/mcjournal/article/viewArticle/24.

Yeh, J. H.-Y. (2009) 'The embodiment of sociability through the tourist camera', in M. Robinson and D. Picard (eds) *The Framed World: Tourism, Tourists and Photography*, Aldershot: Ashgate (199–206).

**Round-the-World Travel Blogs**

*Everything-Everywhere*: everything-everywhere.com
*Follow Our Footsteps*: www.followourfootsteps.com
*Forks and Jets*: forksandjets.com
*Go Backpacking*: www.gobackpacking.com/blog/
*I Should Log Off*: ishouldlogoff.com
*Legal Nomads*: www.legalnomads.com
*Nerdy Nomad*: www.nerdynomad.com
*Nomadic Matt's Travel Site*: www.nomadicmatt.com

*The Lost Girls*: www.lostgirlsworld.com
*The Wide Wide World*: http://thewidewideworld.com/rtw/2009/
*World Effect Blog*: www.theworldeffect.com
*The World is Not Flat*: www.theworldisnotflat.com
*Where the Hell is Matt?*: www.wherethehellismatt.com

# Index

Lightning Source UK Ltd.
Milton Keynes UK
UKOW06f2239030817
306644UK00012B/230/P